THE TRANSFORMATION OF
LABOUR RELATIONS

The Transformation of Labour Relations

Restructuring and Privatization in Eastern Europe and Russia

J. E. M. Thirkell, K. Petkov, and S. A. Vickerstaff

Oxford   New York
OXFORD UNIVERSITY PRESS
1998

Oxford University Press, Great Clarendon Street, Oxford OX2 6DP

Oxford New York

Athens Auckland Bangkok Bogotá Buenos Aires Calcutta
Cape Town Chennai Dar es Salaam Delhi Florence Hong Kong Istanbul
Karachi Kuala Lumpur Madras Madrid Melbourne Mexico City Mumbai
Nairobi Paris São Paolo Singapore Taipei Tokyo Toronto Warsaw

and associated companies in
Berlin Ibadan

Oxford is a registered trade mark of Oxford University Press

Published in the United States
by Oxford University Press Inc., New York

British Library Cataloguing in Publication Data
Data available

Library of Congress Cataloging in Publication Data
Data available
ISBN 0–19–828979–0

1 3 5 7 9 10 8 6 4 2

Typeset in Great Britain by Hope Services (Abingdon) Ltd.
Printed in Great Britain
on acid-free paper by
Biddles Ltd., Guildford and King's Lynn

PREFACE

The aim of this book is to review and explain the impact of political and economic transformation on the labour-relations models of Eastern Europe and Russia. This has been a relatively neglected area of research concern. The literature which exists tends to focus either upon particular trends *within* specific countries or on comparisons of two or three countries. There is a lack of genuinely comparative discussions based upon trends in a range of countries. This is the second book to arise out of a collaborative research project conducted over a five-year period, 1991–6, which investigated enterprise-level changes in labour relations in Eastern Europe and Russia. The original research design and methodology were agreed by the international research team at the beginning of the project. The empirical research was based upon in-depth enterprise case studies in Bulgaria, the Czech Republic and Slovakia, Hungary, Poland, and the Siberian region of Russia. The project was funded by a grant from the Economic and Social Research Council under its East–West Initiative and has provided an unique opportunity for genuinely comparative research into contemporary labour-relations changes in Eastern Europe and Russia.

This volume moves beyond the task of describing and analysing changes within each of the countries to address the fundamental questions of similarities and differences in the ways in which labour-relations models of Eastern Europe are evolving; the approach is thematic, considering, in turn: the political and economic legacy and context for transformation; the role of international institutions in economic reform strategy; patterns of privatization and ownership change; trade unions; distribution and collective bargaining; enterprise strategy, and foreign ownership. In so doing the discussion links changes at the national or societal level to patterns of change and development at the level of the individual enterprise, another relatively neglected area. The volume benefits greatly from the fact that it is a collaboration between insiders and outsiders to the change processes being analysed. Many of those involved in the research are specialists who have been involved in tracking developments in labour relations in the individual countries since the 1970s. This expertise has been especially valuable in understanding the nature of labour-relations legacies and their impact upon current developments (see the discussion in Chapter 1). The authors of the present volume are indebted both to the high quality of research from all those involved in the original project (see Appendix A) and to the considerable intellectual stimulation from working with such a distinguished team. In particular the authors wish to acknowledge the invaluable contribution of the following: Ludovit Cziria, Michał Federowicz, Vladimir Gerchikov, Grigor Gradev, Lajos Hethy, Wiesława Kozek, Richard Scase, Ferenc Ternovszky, and Witold Morawski.

CONTENTS

LIST OF FIGURES AND TABLES

FIGURES

TABLES

ABBREVIATIONS AND ACRONYMS

AGM	Annual General Meeting
BSP	Bulgarian Socialist Party
CEET	Central and Eastern European Team
CFTUOB	Community of Free Trade Unions of Bulgaria
CITUB	Confederation of Independent Trade Unions in Bulgaria
CMEA	Council for Mutual Economic Assistance
CMKOZ	Czech and Moravian Trade Union Confederation
CSKOZ	Czech and Slovak Trade Union Confederation
EBRD	European Bank for Reconstruction and Development
ECE	Economic Commission for Europe
Edinstvo	Unity (Bulgarian Trade Union)
ESRC	Economic and Social Research Council
ETUC	European Trade Union Confederation
ETUI	European Trade Union Institute
EU	European Union
FITUR	Federation of Independent Trade Unions of Russia
Fratia	'Brotherhood' National Free Trade Union Confederation of Romania
GDP	gross domestic product
HRM	human resource management
ICCEES	International Council for Central and East European Studies
ICFTU	International Confederation of Free Trade Unions
IFI	international financial institutions
IIRA	International Industrial Relations Association
ILO	International Labour Organization
ILO-CEET	International Labour Office/Organization—Central and Eastern Europe Team
IMF	International Monetary Fund
KOZ	Slovak Confederation of Trade Unions
Liga	The League (Hungary)
MNC	multinational company
MSzOSz	National Federation of Hungarian Trade Unions
NATO	North Atlantic Treaty Organization
NCRI	National Council for the Reconciliation of Interests (Hungary)
NEM	New Economic Mechanism
NEP	New Economic Policy
OECD	Organization for Economic Cooperation and Development
OPZZ	Association of Polish Trade Unions

PHARE	Poland and Hungary Assistance for the Reconstruction of the Economy
Podkrepa	Support (Bulgarian Trade Union)
RTK	Russian Trilateral Commission
SOTSPROF	Association of Socialist Trade Unions (Russia)
SZOT	Central Council of the Trade Unions (Hungary)
TACIS	Technical Assistance for the Commonwealth of Independent States
UDF	Union of Democratic Forces (Bulgaria)
UN	United Nations
VGMK	enterprise work partnership (Hungary)

1

Eastern European and Russian Labour Relations in Comparative Context

This volume seeks to explain the dynamics of labour-relations changes in a number of Eastern European countries: Bulgaria, Hungary, the Czech Republic and Slovakia, Poland, and Russia. It was generally assumed, both inside and outside the countries of Eastern Europe and Russia, that market-ization, and in particular privatization, of the economies would rapidly transform the structure of authority and interests, the institutions, and the patterns of behaviour that had characterized the previous period of soviet labour relations. There were high expectations of an inflow of foreign capital, technology and expertise, and aid from international agencies which would smooth the transition to a market economy. These presumptions about the rapid move towards a 'normal' economy resulted in labour-relations issues being seen as contingent upon wider economic and political change and not of strategic importance in themselves. A further expectation reinforced this neglect—namely, that a fast transition to a market economy would depoliti-cize the enterprise and take the politics out of labour relations. Hence, it was assumed that labour relations would also be 'normalized'.

In practice the political changes in Eastern Europe have been accompanied by the attempted transfer, imposition, and imitation of some industrial-relations institutions and mechanisms from other market economies, primarily, of Western Europe. These developments have themselves had a role in the form and progress of economic and political transformation. This book will address the extent to which these transferred labour-relations institutions are likely to take root and whether Eastern Europe is fertile ground for the establishment of Western-style labour relations. In order to do this the volume explores the role of labour relations in the wider transformation of these societies and the interaction between the national level of political and economic reform and processes of change at the level of the enterprise.

In analyses of the processes of economic and political transformation in Eastern Europe and Russia the enterprise as a level of investigation has generally been neglected. One notable exception to this is the work of Clarke and his colleagues who have undertaken extensive case-study research in Russia (for example, see Clarke *et al.* 1993; Clarke *et al.* 1994). However, many studies of privatization have tended to concentrate upon the framing of laws and regulations (see Chapter 4), whilst commentators on political change have focused upon the developing machinery of liberal democracy at the national level. A key focus of this volume is processes of change at enterprise level. The enterprise was a key institution of the previous system of economic and political regulation and thus constitutes a very specific legacy. In the context of the removal of the old communist-party structures within the enterprise and the recognition of trade unions as legitimate and independent actors, there has been a freeing-up of interests at enterprise level, creating the space for new labour-relations strategies. Debates over privatization strategies, replacements of enterprise directors, wage conflicts, and disputes between the emerging plurality of trade unions have all contributed to the day-to-day reality of change in these societies.

This opening chapter has three main functions. It begins by considering, briefly, how labour relations were viewed under the command system and introduces the concept of legacy which will be used throughout the book. Secondly, it locates the discussion in the context of existing comparative labour or industrial-relations research. Thirdly, it establishes the structure for the discussion in the following chapters.

THE LEGACY OF THE SOVIET MODEL OF LABOUR RELATIONS

In socialist theory, property was the dominant topic in explaining labour relations. Indeed, before the 1980s, labour relations, as such, with the exception of those in Yugoslavia, typically were not separated from the category of production relations which derived from the ownership of the means of production. From the 1980s, economic reforms in the Soviet Union and Bulgaria led to a reconceptualization of labour relations focused upon the relationship between four parties: the workers, the enterprise, the labour collective, and the trade union (Hethy 1991: 348; Petkov and Thirkell 1992: 2–3). This is in comparison to the Western characterization of labour-relations models in terms of the relations between the trade union, the employer, and the state (e.g. Moerel 1994: 4–9).

Moerel has noted that the political dominance of the Soviet Union across Eastern Europe led to a relatively homogenous model of labour relations across the region (1994: 137; see also Clarke and Fairbrother 1994*b*: 394). Slomp characterized it in the following terms: 'The model combined strong state and managerial power over labor conditions and a complete lack of union autonomy' (1990: 95). Labour codes provided the normative regulation defining labour conditions and welfare provisions, specifying the role of the unions, and, although strikes were not prohibited, neither were they allowed (Slomp 1990: 166–7; 1992: 21–4). The main internal challenges to the model came first from the Yugoslav path of 'self-management' in the 1950s (see, e.g., Slomp 1990: 171–9) and then from Solidarity in Poland in the 1980s. There were also increasingly significant differences between Eastern European countries in the institutions for employee participation developed in the 1970s and 1980s (Slomp 1990: 197–200; Thirkell *et al.* 1995*a*: 21–3).

The significance of the enterprise in the command economies of Eastern Europe had a number of important dimensions. First, the Communist Party organization and its membership were based on the enterprise as the place of work and the enterprise provided not only earnings and employment but a whole range of social, welfare, and other services. The official trade unions as a transmission belt for Party policy supported management in encouraging productivity and also developed into the main agency for the distribution of enterprise-based services. As a result of this pivotal role in the delivery of social and welfare policy, although trade-union membership was voluntary, in practice virtually everyone was a member. By contrast, the role of senior management within the enterprise was focused less on the internal running of the plant and more on the external role of bargaining with the planning ministries.

In the centrally planned economy the nature of the planning process shaped the role of senior enterprise management. Plans, prepared by the ministries but approved by the Party, had legal status. Their content was the outcome of bargaining at ministerial levels between enterprises and ministries. Revisions were frequently imposed from the higher levels. Implementation was the responsibility of the parallel structures of the ministry and the Party: vertical control by the ministry was supplemented by horizontal control from the territorial Party organization. The role of senior management in enterprises was focused upon bargaining with these external agencies.

The internal enterprise organizational structures and the mechanisms of labour relations were designed from above, leaving limited space for management to initiate internal strategy within the enterprise, thus confining it to operational issues. The role of enterprise management in bargaining to secure a good plan target had consequences for labour relations. As Mako and Novoszath (1995: 260) remark, this typically led to company-level cooperation: 'The management and workers (trade unions) organized themselves into a coalition of interests in a continuing struggle with central organizations (ministries etc.) over the distribution of centrally supplied resources . . .' (see also Clarke and Fairbrother 1994*b*: 369–73).

Burawoy and Lukacs (1992: 96–100) argue that in the command system the role of middle managers (for example, departmental managers) was contradictory, with real managerial power residing above and below them. Senior managers were responsible for bargaining with the Party state and first-line managers had discretion over allocation of work and the distribution of bonuses in order to try and meet plan targets at operational level. It has often been noted that this pattern of internal organization led to considerable shop-floor autonomy and a considerable degree of worker control over the labour process, at least by Western standards (see, e.g., Petkov and Thirkell 1991: 160–8; Burawoy and Krotov 1992: 25–8; Burawoy and Lukacs 1992: 65–78). This flexibility at shop-floor level was necessary to cope with shortages in supplies and poorly maintained or inadequate machinery and technology.

It is this apparently indulgent style of labour relations which many Western economists have expected privatization and the institution of 'real owners' rapidly to overcome (see Chapter 4 below). The key question for the labour-relations researcher is the extent to which, and in what manner, these earlier specific forms of organization constitute an enduring legacy in the present. In earlier work the authors referred to the path-dependent character of labour-relations transformation, pointing to the impact of different mechanisms of 'self-management' in the 1980s for contemporary trade-union caution towards participation mechanisms other than collective bargaining (Thirkell *et al.* 1995*b*: 180). Although it was useful to identify such orientations as part of a legacy, the notion of 'path dependency' turns out to be too rigid to capture the continuing, but disjointed, influence of legacies from the past. Nielsen *et al.* (1995: 6–7) have suggested the term 'path shaping' as a less deterministic formulation (see also Hill *et al.* 1997). There is an important rhetorical significance in using these terms—path dependency, path shaping, or legacy: it makes the necessary point that change in the present is inevitably built upon the fabric of the past. However, it is equally clear that the countries of Eastern Europe are not entirely prisoners of their history. As Hyman (1994*a*: 4) has commented in a different context: 'the relative importance of change and continuity can alter; and it is for this reason that historical analysis can plausibly speak of turning-points . . .'. The task for researchers is to be able to use the notion of legacy in a way that allows the identification of enduring patterns from the past but also shows the limits to such continuity. Thus, the notion of legacy here is seen as composed of patterns of authority and interests (power relations), institutions and behaviour and beliefs from the previous regimes which, depending upon the specific conjuncture of events, may or may not continue to influence and shape the present. Thus, legacies may constrain or facilitate certain developments and may result in the modification or corruption of policies and approaches imported from outside or they may be irrelevant in changed circumstances.

Other commentators have outlined the broad contours of the political and economic legacy bequeathed to the new generations of leaders in Eastern Europe and Russia. Kornai (1992: 577–80), for example, points to the backward state of machinery and technical know-how, poor human capital, and the legacy of inherited institutions. Ernst *et al.* (1996: 8–10) consider the differential impact of economic and industrial 'misdevelopment' and macroeconomic imbalances. Dittrich (1994: 159) argues that four remnants from the past will be enduringly significant: the Soviet structure of economic sectors; the lack of integration into the world economy; weak currencies, and external debt. These analyses are useful in pointing the way towards explanations for the variations in policies and their success in the different countries in the region. In this discussion the concern is with the impact of legacy on the specific institutions of labour relations and on the orientations of the main actors in labour relations. As Schmidt (1995: 6) has commented: 'On the one hand institutions provide continuity, reliability and resistance to change, yet on the other hand, in modern differentiated societies they are often the most important agents and mediators of change, and are able to undergo stages of change both by adaptation and innovation.'

This provides a starting point, for example, in understanding the role of some of the reformed trade-union confederations in Eastern Europe, in which such agencies from the past have been able to move into new functions taking many of their previous organizational resources and members with them (see Chapter 5). Part of the work in this volume is to try to uncover and explain the impact of legacy on current and future developments in labour relations. From the above discussion we can pinpoint a number of legacies of the soviet period which might be expected to continue to exert an influence over the shape and direction of change in the period of transformation. At the level of power and authority, the state is unlikely to be able to divest itself of its key economic role quickly and the relative weakness of capital may inhibit the rapid development of the capitalist class. At the level of institutions, the significance of the enterprise as a foundation for not only economic but also social and political organization may constrain attempts to depoliticize employment relations. Traditions of self-management, though varying from country to country, may complicate attempts to privatize enterprises as well as conditioning different actors' views of desirable mechanisms of employee participation. The legacy of political criteria for success and promotion in managerial positions may bequeath a managerial stratum whose skills are at odds with the emerging demands of a market economy. At the level of behaviour and beliefs, the Soviet commitment to full employment, the relatively egalitarian wage structure of the past, the privileging of manual over mental labour, and the habit of cooperation between management and workers at enterprise level *vis-à-vis* the ministries outside may all prove significant in structuring the perceived interests and strategies of actors. The empirical task in this volume is to show when or if such legacies constrain or facilitate adaptation and change.

COMPARATIVE LABOUR RELATIONS

Comparative-labour-relations research was traditionally concerned with the extent to which labour-relations models converge on a standard pattern according to the level of technological development of the economy of which they are an element (Dunlop 1958; Kerr *et al.* 1960). In recent times European integration has spawned discussion about the scope for the development of a pan-European approach to industrial relations which minimizes differences between member states (see, e.g., Streeck and Schmitter 1991; Streeck 1992; Hall 1994). The collapse of the Soviet model of labour relations also raises questions about the extent to which marketization and privatization of the

Eastern European economies will result in the convergence of labour-relations models with Western European patterns over time.

Within the Western European literature there are a number of conceptualizations of how to compare and classify labour-relations models. Slomp (1990; 1992) uses a three-parties and three-levels approach: employer organizations, worker organizations, and the state, and then patterns of decision-making between the parties at central, sector, and enterprise levels. This results in three broad clusters or models: the British, the German or Northern European, and the French. Similar distinctions are made by other authors—for example, between the 'Anglo-Saxon' model and the 'continental' model of collective bargaining (Martin *et al.* 1996); or between 'contestation' and 'corporatism' (van Hoof 1992). In one of the most thorough and impressive attempts to understand the diversity of models within Western Europe Crouch (1993: 350) argues for an approach which acknowledges that: 'differences in industrial relations systems reflect deeper historical differences . . .'. He provides a theory of exchange in industrial relations which cross references the power of organized labour (low to high) with the level of organizational articulation of both capital and labour (low to high), resulting in four 'varieties' of system: (1) pluralistic bargaining or contestation, stable; (2) pluralistic bargaining or contestation, unstable; (3) neo-corporatism with strong labour; and (4) neo-corporatism with weak labour (1993: 43). Such models may provide a starting point for analysis of change in Eastern Europe (e.g. Slomp 1992), though, as Hethy (1991: 349) comments, they do not provide clear blueprints to follow. More negatively, the search for models may lead to a neglect of what are historically specific patterns of development in these countries (for further discussion, see Thirkell *et al.* 1995*b*: 176–86).

The transference, imitation, or redesign of labour-relations institutions between countries and types of society raise several questions about the prospects for such developments. In principle, transferred institutions may develop or decay, be eroded, or take on new forms. There is also the question of the extent to which transfer or imitation is accompanied by the transformation of existing indigenous institutions and their evolution or decline. The answers to such questions have to be set in the context of several factors. These include: the political and economic conditions under which such transference and imitation occur; the patterns of political and economic institutions which arise after the regime changes; and the legacy of existing labour relations.

It has been noted that a distinguishing feature of the changes in Eastern Europe, in contrast to, for example, post-war Germany or post-Franco Spain, is that there is no legacy of capitalist financial institutions and no clear separation between the mechanisms of political and economic management (Offe 1996: 131). The transfer and imitation of industrial-relations institutions found in developed market economies have, therefore, taken place in Eastern Europe in conditions where markets are being created. The principal institutional changes that emerged rapidly after the political changes were as follows: the autonomous emergence of new independent trade unions and the separation of established unions from the communist party state; the legalization of collective bargaining for the determination of wages and conditions of employment; and the establishment of national tripartite institutions, especially for the determination of wage policy.

The outstanding condition common to the different economies in Eastern Europe in 1989 was economic crisis and the need for macroeconomic stabilization. This was interpreted as requiring policies for the general depression of wages (see Chapter 6). In these conditions the maintenance of social peace was seen by governments and the international financial institutions (IFI) as an essential condition for the development of the programmes of economic reform through privatization and the restructuring of the economy. Tripartism was seen as one very important means for securing social consent in the context of macroeconomic stabilization. At a formal level it appears both that there is a remarkable similarity in the patterns of development from one country to another and that some institutions characteristic of Western industrial-relations systems have been transferred into Eastern Europe. However, as Offe (1995: 57) cautions: ' "copied" and transplanted institutions that lack the moral and cultural infrastructure on which the "original" can rely are likely to yield very different and often counter-intentional results'.

This suggests that it may be possible to transfer an institution but it is much more difficult to imitate the context in which it has flourished. Trade unions, labour ministries, and political parties in Eastern Europe have looked to Western European models of labour relations as potential benchmarks for their own development (see, e.g., Hill *et al.* 1997: 236; Toth 1997: 165). For many trade unions the possibility of imitating a German or Scandinavian neo-corporatist model has looked enticing. Much of the discussion of Eastern European 'transition' is built on the premiss of, often unstated, ideal typical models of Western capitalism. In respect of labour relations, this model comprises a set of interrelated hypotheses: regime change will lead to the establishment of liberal market economies which will result in the depoliticization or destatization of labour relations as the state withdraws from the arena of labour relations other than to provide the basic legislation on worker rights; the withdrawal of the state and the privatization of enterprises enable management to develop strategy at enterprise level and to reassert managerial control in response to the pressures of 'real owners' and hard budget constraints; trade unions now independent of the communist party are in a position to appeal to employees as the genuine representatives of their interests at national, sector, or regional and enterprise levels; depending upon trade-union strength, this allows for the development of free collective bargaining or other mechanisms of exchange or conflict resolution to emerge between private employers and independent trade unions. The logic of such hypotheses is clear: labour relations are dependent upon the prevailing forms of political and economic organization; change the society from a single-party-ruled command economy to a liberal, pluralistic market economy and the institutions of labour relations will follow.

If the destination of this model is apparently clear, the best route is much less obvious. As Crouch (1993) admirably demonstrates, the institutions characteristic of labour relations in the West have been built up over the long haul of history. The extent to which the soviet period represented a decisive break or rupture from pre-Second World patterns of Central and Eastern European labour relations is obviously significant here. This raises the question of whether the similarities between countries subsumed under the Soviet model were more significant than the differences. Clarke and Fairbrother (1994b: 394) have a firm answer to the problem: 'Although the countries of eastern Europe have their own traditions of independent labour organization to which to appeal, the old structures were systematically destroyed in the Soviet period and replaced with the distinctive forms of social organization and control which had been established in the Soviet Union.'

Here it is argued that the imposition of the Soviet model of labour relations was a distinctive breaking point with the past but that the evolution of that model in the different countries has varied. The significance of such differences is an empirical question which the analysis throughout this volume seeks to address. Taking such a historical perspective, it is unlikely that the countries of Eastern Europe and Russia could rapidly replicate the conditions in which Western European patterns of labour relations have developed. Two legacies of the Soviet period are likely to exert their influence on labour relations for a long time: the absence of independent capital and the weakness of employers' organizations; and the continuing significance of the state as an employer and as a principal agent in labour relations. As many have noted, in the first six years of reform we have not witnessed the withdrawal of the state on anything like the scale expected (Dittrich and Haferkemper 1995: 141–3; Martin *et al.* 1996: 3). It is a commonly held tenet of Western analysis that: 'a free market involves a separation of political institutions and the industrial relations system' (Martin *et al.* 1996: 10). Although the change in these societies has resulted in a plurality of interest organizations representing employers and workers, they are far from being the stable, independent, and organizationally robust institutions that would be recognized from Western experience. It is clear that in the first phase of transformation there has not been a rapid depoliticization of labour relations in Eastern Europe and Russia (Thirkell *et al.* 1995b: 176–86). It is for this reason that a number of writers have argued against the implied Eurocentrism of many approaches and have posed the question as to whether Latin America or South East Asia might provide more appropriate models; contexts in which the state has had a more dominant influence on economic development than in western or northern Europe (see e.g., Amsden *et al.* 1994; Henderson *et al.* 1995). A quotation may amply demonstrate the point:

it must also be recognized that the risks of abuse of authority remain very real . . . as they are born of a cultural tradition which cannot simply be eliminated by decree or by a change of political thinking of the times. Moreover, one can reasonably wonder whether the forces at work in the industrial relations system are sufficiently stable to interact without state intervention; indeed judging from the weakness and fragmentation of the trade union movement in a number of countries, such doubts seem to be justified. Another reasonable question is whether the social partners are quite ready fully to take on their responsibilities in an industrial relations system with minimal state intervention, or whether they still need the State's guiding hand, for the same reason as individual workers do. (Bronstein 1995: 176)

Although, apparently, an insightful judgement of the Eastern European situation, these comments were actually made about industrial relations in Latin America. Equally, commentators on Russia have wondered whether, in the context of the tradition of enterprise-based welfare and social policy systems and the legacy of paternalism in Russian enterprises, the Japanese model of enterprise trade unionism is not a more plausible outcome of Russian transformation than anything equating to northern European industrial-relations traditions (see, e.g., Clarke and Fairbrother 1993*d*: 194). Ultimately for the researcher it is not a question of which model to follow but rather how best to understand the dynamics of change.

If conditions in the countries look unlikely to lead rapidly towards the institutionalization of Western patterns of labour relations, it is still possible that similar structures might be imposed or transferred from outside. Transplanting labour-relations conventions from one institutional or cultural context to another has been a perennial topic of comparative industrial relations, most recently discussed in respect of the success of multinational companies in transferring institutions and procedures from one country to another (see, e.g., Marginson and Sisson 1994, 1996). In Eastern Europe there have been three potential avenues for transplanting labour-relations ideas and practices: through exhortation and imposition, when international agencies like the World Bank or the International Monetary Fund (IMF) may tie financial support to acceptance of certain policies; through imitation, where governments, trade unions, or managers may try to copy policies or approaches they have seen or experienced in other countries; and, lastly, through example in foreign takeovers or joint ventures, where managers, techniques, and philosophies may be transferred into eastern Europe. The exceptional case has been eastern Germany, where the existing institutions of western Germany were imposed on the east. Even in this extreme example it has been argued that, although institutions may have been transferred, their impact or role may be different as they are adapted and used in the prevailing local circumstances (Offe 1995; Hyman 1996). This confirms the need for detailed empirical work and the importance of analysing the enterprise level. As Niland and Clarke (1991: 173) observed: 'The best test of alleged "change" is whether it significantly affects the relations of management and workers and the terms of employment at the workplace itself.'

Other recent work in the field of comparative labour relations in the West also suggests the need to focus on the enterprise. It is perhaps particularly ironic that, just as trade unions in the East glimpse the possibility of obtaining some of the advantages of Western European systems, scholars in the West are increasingly identifying the fracture and decomposition of Western European models of labour relations in the context of economic globalization (see, e.g., Streeck 1992). Writers such as Locke, Kochan, and Piore (1995: 140) have questioned the relevance of the earlier focus on national traditions, arguing instead that it is no longer so useful to put the emphasis 'on national models as units of analysis'. This approach, in part, arises from the argument that the balance of power between capital and labour in First World labour relations shifted in the 1980s, putting employers firmly in the driving seat of change (Clarke and Niland 1991: 172; Martin 1992; Hyman 1994a: 11). In an increasingly global economy, the key differences in industrial-relations practice may be from sector to sector and from enterprise to enterprise, depending upon the specific competitive conditions and the strategic choices made by managers. But strategic choice will be filtered or constrained by varying institutional mechanisms from context to context (Kochan *et al.* 1986: 11–12; Locke *et al.* 1995: 140–1). Nevertheless, this suggests that the unit of analysis for industrial-relations specialists becomes the enterprise situated in its historical, national, market, and organizational context. Such an approach has both advantages and disadvantages for the analysis of events in Eastern Europe and Russia. It is problematic, because the position of 'employers' is very diverse and the state remains the most significant employer in many countries. The continuing involvement of the state in day-to-day management of enterprises may indeed, as Martin, Vidinova, and Hill (1996: 13) suggest in the case of Bulgaria, weaken management's position:

In market economies, declining product markets and fears of increasing unemployment are associated with perceptions of increased managerial bargaining power, even if this increased power is unevenly distributed between employers. However, the specific political and economic environment during the transition in Bulgaria *reduced* managerial authority.   (Emphasis in original.)

However, with the increasingly differentiated nature of ownership structures in eastern Europe and Russia—encompassing multinational companies (MNCs), joint ventures, new private small and medium-sized enterprises, remaining large state-owned enterprises, new employee-owned and many forms of privatized enterprises—the focus on the enterprise and the scope for differentiation of practice *within* nations is instructive, perhaps especially at a time of such economic and political turbulence.

In researching change in labour relations in Eastern Europe and Russia it has, therefore, been necessary to consider both the national level of changing normative regulation and developing political bargains but also, crucially, what has been happening at the level of the individual enterprise. The search for a new 'model' of labour relations may only serve to obscure the emerging heterogeneity of practice in individual enterprises—hence, the importance and value of combining a case-study approach with a wider analysis of the political and economic context of labour relations. It is hoped that, by comparing 'almost identical countries' in comparative terms (Moerel 1994*a*: 24), the discussion here will benefit from being able to analyse why certain transplants or imitations have had salience in some countries and not others. It will also be able to uncover the subtleties of transformation and the deviations from apparently similar starting points in each case.

It is clear from the above that it will be argued here that current developments in labour relations in Eastern Europe and Russia can be understood only by reference to the legacies from the past; however, although it is necessary to consider the past, it is not sufficient for an understanding of the present and the future. Many of the questions and issues raised so far can begin to be resolved only by an empirical analysis of transformation. This requires the specification of the levels, agents, and dynamics of labour-relations change. In the past the principal agents in labour relations were the parallel structures of the party and the state ministries, enterprise management, and the labour collective. The main levels of interaction were the branch (sector) and the enterprise. In the period of transformation, with the collapse of the communist party state, the key agents were expected to become the state, the employers and management, and the reformed or new trade unions, operating at three levels: national, branch, and the enterprise. The dynamic of developments is provided by the interaction of environmental pressures with the strategic choices of the principal agents (Kochan *et al.* 1986: 5). The collapse of the Soviet model and the command structure it entailed frees up interests previously suppressed and creates spaces within which such interests can be pursued. As Hyman (1994*a*: 11) has put it, 'strategic choice exists, not because of the absence or weakness of structural determinations but because these determinations are themselves contradictory'.

In order to operationalize the notion of strategic choice we need to specify not only the agents in labour relations—governments, ministries, employers, managers, trade unions, employees—but also the concepts of resources and space. Resources refer to relative power; the agents in labour relations rarely meet in an arena where power is shared equally. In a capitalist economy it is the asymmetry of power between capital and labour that precipitates labour's collective organization (Crouch 1993: 31). Resources can refer to organization, mobilization, institutions, finance, support, indeed any of the means by which agents seek to achieve their aims. Space refers to conjunctions of events and circumstances in which agents are able successfully to use their resources to pursue strategies. The task here is to uncover the continuing influence of legacies from the past and how in the context of contemporary circumstances the principal agents of labour relations are developing new patterns of inter-actions and new strategies. To do this it is necessary to start with the broad environment in which labour-relations change is situated—the political and economic context. Simply put, for how long do attitudes, values, and institutions relating to the past persist in the context of changing material circumstances, under what conditions can institutions from the past reinvent themselves as effective institutions in the present, and to what extent are new institutions successfully transferred or imitated from outside?

STRUCTURE OF THE BOOK

This volume addresses the questions of change and development in Eastern European and Russian labour relations thematically. Although country-by-country comparisons can be instructive, they tend to remain at the level of description and often fail to provide the analytical insights that can emerge from comparing the similarities and differences in institutions and practice between countries. In the chapters which follow a series of interrelated hypotheses are investigated. Chapter 2 considers the political and economic context for labour-relations change in the different countries. As stated earlier, it has been a taken-for-granted assumption of much economic analysis of transformation that labour relations are contingent upon the political and economic environment. This discussion will consider the extent to which labour-relations events are a constituent element of political and economic reform. A second-order assumption of much of the existing literature is that a change in the political and economic regime will lead rapidly to the depoliticization or destatization of labour relations. The second chapter also investigates the extent to which this has happened.

Chapter 3 considers the role of international agencies in fostering and supporting particular reform projects. These agencies are seen as 'shadow partners' in the development of the reform agenda. The hypothesis that international agencies will force the transference of certain models of economic and political reform in exchange for aid and support is investigated and the implications of this for labour relations are discussed. The prospects for choice and the success or failure of these strategies from outside are considered.

Chapter 4 discusses privatization and its pivotal role in the reform strategies of Eastern European governments. It has been assumed by the architects of privatization both outside and within the countries of eastern Europe that a change in ownership will lead to new patterns of corporate governance resulting in a shift in managerial behaviour as they begin to act on behalf of 'real owners'. In this scenario privatization is expected to be a central mechanism in the reform of enterprise-level labour relations. This chapter tests these suppositions in the light of the real empirical process of ownership change in Russia and Eastern Europe. Building on the discussion in earlier chapters it outlines the contested nature of privatization projects.

In the next chapter the developing role of the trade unions is considered. With the removal of the Communist Party and the reform of its dependent unions it is expected that the trade unions will become genuine independent representatives of the workers—that is, become more like Western trade unions. However, it might also be predicted that the break-up of the command economy could lead to a fragmentation of trade unions. In the context of economic dislocation and rising and persistent unemployment it is also probable that trade-union membership will decline, aggravated further by the impact of an increasingly privately owned economy and the increase of employment in small firms. The strategies and prospects of the different trade unions will be discussed.

Chapter 6 looks at the key areas of distribution and collective bargaining and the scope for the development of 'normal' labour relations and independent collective bargaining between employers and trade unions. Marketization is expected to disrupt the pattern of differentials that were politically prescribed in the Soviet era, as staffing levels and reward structures are redesigned to reflect market conditions. The extent of change is assessed in the light of the continuing role of incomes policies.

Chapters 7 and 8 discuss enterprise-level case studies. The focus is on processes of change and the interaction of the enterprise with its environment. The first compares eight cases, three Russian, three Polish, and one each from Bulgaria and Slovakia. The discussion explores the process of enterprise change and the extent to which changes in ownership have provided management with the opportunity to develop new strategies in labour relations. The second looks specifically at cases of foreign ownership to investigate the extent to which this results in a genuine transfer of Western policies and approaches to labour relations. The chapter is based upon five cases, one Slovak, two Hungarian, and two Bulgarian.

The volume ends by drawing these themes together in the conclusion and summarizing the similarities and differences in developments between the countries. A final assessment is made of the current and likely future success of the transference and imitation of labour-relations institutions from outside and the prospects for the convergence of Eastern European labour relations with those of the rest of Europe.

2

The Transformation of Labour Relations: Political and Economic Contexts

The function of this chapter is to situate developments in labour relations in their broader national, political, and economic contexts. The scope for reform of the labour-relations model is highly contingent upon the prevailing political and economic environment, although the influence is not all in one direction. A basic assumption behind neo-liberal models of 'transition' is that the change in regime to a liberal market model will result in the depoliticization of labour relations and the withdrawal of the state from enterprise administration and management. In this sense, major changes in labour relations are seen as logically subsequent to other political and economic change. This chapter explores the validity of such assumptions; the discussion is organized in three parts. The first section aims to explain, briefly, the nature of the Soviet model of labour relations and its dependence on the economic and political structures of the Soviet model of socialism. This model, developed in the Soviet Union in the 1930s, was imposed on the countries of Central and Eastern Europe after the Second World War. However, especially during the 1980s, there were variations in the patterns of development between countries and this had some influence on the development of their economies and politics after the political changes and impacts upon their labour relations. The second section aims to show how the development of political pluralism and the market economy has been influenced by the imposition of the neo-liberal model of economic transformation. The imposition of this model was a process fostered by the IFI (as discussed in Chapter 3), but also by key groups of economists and politicians within the countries themselves. There were a number of principal elements in this model: macroeconomic stabilization, the development of institutions suitable for a market economy, including privatization of state property, and restructuring and diversifying the economy; however, the implementation of the model varied from country to country. In this section each country is treated as an individual case, showing the strategic choices and turning points in the patterns of development and the differences between the countries. The third section concludes by comparing the patterns of development in the different countries.

THE SOVIET MODEL OF LABOUR RELATIONS

The Soviet model of labour relations was transferred to and imposed on the countries of Eastern Europe in the late 1940s and there was a similar, though not identical, model throughout the region. The principal components of this model were created with the establishment of the administrative command system of political and economic management at the beginning of the 1930s. The model was designed to reflect certain values regarded as fundamental features of socialism. Thus, one of the central values of the socialist system was the maintenance of full employment (which has been a central problem for capitalist economies), which was underpinned by the operation of the planning mechanisms. For the development of the planned economy the working class was given a leading role and accompanying this was an egalitarian approach to wage distribution which also favoured physical labour relative to mental labour.

Officially the foundation of the planned economy was the state ownership of the means of production, so that state property was the basis of 'production relations' (the concept of labour relations became gradually recognized only during the 1980s) (Petkov and Thirkell 1991: 1–3). It has been argued by Kornai (1992: 361–2), however, that the power of the communist party and its ideology were more important than the state ownership of property in the socialist system. The organizational basis of the communist party was certainly in the workplace and its members affiliated there. The party's main functions at this level derived from its accountability for plan fulfilment and the operation of the cadre system for appointments and promotions. It was not officially a party in labour relations but, in practice, it was not unusual for the party organization to play a role in resolving internal organizational conflicts and in maintaining the pattern of cooperation between managers and the workforce.

The nature and functions of the other institutions of labour relations were mainly derived from the centralized system for the planned management of the economy. Plans were implemented organizationally through the structures of branch-based ministries to which all enterprises were affiliated, but the territorial party and trade unions had an important role in exercising control over plan fulfilment. Enterprise organizational structures were centrally prescribed, as were the tariff grade structures (usually on a branch basis) which determined the rate for each job. Wage policy, through control of the enterprise wage fund, was enforced.

The trade unions were organized on the branch principle, but were primarily accountable to the territorial organization; they were subordinate to the party and operated according to the rules of democratic centralism. Their main, dual, functions were those of promoting production (especially through the mechanisms of socialist emulation) and the distribution of social welfare. The enterprise collective agreement signed annually by the director and the trade-union president did not include wages and was mainly focused on measures to fulfil the production plan and its relationship to the provision of social welfare. Although the consent of the trade union was required for the dismissal of individuals, its function was not that of representing the interests of the workforce as a whole. A key feature of distribution was the success of the enterprise director in securing plan indicators in negotiations with higher levels in the ministry and in this aspect he or she could be seen as representing the interests of the workforce. Substantive standards for different aspects of the employment relationship were set out in the labour codes and associated regulations.

The Reform Process of the 1980s

Changes in the 1980s differed significantly between countries. In the Soviet Union and Bulgaria and subsequently Czechoslovakia the reform process was initiated from the top. Its basic assumption was that the goal of improving production and productivity was to be addressed in terms of motivating the workforce rather than the management. Hitherto, improvement had been seen as essentially a technical and engineering problem, but now the 'human factor' of the workers at the base was identified as the critical consideration (Zaslavskaya 1986). Although reform of the wage system was attempted at this time (Filtzer 1994) in respect of wage control, the wage fund and wage structures remained. Other mechanisms for motivational change came to be incorporated within the concept of self-management. This involved giving powers to the labour collective, for example, in the elections of directors and supervisors, and especially in changing the labour process through the brigade organization of work. The brigade organization of work, which was promoted especially in the 1980s in the Soviet Union, Bulgaria, and Czechoslovakia, involved the payment of wages to the brigade as a collective (team) instead of to individual workers. Commonly, the decisions on the distribution of earnings within the brigade were made by the members of the brigade or their representatives on the brigade council. Ownership change was also seen as a potentially important motivator, and the introduction of *arenda* (leasing) in 1989 was a further stage intended to improve the motivation of both managers and workers.

In the Soviet Union the powers given to the Council of the Labour Collective in relation to the distribution of social funds was potentially a threat to the partnership between the Director and the Trade Union Committee which had shared control over them. Generally, therefore, directors and the trade union were not in favour of the transfer of these functions to the Council of the Labour Collective (Voeikov 1997).

The distinguishing feature of change in Poland was, of course, that it derived from below, through Solidarity, which challenged the Party at its base in the workplace, so that this level became the focus of politics (personal communication, W. Morawski). In Poland the concept of self-management was used as a framework for political opposition to the Party and the state and displaced the political salience of motivation found in the Soviet Union, Bulgaria, and Czechoslovakia. The pressure from Solidarity resulted in significant changes in the model of labour relations through the creation of enterprise councils and in the reconstitution and reform of the established trade unions. However, there were only limited developments in marketization: prices were nominally freer than in Hungary but reforms did not break the central allocative system (Myant 1993). There was, therefore, a major change in politics and the institutions of labour relations without major changes in economic organization.

In Hungary, reform was an incremental process led politically from the top and focused upon changes in economic mechanisms. As early as 1968 there was an explicit emphasis on the importance of managerial leadership as the key agent in the process. The changes in the planning process led to an increase in enterprise autonomy. Although the core industrial structures remained monopolistic, there was significant development of the second economy in which there were elements of competition. Changes in labour relations, especially at the level of the enterprise, were generally derived from changes in economic mechanisms. They included a representative role for shop stewards and the right of trade unions to veto managerial decisions. At national level, trade unions were not independent of the party but claimed a measure of autonomy. National control over wages remained, although it was debated. There was, however, a conscious attempt to limit its constraint on motivation through the enterprise work partnerships (VGMKs), which operated outside the central wage control. The establishment of enterprise councils and managerial elections in 1985 reduced the role of the Party organization in the enterprise.

It is clear from this discussion that at the point of regime change in each of the countries there had already been some shift away from the classical model of Soviet labour relations and that the nature of such changes varied from country to country. In particular, there were differences in the significance and power of institutions of self-management and variations in the degree of enterprise autonomy. These contrasts provide the specific legacies of each case and influenced both the nature of regime change and the continuing development of their labour-relations models.

Underlying all the changes introduced in labour relations during the 1980s was the relative economic failure of the centrally planned economies in terms of a range of economic criteria, including growth of GDP, productivity, and the level of real wages. Attempts at extrication from the crisis became the driving force for both the search for the market economy and the development of political pluralism which led to the imposition of a neo-liberal model of economic transformation.

THE DEVELOPMENT OF POLITICAL PLURALISM AND THE
SEARCH FOR A MARKET ECONOMY

This section considers how each of the countries have been influenced by, and
have responded to, the imposition of a neo-liberal model of economic transformation. There are a number of common elements in this model. The first
was macroeconomic stabilization as the means for reducing the economic crisis which was common to all countries (the various aspects of stabilization are
discussed in Chapter 3). The second was the development of the institutions
suitable for a market economy including the privatization of state property.
The third element was diversifying the structure of the economy by encouraging the development of privately owned small and medium-sized enterprises and the provision of services. This implied the significant restructuring
of industrial branches and of industrial enterprises and their exposure to competition. In the presentation of the country cases the first aim is to explain the
political processes in terms of the stability or instability of governments, their
strategies, and the nature of their popular support. The second aim is to
explain the processes of economic reform especially in relation to economic
stabilization and restructuring through privatization and in relation to the
political processes. The third aim is then to discuss those aspects of labour
relations which were determined directly at national level, especially tripartism and labour legislation, and those which contributed to the shaping of
processes at that level. The latter relate particularly to the occurrence or
absence of industrial action and the maintenance of social peace which has
been regarded as an essential precondition for economic reform. Contrary to
the assumptions built into the neo-liberal model that regime change will lead
rapidly to the depoliticization and destatization of labour relations, we
explore the difficulties of achieving such a separation in practice.

Poland

In 1989, when Solidarity entered the Round Table negotiations on political
change with the government, the immediate legacy was an economic crisis.
There was hyperinflation, resulting from the government's attempt to
maintain consent since 1985 by substantial wage increases, fuelled further
by continuing wage pressures, massive shortages, and a large foreign debt.
The political climate was characterized by a widespread sense of economic
failure. The Round Table negotiations which led to the agreement of 5 April
were focused on three main issues: the political legitimation of Solidarity;
the development of the private sector but not privatization; and wage indexation and social benefits. Thus, labour relations were both a contested and a
substantial part of the process of exchange in the political transformation
deal.

In the June election the triumph of Solidarity was unexpected (Balcerowicz 1995: 293). This presented a challenge for the new government, which had no developed programme for economic reform although it was the central political issue. In these circumstances there was an opportunity for the group of 'technopols' headed by Balcerowicz to occupy the political space and formulate the strategic choice of economic policy under the protection of the Prime Minister Mazowiecki. Balcerowicz acknowledges that most Polish economists would have favoured a more gradual approach than the rapid shock therapy and stabilization package prepared by his team and discussed with the representatives of the IMF. The IMF had no reservations about it and the critical international loan was quickly forthcoming. The rejection of gradualism was a turning point. Balcerowicz presented the political choice as one shaped by the need 'to shut our eyes and jump into the hole without checking either the state of the water or the depth of the drop' (Myant 1993: 84). Listening to Sachs (an economic adviser to the Mazowiecki government), a Solidarity economist commented to Kuron that this was nonsense, to which Kuron replied 'I don't know much about what he is arguing for, but listening to it I know that it has political value' (Myant 1993: 85). Shock therapy filled the policy vacuum for a government with no economic programme. The strategic choice of shock therapy as the economic reform policy was, therefore, the product of a very specific configuration of political agencies. Balcerowicz uses the concept of 'extraordinary politics' for the period 1989–90—a period characterized by the clear discontinuity in a country's history, a deep economic crisis, the breakdown of the institutional system, and liberation from foreign domination. In extraordinary politics there is space for technopols—that is, people like Balcerowicz. If they are not there, the opportunity will be missed. There is soon a return to normal politics: parties and interest groups, institutional constraints, and less willingness to act for the common good.

The subsequent development of the political process in Poland was one of frequent elections and changes of government in 1991, 1992, and 1993. Political instability was related to the fragmentation of political parties and their inability to maintain popular support during the economic transformation. In fact, there was a continuing pattern of strikes which contributed to the precariousness of governments. Thus, the fall of the Suchodska government in 1992 was influenced by trade-union, as well as by direct political, pressures. (The significance of elections as turning points for Solidarity is discussed in Chapter 5.) The initial conception of Solidarity as providing the counter political élite and as the umbrella for economic reform was constrained by divisions within the organization. The process of political change in Poland was one in which Solidarity became the mass social and political movement united by opposition to the Communist government, but when the Party lost power the main unifying force of Solidarity disappeared and the divisions developed rapidly. As a movement it depended on the active participation and mobilization of the industrial working class, which was the product of socialism and became its gravedigger in Poland, but 'these were the workers who had to face the negative consequences of the transition to a market economy, the first being the actual or potential unemployment' (Balcerowicz 1995: 294). Simultaneously, Solidarity's intelligentsia became the counter élite and separated from the workers at the base. These features are central to understanding subsequent developments in Poland—elsewhere there was no large-scale mobilization of the industrial working class in the process of political change. This was a factor which limited the time span of the political consensus in support of the reform package introduced in January 1990. The other distinctive political features of Poland which influenced the economic reforms, as compared with the Czech Republic and Hungary, were characterized by Balcerowicz (1995: 322) as 'strong and rather aggressive trade unions; frequent elections and a fragmented party system'.

The shock-therapy package of January 1990 was especially directed to the control of inflation and consisted of price liberalization, balancing the budget, and tight monetary and wage control. The results of the package are a matter of controversy (the worst recession, or not so bad as Balcerowicz argues). An alternative would have been to have adopted a more gradual approach focused on systemic change and especially the break-up of monopolies (Myant 1993: 86). Shock therapy was assumed to lead to rapid adaptation and speedy recovery. It produced the deepest depression and failed to produce adaptation and restructuring in manufacturing industry (Myant 1993: 107).

The continuation of neo-liberal policies was not officially abandoned but attempts to soften their application was a continuing political issue. Balcerowicz, as architect of these policies, left office in December 1991. The left government elected in 1993 accepted the principles of the neo-liberal package but was sensitive to the need to seek consent for their implementation. A continuing contested issue in the political arena from 1989 was the privatization of large enterprises as a means of structural economic reform. The Law on Privatization of July 1990, patterned on the UK model (Ernst *et al.* 1996: 105), set up the framework and procedures for the privatization of state enterprises, but implementation was repeatedly delayed. The provision that the employee council should be dissolved on the completion of privatization was one factor influencing trade-union and employee resistance.

The government had recognized as early as the middle of 1990 that social and industrial protests were likely to occur which would require a framework for the resolution of labour-relations disputes, and a package of laws on trade unions, employers' organizations, and disputes procedure was eventually passed in May 1991. The underlying assumption was that, with a rapid transfer to a capitalist economy, it would be possible for the state to stay outside labour negotiations and strike pressure, but this proved completely impossible. 'The fundamental mistake was the elites' belief that the enactment of the legislation would somehow in itself constitute a breakthrough in the process of building a system of interest representation appropriate to a market economy. But this did not happen because . . . actual changes in economic and political relations lagged far behind the assumptions made in the legislation.' (Hausner and Morawski 1994: 1). Most conflicts required the government to intervene. This showed the anticipatory nature of labour codes and legal frameworks in conditions of labour turbulence.

During 1991, and especially from 1992, social and industrial protests against the effects of the recession intensified. The wage tax (*popiwek*) was a continuing issue, but much of the trade-union and employee action was about the threat of unemployment (Kloc 1994: 130). Although key sectors such as mining and transport were involved, there was action and pressure from other branches and regions. This unrest had consequences at the national level in relation to changes of governments and in the recognition of a need to create new structures and mechanisms to secure political consent.

During 1992 there was increased discussion of the need for some form of social pact with tripartite institutions as a mechanism for linking, and solving, major political, industrial, and social problems. The result became known as the Kuron Pact on State Enterprises, after the Minister who facilitated its creation. The pact aimed to encourage privatization and to secure industrial and social support for national wage policies (including the abolition of the *popiwek*), and also to function as a mechanism for resolving differences within Solidarity. The salience of labour relations in Poland thus resulted in the most comprehensive institutional package of any Eastern European country. The pact had three main parts: privatization; the financing of state enterprises including wages; and social-collective agreement on social insurance and application of International Labour Organization (ILO) standards on health and safety. A law on mass privatization was passed in April 1993 but its implementation has been slow. The tripartite commission started work in March 1994 and the new left-wing government elected in September 1993 has continued to use it, but the Commission has been primarily concerned with pay negotiations (Morawski 1997: 310).

The outcome of the economic reform process and its political constraints are contested. For some, Poland, despite significant economic problems, 'is rapidly becoming a "normal" country' (Ernst *et al.* 1996: 79). However, Sylwestrowicz (1995: 31) reported on a conference of Polish economists early in 1995 of whom the majority concluded that 'capitalism is still a long way off'. The shortage of capital is a key factor which constrains further privatization. 'The basic regulator is still the state', which distributes more than 80 per cent of GDP (Sylwestrowicz 1995: 31). However, the 1995 government was formally committed to the continuation of the economic reform and privatization. By 1996 there were no significant differences between the main political organizations on the issues of the transition to capitalism, early entry to the European Union (EU), and membership of the North Atlantic Treaty Organization (NATO).

To summarize the discussion on Poland it is necessary to pick out the following key points. The unexpected victory of Solidarity in the elections created the opportunity for the Balcerowicz group to occupy the strategic space and promote the choice of shock therapy and neo-liberal reform. It was recognized at the outset both that there was popular support for the 'dash to the market' but also that the prestige of Solidarity (as a movement and as a trade union) was necessary to maintain this support. The role of Solidarity as an institution for securing social consent meant that the process of political exchange between the leading agencies in the first phase was bipartite rather than tripartite. However, the consequences of economic reform led to significant protest action, reflected in pressures within the political parties and the fall of Balcerowicz in 1992. As a result, tripartism became essential to the progress of reform, in terms of consent for wage policy and acceptance of the process of privatization. The 1991 framework of labour-relations law was based on the anticipated, but unrealizable, assumption that the state could withdraw from labour relations. Changes of government in 1993 and 1995 influenced the intensity of the stabilization package but did not alter the general direction of economic reform in the absence of any concerted alternative economic programmes. The only opposition came from sporadic sectional labour resistance.

Hungary

From 1968 onwards Hungary came to be regarded as the leader of economic reform in Eastern Europe, although significant political change did not occur for another twenty years. The shift to what has been termed 'a liberalized planned economy' (Hethy and Csuhaj 1990: 14) took place with the decision to introduce the New Economic Mechanism, which ended quantitative central planning policy, increased enterprise autonomy, and focused on profit maximization. In contrast to that of other countries, which emphasized worker motivation, the Hungarian approach was managerialist—the reform depended on 'the two to three hundred thousand executives' and not on the workers (Kadar 1984: 254) and there was no attempt to change labour relations. During the 1970s and early 1980s the general trend was towards greater enterprise autonomy, although there were times of recentralization, as, for example, in 1972. There were elements of marketization especially in relation to prices. Prices of consumer goods were related to costs and there was a wider availability of consumer goods than elsewhere in Eastern Europe.

In labour relations there was a process of incremental change at the level of the enterprise. The focus of collective agreements shifted from plan fulfilment to employment issues. Enterprise trade unions received the right to veto management decisions regarded as injurious to workers' rights and shop stewards had the right of consent over a range of workplace issues in the changes of 1977–80. Although the ILO report of 1984 confirmed that the trade unions were not independent of the Party, it accepted that they had in practice an element of autonomy. However, overall the changes were greater at the level of the enterprise than at the national level. This was equally true of the management of the economy.

During the 1970s international credit had become important for the economy. In 1982 there was a severe liquidity crisis and Hungary became the first East European country to join the IMF and the World Bank. From 1985 there was a series of changes in the organization of enterprises. Elected enterprise councils reduced the power of the Party organization at this level. Enterprise autonomy was now significant and this was followed by reform of the banking system in 1987, both characterized as the delayed second stage of the New Economic Mechanism.

The positive aspects of the socialist legacy were the incremental development of reforms associated with changing economic institutions and the opening-up of the economy over many years. These were paralleled by the reforms of the system of labour relations. The main negative legacy was the size of the foreign debt. Nevertheless, it was not uncommon for outside observers to conclude that Hungary was the best-placed country to make a successful transition to a market economy. Managers were better prepared because of earlier decentralization; the second economy was well developed and trade and price reforms were significant. In Hungary the period of 1988–9 was of decisive importance. The Party made the strategic choice to initiate political reforms as the stage essential for the transformation of the economy (Bruszt 1995: 274), in the absence of any significant political opposition pressure or labour unrest. The period is of special analytical importance because of the linkages between events and processes in different fields—political, economic, and labour relations. A Round Table was the forum for the process of political exchange involving political and economic groupings. The Party led the proposals for political pluralism in 1988, and formal independence of SZOT (the Central Council of the Trade Unions) came in the autumn of 1988. There was a rapid emergence of new unions using the terms of the draft law on associations which permitted the formation of trade unions as well as of political organizations. Some of the new unions developed links with the new parties but, in contrast to Poland and Bulgaria, neither they nor established unions were significant agencies in the process of political change. However, the political and economic crisis of 1988–9 undermined the 'system of labour relations' (Hethy and Csuhaj 1990: 18) and led to revisions of the Labour Code and the politically contested Strike Act which was passed in March 1989.

A continuing issue during the 1980s had been that of centralized control over wages which remained until 1989. The development of VGMKs from 1982 had provided a mechanism for increasing wages and gave a minority of groups inside the enterprise entrepreneurial experience. There were also substantial changes through the experience of many workers supplementing their earnings in the second economy, the largest in Eastern Europe. In October 1988 the National Council for the Reconciliation of Interests (NCRI) was created as an institution for tripartite discussions on the removal of administrative control over wages.

The Antall government elected in May 1990 had a substantial majority in parliament and, as its term was not due to end until 1994, it had a prospect of the stability widely regarded as necessary for the initial transformation of the economy. A major economic legacy was the very high foreign debt which made it highly dependent on IMF loans. The economy was hindered by a number of external shocks and in 1991 there were important reductions in enterprise employment but there was no economic crisis of Polish or Bulgarian proportions. The economic reform has usually been characterized as gradual in contrast to shock therapy. There was, however, a core group around Antall which strongly favoured the pursuit of a range of neo-liberal economic policies, including the further liberalization of prices, wages, and imports, which have been characterized as 'shock therapy' (Henderson *et al.* 1995). However, by the autumn of 1990 this had been abandoned as the result of growing discontent. Adverse results in the local elections, the taxi and truck drivers' blockade of the Danube bridges in October protesting against the increase in fuel prices, which paralysed the country for three days, and the threat of industrial action from the trade unions all contributed to a moderation of policy (Szabo 1992: 357–81). In this unforeseen crisis the NCRI played a significant part in the resolution of the dispute, and the government made the strategic choice, in the field of labour relations, to consolidate the institutional status of the NCRI and not to abolish it as a relic of socialism. Subsequently, there was incremental development of this institution until political pressure to restrict its activities emerged in the autumn of 1995. After the autumn of 1990 there was only very limited industrial action and social protest. Hethy (1992) suggests that the legacy of the experience of the second economy contributed to this.

In the political arena there was a government reshuffle and the relaxation of shock therapy, but the political crisis had important consequences for economic policy formulation: 'From early 1991 through to its defeat in mid-1994 the formation of and implementation of economic policy—and with it the privatization and management of state assets—degenerated into power struggles between competing ministries, agencies and individuals, all of whom reflected shifting vested interests' (Henderson *et al.* 1995: 90).

Rapid and extensive privatization had been an explicit goal of the government, but in practice the privatization process was very protracted and was contested within the political arena, leading to frequent shifts in the approach. Spontaneous privatization of some state enterprises had occurred before the political changes (see the Promed case in Chapter 8) and the Antall government attempted to establish central control over the privatization process by creating an agency for this. The strategic choice was to sell state property, and this was associated with securing the highest proportion of direct foreign investment, in the early years of transformation, of all the countries in Central Europe. Privatization has been a continually contested issue and there has been a succession of laws and regulations on privatization reflecting the balance of power in the political arena.

In the field of labour relations there was an incremental development of tripartism, in terms of its functions, at national level until 1994. These were extended from the original function of wage determination to include the formulation of social and public policy, the preparation of labour legislation, and the development of labour-relations institutions. However, other aspects of labour relations were more contentious, especially in relation to the place of the trade unions, which the government was reluctant to legitimate. Initially some leaders of the established unions feared that the government might imprison them. The government faced awkward political choices over the conflicts between the established and the new trade unions, especially over the division of trade-union property and the general legitimacy of trade unions. In the initial proposals for the revision of the Labour Code of 1992, which set up the framework for labour relations, collective bargaining, and consultation, the government sought to make works councils the agencies for collective bargaining rather than the trade unions, but had to abandon this proposal. Nevertheless, Hungary is alone in Eastern Europe, because the institution of consultation through works councils remained in the legislation. In the 1993 elections to the works councils and to the Social Security Boards (for Pensions and Health Insurance) the unions affiliated to MSzOSz (the National Federation of Hungarian Trade Unions) were generally most effective in securing support.

There was never mass consent for the economic policies of the Antall government and its defeat in 1994 confirmed the evidence of opinion polls in earlier years. The Horn government faced ongoing financial problems which required continuing stabilization and consequently significant dependence on the IFI. Initially there was the prospect that the arrival of a social-democratic government could provide the basis for a social pact in which the trade unions could participate. The concept of the pact was focused on a longer time scale than the customary one-year tripartite agreements. However, agreement on such a basis could not be achieved (Hethy 1995). The government was under international pressure (and from some Hungarian economists) to implement macro-stabilization measures and to reduce employment-related social costs (the highest in Eastern Europe), and this led to moves to restrict the role of tripartism in this field. Social policy became the dominant issue in national-level labour relations. Tripartism experienced some revival in 1996 partly as a consequence of the tradition of institutional practice built up since 1988.

To conclude the discussion of the Hungarian case the following points are to be noted. The legacy of economic reform meant that it was often regarded as the most advanced on the road to the marketization of the economy. The bargained nature of the political transformation took place in the absence of significant economic crisis, and labour relations were not an active constituent in the process. The political outcome of the transformation was a government with a sufficient majority to achieve its four-year electoral term. In response to the early challenges from the base (the taxi drivers' strike and local elections), the government modified its economic strategy and articulated the concept of the social-market economy. There was significant incremental development, as well as institutionalization of tripartism. This functioned as an important mechanism for securing labour consent at the level of representative institutions but not for positive popular political consent. The absence of such positive support underlay the change of government in 1994. However, the lack of sufficient improvement in the functioning of the economy increased the government's dependence on IFI policies and these shifted the direction and intensified the pressures on aspects of labour relations, especially wages and social policy. Notwithstanding this, the only labour-relations response was sectoral, and at the political level the predominant consensus was that an alternative economic strategy was not feasible.

The Czech Republic and Slovakia

The outstanding feature of the Czechoslovak legacy in 1989 was the absence of significant economic reform in the 1980s and of any private sector. However, some aspects of the economy were relatively well developed and there was no foreign debt. In terms of management and labour relations, changes were confined to the 1987 Law on State Enterprises and the brigade organization of work, both reflecting changes in the Soviet Union; the structure and functions of trade unions remained unchanged. In the political transformation crisis, the main agencies were political movements (Civic Forum and Public Against Violence). The action of these movements was paralleled by the formation of strike committees, sometimes spontaneously inside enterprises and sometimes prompted by movement representatives from outside. The strike committees organized the general strike of 27 November 1989, a turning point in the process of political change. They continued to focus on the replacement of the existing trade-union position holders and the takeover of the established organizational structures and the substantial properties they controlled. The transfer was consolidated when the new confederation was constituted in March 1990.

In the political arena Klaus established himself as the leader of Civic Forum and as a committed advocate of a rapid transition to a market economy involving shock therapy, although other leading economists argued for a gradual approach with more attention to restructuring. His success in the elections of June 1990 showed that 'the population is ready to bear the possible social consequences' (Dlouhy quoted in Myant 1993: 175). 'Thus, as in

Poland, one of the paradoxes was that a gradual approach, aiming to be polit-ically acceptable, was actually out of tune with a political atmosphere and the popular desire to feel that, at last, real change was under way' (Myant 1993: 171).

The Trade Union Confederation's acceptance of the broad principles of economic reform reflected popular attitudes, but in the establishment of the institutional framework of labour relations in 1990 it successfully contested the first draft of the law on strikes, and secured legislation on collective bar-gaining, but lost the previous rights to participate in management. There was cooperation in the establishment of national-level tripartite institutions. The context of this package was the prospect of price liberalization and wage cuts as the start of the shock-therapy package. This was due to start at the begin-ning of 1991 and was judged to need trade-union acceptance to ensure social consent. Although formally there were negotiations between the partners, in fact the government more or less imposed the terms, as the trade unions feared that resistance might lead to a campaign accusing them of collaborat-ing with the old regime (Adam 1995: 201).

The results of shock therapy were comparable with those of Poland except for a low rate of unemployment but, unlike Poland, social peace was main-tained and there were few strikes. However, there were consequences in the political arena as Klaus created his own party within the Civic Forum strongly committed to the neo-liberal conception of economic reform. The strategic choice of a mass voucher scheme as the principal method of privat-ization had already appeared in the Klaus programme of April 1990 and it became a major, and popular, element in his successful campaign for the 1992 election. One consequence for labour relations was that it helped to eliminate any threat of worker resistance to privatization.

Myant (1993: 195–6) suggests that four main factors contributed to the maintenance of social peace despite massive wage cuts: redundant workers in big cities could find jobs; the union officials were new and did not want to be tainted with the past; the union membership wanted radical change; and pro-tective government policies delayed bankruptcies and promoted some job creation. Trade-union participation in the national tripartite negotiations produced little of substance. It is possible to argue, however, that there was an implicit rather than an explicit social contract: government control of wages was important for allowing enterprises to maintain employment and thus keep unemployment low. The trade unions recognized the value of this trade-off and as organizations they retained their valuable properties.

By the middle of the 1990s there was a shift in the relations between the government and the trade unions in the Czech Republic. In 1995 Klaus declared that the economic transformation had been completed and would be followed by the social transformation in the fields of pensions and social secu-rity. The issue of pensions triggered a major demonstration in Prague and conflicts in the budget sector, suggesting that a challenge to the neo-liberal strategy comes from the public (budget) sector and in relation to social policy. For the 1996 election the Klaus manifesto, derived in part from the agreement with the IMF, declared in favour of ensuring that corporate interests should not override the interests of citizens as individuals and aimed to facilitate individual as opposed to collective labour relations. The loss of an overall majority in the elections and the unexpected success of the Social Democratic Party has affected policy in this area.

To summarize the discussion on the Czech case the following can be concluded. The electoral success of Civic Forum, with Klaus as the dominant leader favouring the strategic choice of a rapid transformation of the neo-liberal type, was based on initial electoral and social support for the economic transformation, and social peace was never seriously challenged. Nevertheless, there was rapid formal acceptance by Klaus of the principles of tripartism as a necessary/desirable condition for ensuring stability. Underpinning social peace was the implicit social contract of low unemployment in exchange for wage restriction. The strategic choice of citizen-based voucher privatization was a factor in maintaining the popular and electoral support for Klaus in 1992.

The wage policy directed by the government was not seriously challenged, but Klaus's declaration in 1994 that the social transformation would follow the completed economic transformation provoked what was regarded by Klaus as significant protest action, and this was a turning point for the trade-union confederation. The relative success of the Social Democrats in the 1996 election was not foreseen and was the first indication of discontent with the programmatic development of economic reform, carried out with the political continuity accruing to the longest serving political leader in Central and Eastern Europe. This political stability was made possible by popular support and was a precondition for the programmatic development of economic reform.

Slovakia

The Czech Republic and Slovakia constitutionally separated at the beginning of 1993, at a time when the main legal framework for labour relations was already well established, together with the institutions of tripartism, and a common model of privatization had been adopted. The federal nature of Czechoslovakia had led in 1991–2 to the existence of 'three separate Councils simultaneously: the Federal, the Slovak and the Czech' (Cziria 1995: 148), so that a Slovak institution was in existence before the separation, though it was subsequently confirmed by Slovak legislation. In a similar fashion, the federal trade-union structure lapsed, leaving the two republican centres. Comparison with subsequent developments in the Czech Republic raises the question of the extent to which Slovakia has diverged from the Czech trajectory and the reasons for this. The most significant difference is that the national tripartite process on wages and other issues, despite disagreements and delays, continued to function regularly until March 1997. Thus, Meciar did not attempt to follow Klaus in devaluing the content of the process, which is an illustration of how strategic political choice can influence the pattern of labour-relations development. At the International Conference for Ministers of Labour from Eastern Europe organized by the Belgian Ministry of Labour and Employment in Brussels in May 1997, the Slovak Minister of Labour's paper emphasized the importance the government attached to the social dialogue and its positive contribution to social peace. The economy has continued to develop, and the influence of the IFI appears less salient. In Slovakia, trade unions have avoided fragmentation and have retained perhaps 60–70 per cent of their membership, their property, and their social funds. Revision of the inherited Labour Code was expected to take place in 1997. Issues included the possibility of including provision for participation (opposed by the trade unions but of potential significance in non-union firms), and whether the restrictions on collective bargaining in the Labour Code should be retained.

Bulgaria

During the 1980s there was a steady decline in the economy and consequently the issue of economic policy became more urgent. For the political leadership the search for solutions which did not breach the ideological commitment to full employment and the predominance of state ownership became increasingly imperative. Politically Bulgaria was distinguished by the continuity of Zhivkov's leadership, which spanned the period from 1956 to 1989, comparable to Kadar's period of leadership in Hungary. None the less, there was discontinuity in the circle of his advisers, who were changed about every four years, the changes being associated with the enunciation of new policies.

The labour-relations model was essentially similar to that transferred from the Soviet Union in the late 1940s, and the first major change, the introduction of the brigade organization of work in 1978, was influenced by developments in the Soviet Union, as were mechanisms such as counter-planning and worker proposals. Internally the pressure for such changes derived from the goal of improved economic efficiency and better labour utilization/productivity. However, the external example of the emergence of Solidarity and its challenge to the political system in Poland strongly influenced the leadership's perception of the potential threat to the political system from labour relations. The choice was to promote the head of the trade unions as a candidate member of the Politburo and to redefine the function of the trade unions, not to that of protecting workers' interests but as 'organizers of the labour collective'. In implementing this function the trade unions became responsible for extending the brigade organization throughout industry and for the introduction of councils of the labour collective. This was set within the concept of 'self-management' introduced, not, as in Poland, as a mobilizing concept deriving from the base, but from above. The change was, however, intended to mobilize pressure from the base in the economic context of the new economic mechanism which aimed to decentralize some decision-making to enterprises.

The Labour Code of 1986 legalized the institutions of self-management. The conception of agreements between brigades and the director, introduced in 1986, recognized differences of interest between different members of the collective; up until this point the theory had been that there was congruency of interests. The issue of property re-emerged in 1988, when there was a short-lived attempt to transfer the property of the enterprise to the labour collectives, who, however, did not respond to the increase in responsibility without power. The next step was Decree 56 of January 1989, which replaced the labour-managed enterprise by that of a firm in which the rights of management were restored, and allowed private individuals to register firms. In 1987 an attempt within the trade-union organization to alter its function from that of organizer of the labour collective to that of interest representation of the workforce was rejected by the Party leadership. In effect, this would have been a variant of the classical Western model of trade unions.

The legacy of the 1980s in Bulgaria can be summarized as follows: there was no real change in politics and no dissidents; change in the economic mechanisms was limited; the issue of property was identified but only in a very restricted form; and labour relations were a significant field of action but there was no real pressure from the base. On the economic side there was considerable foreign debt.

The political changes initiated from within the Party leadership in 1989 were closely associated with the emergence of ethnic conflicts with the Muslim population, which at one stage threatened to become a civil war. These conditions created space for the emergence of alternative organizations in the political and trade-union fields. Thus, *Podkrepa* (Confederation of Labour 'Support') registered as a trade union to represent Muslim ethnic interests. With the rapid eruption of strikes in some industrial sectors and the budget sectors of health and education, *Podkrepa* shifted to the industrial sphere, which provided space for its anti-communist activities. The Round Table which operated from January to March 1990 was the forum in which the competing political centres brokered the political transformation and the restructuring of the Communist Party and its exit from the enterprise. The established trade unions which had separated from the Party and *Podkrepa* were participants in the Round Table.

The Confederation of Independent Trade Unions in Bulgaria (CITUB), the successor to the communist trade unions, chose to play a proactive role in the resolution of the industrial conflicts which threatened the political process. Consequently, it was in a position to take an active part in the design of the institutions of labour relations, especially the National Tripartite Council, the Law on Disputes, and the recognition of collective bargaining.

By March 1990 the main Bulgarian labour-relations institutions were complete and these structures still persist. Nevertheless, there was no explicit action in the economic field. Although there was considerable expectation that the opposition would win in the election of June 1990, in fact Lukanov's Socialist government was re-elected. He recognized the severity of the economic crisis and, although he declared a moratorium on the repayment of interest on the foreign debt, he was ready to prepare the steps for a foreign loan based on a programme drawn up by American economists. However, he was unable to carry the socialist party with him. Lukanov facilitated trade-union opposition as an exit strategy which brought the government down and opened the way for the coalition government which had to carry through price liberalization. The ensuing coalition for macro-stabilization was successful in securing popular consent for nine months, but the need for trade-union support for social peace was essential and the IMF required trade-union endorsement as a condition of support. In the election of September 1991 the neo-liberal and anti-trade union government of the Union of Democratic Forces came to power but eventually fell within two years because of withdrawal of trade-union support.

The Berov government of technocrats in 1993–4 had to impose a wage freeze to get IMF support, while the trade unions were able to get the revision of the Labour Code they had been seeking, which gave a legal basis for the tripartite institutions. The Socialist government of Videnov, elected with an overall majority in December 1994, chose to follow neo-liberal policies, especially in relation to the reform of social security. It did not wish to be constrained in its policies by tripartite negotiations and hoped that it could secure results without short-term popular support. At the end of 1996 the economy was in crisis, Videnov resigned, and protests aimed at early elections were growing. Elections took place in April 1997.

The political process has been one of turbulence and instability, with seven governments since 1989. Changes in governments have been turning points in the direction of economic reform, in relation to international loans and with regards to the trade-union confederations. Two changes of governments have been connected with trade-union opposition, but dependence on IMF loans has also constrained governments' room for manœuvre. Economic performance has been considerably hampered by three external events: the Bulgarian economy was closely linked to the Soviet Union through the Council for Mutual Economic Assistance (CMEA) and suffered greatly from its demise; the Gulf War prevented the repayment of Iraqi debts; and the embargo on trade with Yugoslavia had negative results.

One result of political instability has been that privatization plans have been repeatedly proposed and planned only to be deferred for political reasons. Thus, the Union of Democratic Forces (UDF) government placed restitution first as a deliberate choice, as a result of internal pressure and so that a Bulgarian group with funds could be created. Privatization in agriculture was expected to weaken support for the Socialist Party in its rural base. The repeated deferment of large-scale privatization until 1995 was a major sequence issue which had consequences for labour relations in large enterprises.

To summarize the Bulgarian case, the following issues can be noted. The issue of strategic choice in relation to economic reform has been repeatedly postponed, principally because of the absence of coherent (relatively united) and dominant political agencies and the consequent instability of governments. Thus, the management of recurrent economic crises required coalitions in 1991, 1993, and for a time in 1997. The attempt by Videnov to act as a decisive agency for reform in the period 1994–6 was undermined by the lack of economic success. The specific nature of the political transformation crisis of 1989/90 provided the opportunity for the trade unions to operate as a leading agency and to establish the formal framework for labour relations. Trade-union consent was essential for price liberalization and the lack of it undermined the UDF in 1992. However, by 1996, despite the continuing economic crisis, there was no prospect of general and active labour unrest.

Russia

The process of political and economic change in the Soviet Union and Russia was both protracted and sharply contested within the Soviet regime. The critical turning point for both political and economic change was the attempted *coup* of August 1991. *Perestroika* as an umbrella concept for reform of the Soviet economy was declared as a central political goal in 1985, soon after Gorbachev came to power. Elaboration of the concept took place in several stages until 1990. Initially it was defined in economic terms, but in the second stage (January 1987 to June 1988) the twin political concepts of *glasnost* and democratization were predominant. This was followed by attempts to implement political changes, including the first elections of March 1989. A series of proposals for economic reform led to political controversies within the Politburo, the Party, and other organizations, such as the trade unions, on whether there should be moves to some kind of market economy and on the speed at which such moves should be made. In 1987 the established trade unions declared their independence from the Party and the government as a move against market reform. Political changes and increasing political conflicts between Yeltsin and Gorbachev in 1990 were accompanied by competing programmes for economic reform. Gorbachev's Shatalin Plan of 1990 proposed a radical 500-day reform programme devolving more power to the republics and legislative proposals for the establishment of a market economy. This was rejected by the Supreme Soviet, reflecting resistance from the vested interests of the ministries and the enterprise directors.

The management of enterprises and their labour relations under *perestroika* had been the subject of reform initiated from the top and promoted under the concept of self-management. Thus the 1987 Law of Enterprises aimed to increase enterprise autonomy by freeing it from some ministry controls, and establishing direct links with customers and suppliers. At the same time the powers of the labour collective—for example to elect managers—and of the enterprise council were increased. (However, managerial pressure led to the removal of the power to elect managers in 1990.) The possibility for the labour collective to approve the leasing of the enterprise from the ministries (from 1989) provided a further opportunity to increase autonomy, whilst the law on cooperatives of 1989 gave management the possibility to create cooperatives within their organization, which operated outside the national rules on wages and taxes. Although these changes increased managerial autonomy, the labour-relations philosophy of the *perestroika* period was based on the assumption that the fundamental issue for economic reform was the motivation of labour: 'In my opinion, the hardest problem to resolve in the *perestroika* of the economic system is to ensure the direct interest of working people in the final results of their labour' (Aganbegnyan 1988: 119). The legacy in labour relations was, therefore, based on the Soviet model discussed above, combined with some recent modifications.

Some of the changes deriving from *perestroika* were accompanied by increases in industrial conflict in 1987 and 1989 (Clarke and Fairbrother 1993a: 126–7), but the miners' strikes in 1989 were regarded by the authorities as a serious challenge to *perestroika*. The strikes were primarily economic but were also against ministerial control and in favour of moves to a market economy, which the miners considered would be in their interests. The miners' strike in the spring of 1991

had a decisive impact in bringing the crisis of the Soviet system to a head. It was the miners' strike which forced the realignment within the ruling stratum in which the balance of power shifted decisively in favour of the reformist faction as Gorbachev ended his vacillation and Yeltsin showed a willingness to compromise. . . . The eventual outcome of the miners' strikes was the collapse of the Union, the replacement of Gorbachev by Yeltsin, and the introduction of the neo-liberal 'shock treatment' at the beginning of 1992. The miners backed all these developments. (Clarke and Fairbrother 1993c: 167–8).

Thus, labour relations set in motion the chain of events which led to political and economic change. In July 1991 Yeltsin decreed the end of Party organization in the enterprise. The Federation of Independent Trade Unions of Russia (FITUR) leadership sought and received assurances from Yeltsin that the enterprise trade unions would not be abolished (Connor 1996: 24).

At the start of the August *coup* Yeltsin and Khasbulatov issued a decree against it calling for a 'general strike' (Khasbulatov 1993: 142)—the only case of a government in Eastern Europe attempting to use this weapon. Steele (1994: 71) is sceptical about worker support in Moscow, but Khasbulatov (1993: 147) refers to reports of many strikes and demonstrations in response to this call. Whether this support would have grown significantly if the crisis had not been speedily resolved is difficult to assess, but it is plausible to see support from workplaces as the response of individuals and not of organizations and certainly not of the established trade unions. The failure of the *coup* was a clear turning point in political and economic development. With the end of the Soviet Union and its state, Yeltsin was now in the leading position. The issue of the economic strategy and the reform was rapidly accelerated and the strategic choice was made by the end of 1991 with the appointment of Gaidar and his group. Steele (1994: 295–306) argues that Gaidar was determined to smash the existing political and economic system and was perhaps conscious of the forces which had stopped the Shatalin Plan. The centrepiece was price liberalization, which smashed the planning system, together with mass privatization and a single exchange rate for the rouble. It was the transfer of the Polish model to Russia, without taking account of the different Russian conditions. Large-scale privatization was to be carried out mainly in the course of that year, but, in a clear recognition of the potential importance of the workforce and the necessity of securing their consent, there was extensive provision for insider shareholding (see details in Chapter 4). The ECE (1993: 160) identifies three reasons as particularly important for the failure of the Gaidar strategy: 'given the specific conditions of the Russian economy the initial reform programme was not conceptually adequate and was too narrowly focused on stabilization goals alone', 'the government lacked the political support needed to persevere with drastic and unpopular stabilization measures', and 'the programme has not been supported by an appropriate external assistance package'.

Transfer of the ownership and property rights over enterprises had been a major issue of strategic choice on the political agenda since 1990 and had been part of the Shatalin Plan. The issue of how shares should be distributed—that is, the form and control of ownership (insider/outsider)—was a major political issue. In the Russian context the role given to the labour collective would be significant. However, in practice, relatively little industrial privatization had taken place before the summer of 1992. It was then announced that there would be a rapid programme with provision for substantial insider ownership, a provision generally welcomed by managements.

The lack of political support for shock therapy led to the dismissal of Gaidar at the end of 1992 and the stabilization programme was slowed down. However, the general direction of implementing the neo-liberal model remained unchanged under Yeltsin. Many enterprises were in crisis but were rarely bankrupted and a pattern of subsidization was continued. In 1993 the focus of politics was on the conflict between Yeltsin and the Congress which developed into the White House crisis of September. In the run-up to the April referendum, opposed by the Congress, Yeltsin claimed the support of a number of unions but not FITUR and the result was broadly in his favour (Conner 1996: 117). Later in the summer the FITUR was preparing to call a general strike and did so in the White House crisis, when Rutskoi and

Khasbulatov hoped for mass-strike action in support of them which did not materialize. Subsequently there was no serious political challenge to the economic reform until it was questioned by the Communist Party led by Zyuganov.

National changes in the model of labour relations were directly linked with the introduction of the Gaidar programme. The government judged that the reduction in living standards could well lead to industrial unrest and it was 'interested in extracting itself from the owner–manager–paymaster role as the beginning of a move towards a referee role between the interests of labour and those of the yet-vague category of owners–employers' (Connor 1996: 25). The outcome was the decree of November 1991 'On Social Partnership and the Resolution of Labour Disputes', which led to the setting-up of the Tripartite Commission with wide terms of reference. These included the negotiation of an annual general agreement, and the Law on Collective Agreements was passed in April 1992. The Commission was to deal with the minimum wage (important in cities such as Moscow and Leningrad) and to encourage tripartite branch agreements.

The perceived threat to social peace helped to secure the position of the FITUR trade unions. In July 1991 Yeltsin's decision to end the Party's organization in the workplace had prompted trade-union fears that they might suffer the same fate (Connor 1996: 24). The FITUR unions had distanced themselves from Yeltsin during the crisis of 1991, but the main independent unions (Miners, SOTSPROF) backed Yeltsin as the advocate of market reforms. However, their leverage in the political arena was not large, and, despite their support, they subsequently lost their seats on the tripartite commission, mainly as a result of the deal that Yeltsin did with FITUR. FITUR institutionalization in the tripartite framework enabled the unions to keep their property and to preserve, at least for a time, their role in the administration of social security, though this was a continuing bone of contention between them and governments.

The Party Programme of the Communist Party in 1995 was strongly critical of the neo-liberal model of economic management, and was committed to what was termed the socialist forms of economic management, with extended rights for enterprise labour collectives in all forms of property and management through soviets, trade unions, and workers' self-management (Communist Party of the Russian Federation 1995: 78, 110). In essence this implied a return to the labour-relations model of the 1980s. This was the programme for the Duma elections of 1995 in which it did well, and on which Zyuganov contested the presidential elections of 1996. Yeltsin's majority was greater than had seemed likely from earlier opinion polls. His victory closed off the most serious electoral challenge in Eastern Europe to the neo-liberal model of reform and to the possibility of an alternative model of labour relations.

To summarize the Russian case the following points can be stressed. In the Soviet Union the strategic choices in the field of economic reform were repeatedly postponed, mainly as the result of conflicts within the Communist Party and separatist Republican pressures. It took the crisis of the August *coup* to resolve the log jam and create the space for Gaidar and his colleagues to impose the choice of a neo-liberal model on the Russian federation. There was no expression of popular support for this choice and its absence was identified by the UN as one of the important causes of its failure. Although trade unions never became major agencies in the political arena, national tripartism was set up simultaneously with shock therapy. However, the choice of insider-dominated ownership as the principle form for privatization was influenced by managerial pressure but also recognized the importance of employee consent, and the legacy of the particular status of workers in the Russian enterprise and the paternalist tradition of the Director as the representative of the workforce. The outcome of the White House crisis in 1993 confirmed the continuation of economic strategy and illustrated the compliance of trade unionists irrespective of FITUR criticism of its results. However, in the political arena elections to the Duma demonstrated popular political discontent with Yeltsin, expressed first in temporary support for Zhirinovsky and then for the Communist Party, which in 1995 and 1996 offered an alternative economic model together with a traditional vision of labour relations. Yeltsin's victory, facilitated by Western financial support, confirmed the direction of economic reform.

PATTERNS OF DEVELOPMENT: SIMILARITIES AND DIFFERENCES

In this section, the chapter is concluded by comparing the patterns of development in the different countries. It is obvious that the simultaneity of the processes of transformation involving both political and economic reform has meant that the interactions between the political and the economic have shaped the dynamics of societal development. Thus, the process by which political pluralism was established, and the constitutional forms adopted in the different countries, not only had important consequences for the development and stability of the political system, but was also related to the development of economic reform, to the choice of methods, and to the maintenance of popular support and consent. It is, however, argued that labour relations have been a fundamental and constitutive element of both the political and economic transformations, although their importance has varied between countries and over time. The aim, therefore, is to compare the role of labour relations and the impact of political and economic strategies on labour-relations outcomes.

The relationship between labour relations and regime change in Eastern Europe needs to be considered in two main respects: first, the extent to which the state of labour relations at the time of regime change was a significant feature of the political context; secondly, whether the institutions of labour relations, especially trade unions, were active as an agency in the political arena.

In Hungary, in the negotiated process of regime change, neither the established trade unions nor the new independent unions were active or significant agencies in the process. The political arena was dominated by the Socialist Party and the new political formations. In the collapse of the regime in Czechoslovakia, labour relations as such were not an issue but politically oriented strike committees participated as agencies in the process of regime change and particularly in the displacement of officers of the established unions.

In Poland the Solidarity bloc was the leading agency in regime change in conditions of economic crisis. The Bulgarian crisis of 1989–90 combined political, economic, ethnic, and labour-relations aspects. In these conditions both *Podkrepa* and the established unions were active as agencies. In Russia, *perestroika* had been undermined by industrial action, and, although the process of political pluralization was protracted, the turning point was the crisis of August 1991, when Yeltsin called for a general strike in which the established unions were conspicuous by their silence. Thus, there were major differences in the place of labour relations and of trade unions in the political transformation process, and very few similarities. The role of the trade union as an active agency in the transformation crisis or its absence constitutes a specific legacy in each case. After seven years of the transition there is some evidence that where trade unions were active in the political arena at the time of the transformation crisis, as in Poland and Bulgaria, they have retained some leverage in politics, but if they were not then their leverage has been more limited.

Macroeconomic Stabilization and the Development of the Economy

For the new political regimes in Eastern Europe the initial common characteristic was that of economic crisis associated with the disintegration of the CMEA and the ending of cheap energy from the Soviet Union. There were, of course, variations between countries in the intensity of the crisis: greater in Poland, the Soviet Union, and Bulgaria, less in Czechoslovakia and Hungary. Economic stabilization and the choice of reform strategy, its sequence, and its components were the central issues faced by the new regimes. The pace at which these could be implemented was one of the areas where an element of strategic political choice was possible. This was dependent to some extent upon the intensity of the crisis and the political leadership's judgement about the prospects of organized opposition to a process which was generally recognized as one which would lead to significant falls in the standard of living of the majority of the population. The country cases show the importance of coherent political groupings around leaders with power and commitment to the neo-liberal model (for example, Balcerowicz, Klaus, and Gaidar), although not in the case of Hungary or Bulgaria. Internally and externally the maintenance of social peace, especially during the process of macro-stabilization, was seen as a critical issue for the various incoming regimes.

The distinction is sometimes made between countries where the full rigour of shock therapy was applied for at least a period—that is, Poland, Bulgaria, and Russia—and those where a more gradual approach was followed, as in Czechoslovakia and Hungary. In the latter countries it is certainly the case that the economic crisis was less intense, but they like the others set out to follow the essence of the model of macroeconomic stabilization promoted by the IFI and some groups of influential economists inside the countries. The main components of this model were price liberalization, trade liberalization, and convertibility. At some stage all governments answered the 'siren call of shock therapy' (ECE 1993: 7). In fact no government set out on a gradual approach, although from the autumn of 1990 the Hungarian government's approach became more gradual as a result of the taxi drivers' strike, the threat of trade-union action, and defeats in local elections (Henderson *et al.* 1995). As explained in the country cases, the political leadership in both Poland and Czechoslovakia estimated, with some reason, that in the immediate aftermath of the political change their populations were ready to sacrifice standards for a period provided that results were forthcoming. However, it is notable that both Balcerowicz and Gaidar, the two individuals most personally identified with the goal of rapid change, had lost their positions within two years as a consequence of discontent mediated through political agencies. The 'transformational recession' (the fall in production) was greater than economists anticipated. Kornai (1995) admits that he did not foresee this and he stresses the similarity between countries.

The issue of maintaining social peace and a measure of popular support during the period of macroeconomic stabilization influenced the actions of governments and the legal and institutional models of labour relations that were established, especially in the period of macro-stabilization. There are two principal aspects of institutional change: first, the general laws legitimating aspects of labour relations excluded from or marginalized in the socialist model—the right to strike, the independence of trade unions, collective bargaining, etc.; and, secondly, national institutions of a tripartite form.

Comparison of the different countries shows that, although formally there are more similarities than differences in the laws and institutions, there have been very significant variations in the patterns of legal and institutional development and in the salience and function of these institutions in practice. Thus, in Hungary the establishment of the first national tripartite forum in 1988 and the Law on Strikes in 1989 were not followed by the law on collective bargaining until the enactment of the Labour Code in 1992. In Poland the pattern was reversed—laws on trade unions and disputes first, but nothing on tripartism till 1992. In Bulgaria and Czechoslovakia the two forms were more closely integrated at the beginning of 1990 and in 1990/1 respectively, although the contested issue of the Labour Code in Bulgaria was not resolved until the Berov Coalition of 1993. In Russia, the decisions on shock therapy, ownership change, the establishment of the Russian Trilateral Commission (RTK), and the General Agreement were closely linked in time. However, the key mechanism which expresses the significance of national tripartism is the scope and importance of the General Agreement.

The direct institutional result of shock therapy is tripartism to secure employee consent. Industrial action had a national level effect in Poland and Bulgaria (but only very briefly in Hungary) as a consequence of shock therapy. In Russia, the introduction of shock therapy in 1992 was accompanied by substantial increases in the number of strikes and participants. Although the figures for 1993 and 1994 were lower, the totals for 1995 were the highest ever, reflecting the continuation and consequences of the economic crisis (Voeikov and Milovankina 1996: 92).

Although all of the countries initially signed up to the neo-liberal vision and followed similar macroeconomic stabilization policies, there was considerable variation in the timing and sequence of post-stabilization policies, especially ownership change. In Poland and Hungary industrial privatization is a long-drawn-out and contested process; in the Czech Republic the policy of mass privatization followed the limited shock therapy very rapidly and, although there were debates before the political decision to take the mass privatization route, its implementation was not significantly contested; in Bulgaria, for political reasons large-scale privatization is repeatedly postponed and so was separated from the main shock therapy; whereas in Russia, the outstanding feature is the close sequencing of shock therapy and ownership change.

In Poland and Bulgaria, trade-union centres have participated in the processes leading to the political decisions on privatization. In all countries, the actual forms of privatization have direct implications for labour relations at the level of the enterprise. The essential difference is the balance between insider and outsider control (discussed in detail in Chapter 4). Outsider control, as implemented in Czechoslovakia, excludes direct employee involvement, but insider control, as in Russia, has given possibilities for employee participation, while in Poland employee buyouts have constituted one significant form of ownership change.

The link between the neo-liberal model of economic reform (discussed in Chapter 3) and the consequent economic deprivation, and the relationship of these to elections and changes of government, is not as clear as might have been expected. The unexpected electoral success of Solidarity in 1989 was the turning point for the neo-liberal reform. Successive elections in Poland reflected discontent with the results of this economic policy. The new governments modified the pace and trajectory of reform but not its general trajectory. In Hungary, the defeat of the Antall government in 1994 by the Socialists was not a surprise, as the lack of political assent had been clear in opinion polls. However, the implementation of neo-liberal stabilization measures has been continued by the Horn government without, up to 1997, the apparent loss of political consent. In Bulgaria, price liberalization was delayed by the absence of consent and the unexpected failure of the UDF in the 1990 election, which was therefore not a turning point. Consent for price liberalization required a coalition government in 1991 and again in 1993 to secure an IMF loan. The Bulgarian Socialist Party (BSP) secured a significant majority and sought to use it to proceed rapidly with neo-liberal policies. The economic policies pursued by left-wing governments in Poland, Hungary, and Bulgaria have been characterized as 'Socialist monetarism' and reflect the hegemony of the neo-liberal model analysed in Chapter 3. (Socialist monetarism refers to the continuation of neo-liberal policies by socialist governments.)

In Czechoslovakia, and subsequently in the Czech Republic, Klaus was able to develop and consolidate his political support and so to proceed more programmatically than elsewhere. However, the unexpected success of the opposition in the 1996 election pointed to a reduction in social and political consent. The economic crisis in the middle of 1997, in what had seemed to many observers the most successful case of marketization, underlined the continuing risks to the economic development of countries in transition in Eastern Europe. Although Slovak governments have incurred international criticism on some political trends, the economic development has proceeded steadily.

In Russia, the introduction of the reform package was accelerated by the August *coup* in 1991 which, at least in part, was a reaction to marketization. The 1993 programme of the Communist Party (the only one with a large membership) opposed the neo-liberal economic policy. It was relatively successful in the parliamentary elections of 1995 but this was not translated into comparable support for Zyuganov in the presidential election of June 1996, when the extent of support for Yeltsin was not expected. Thus, politically, the most important potential turning point in the whole region since the crisis of 1993 did not occur and there was no reversal of economic strategy or return to an earlier model of labour relations.

Extraordinary Politics, Economic Reforms, and Labour Relations

Balcerowicz coined the term 'extraordinary politics' to characterize the relation between politics and economics in Poland in 1989–90. In essence it meant that the popular support for marketization and its consumer goods was sufficient to endure the negative effects of stabilization, and to give technopol politicians space to engineer a rapid transition by shock therapy rather than a more gradual transition. This raises the question of the extent to which 'extraordinary politics' were characteristic of the transition in other countries. The evidence from Czechoslovakia is similar in terms of popular support for economic reform which opened the way for Klaus to develop marketization on a programmatic basis. In Hungary, on the other hand, the group who favoured shock therapy lost out as a result of popular pressure in 1990 and, as a result, politics became focused on the interaction of interest-group politics but detached from popular pressure. In Bulgaria, the extent of the transition crisis and of political division precluded extraordinary politics, and price liberalization could come only when a coalition government, with trade-union support, was constructed in 1991. The issue of popular support in Russia and the political conflicts between Yeltsin and the Duma were much more complex. Gaidar's introduction of shock therapy and rapid institutional change was attempted without popular support and in that sense politics in Russia were not 'extraordinary'.

Przeworski has argued (1991: 180) that 'Reforms are least likely to advance when political forces—in particular opposition parties and unions—are strong enough to be able to sabotage them and not large enough to be able to internalize the entire cost of arresting them.' The actual pattern of developments in Eastern Europe has been more complex than this suggests. As will be discussed in Chapter 5, trade-union centres in Poland, Bulgaria, Hungary, and Czechoslovakia endorsed the principle of the reform process and the costs of stabilization on behalf of their membership at a time when other political forces, apart from the Communist parties in Bulgaria and Russia, lacked a membership base. However, trade-union centres distanced themselves from the stage of the neo-liberal reform affecting social policy and enterprise welfare which had been a fundamental feature of socialist labour relations.

3

International Agencies

The previous chapter discussed the influence of legacies from the Soviet period on the political and economic processes of transformation. One way in which legacies may be overcome is through the transfer or imposition of models of development from outside. Another factor in the process of transformation in eastern Europe and Russia has been the transfer of a neo-liberal model of economic stabilization and development from the West and most especially by the IFI. The principal financial institutions are the International Monetary Fund (IMF) and the World Bank and it is these institutions which form the core of the analysis in this chapter. However, there are other institutions including the European Bank for Reconstruction and Development (EBRD) and the Organization for Economic Cooperation and Development (OECD), the Paris Club, and those of the EU which operate to promote the development of market economies in eastern Europe (Poland and Hungary Assistance for the Reconstruction of the Economy (PHARE) and Technical Assistance for the Commonwealth of Independent States (TACIS)). The functions of this chapter are fivefold: to consider the role of the international financial institutions in Eastern Europe; to analyse the transference of the neo-liberal model and the mechanisms by which it is imposed; to investigate the strategic choices of governments and the role of international financial institutions as shadow partner; to look at the economic alternatives to neo-liberalism; and to examine the implication for labour relations.

THE INTERNATIONAL FINANCIAL INSTITUTIONS IN EASTERN EUROPE

The IMF and the World Bank were founded to promote post-war recovery and economic development and to prevent the recurrence of the depression of the 1930s through the regulation of international economic and financial relations, especially in periods of crisis. Institutionally they are joint stock companies and their strategic shareholders are the G7 countries. They were originally important for the management of the monetary systems of the First World, but the privatization of this process in the 1970s reduced this role. The debt crisis of the Third World made it the primary recipient of IMF lending in the 1980s and contributed to the development of its programmes and of the model. The effectiveness of these programmes and the relevance of the model in relation to the Third World have been extensively criticized (see, e.g., Bird 1993: 166–80), and its relationship to the World Bank and other financial institutions has been a topic of debate. The IMF defines itself as an institution which seeks to maintain an orderly system of payments and receipts between nations, whereas the Bank is primarily a development institution (Driscoll 1994: 2). From this it follows that the IMF concern is with the short term, while that of the Bank is with reform and the medium term. However, in practice in Eastern Europe the distinction has at times become blurred.

For the IFI there are currently four types of transition underway in the world economy, of which the 'industrial post-socialist' transition in Eastern Europe is the most recent. The others are the Latin American, the sub-Saharan African, and the Asian rural, which includes China, India, and Vietnam (World Bank 1995: 98–9). The East European transition has a number of characteristics which, as a general category, distinguish it from those of the others. The East European economies have been heavily industrialized over a long period in contrast to the rural economies of many developing countries. More importantly, the primary mechanism of the socialist economies has been the planning system originally created for the process of industrialization, hence the absence of market mechanisms. The framework of institutions and mechanisms established for the planned economy differed substantially from those of developed market economies. Such market mechanisms, including openness to world markets, and the appropriate capitalist institutions existed to a greater or lesser extent in the other types of transition. During the 1980s it had become increasingly clear that the socialist economies were not successful in achieving the growth and productivity rates needed to provide the levels of consumer goods and the higher wages found in the most advanced market economies of the world.

In the East European transition the IFI have promoted the mechanisms of the market economy as fundamental for economic development, although many of the essential institutions which underpin and ensure the operation of market economies have been absent or underdeveloped. From the start of the transition, the objective promoted by the IFI, advisers, and politicians was the need to apply market mechanisms as rapidly as possible and to implement a model of a market economy derived from an ideal end state. The main components of the model have been regarded as fundamental, so that significant alternatives are not to be considered. As the ECE *Economic Survey of Europe in 1991–2* (ECE 1992: 3) noted, despite

the major failure to foresee the revolutions of 1989, they were quickly followed by western advisers explaining why there was no 'alternative' to doing this or that, if the transition to a market economy were to be successful and by politicians declaring that the transition would be swift and painless. . . . The destination is usually described in terms of a unique western model which bears little relation to western reality.

Despite the variations in institutional legacies, the economic instruments applied to the different types of transition are essentially the same and the model can therefore appropriately be characterized as hegemonic. The implementation of the model develops in two stages. The first is the macro-economic stabilization and monetary stage with the liberalization of prices and trade combined with measures to limit inflation. The second stage is the restructuring of the economy and its sectors with ownership change through accelerated privatization as its core. The two stages may overlap in time depending on national policies and conditions. Although the implementation of the different elements of the model are open for discussion with the parties involved, the fundamentals are not. The instruments and controls for implementing the model are discussed below. International financial institutions came to the fore from the beginning of the reforms (see the section on Poland in Chapter 2), and the dependence on international loans has given them a continuing role in supervising the process of transition. The agencies have, therefore, operated in a process which has involved both the exit from the crisis of the planned economies and the creation of market economies in these countries, often in conditions of severe economic difficulty.

The experience of the IFI in other transitions has had some influence on their approaches. Thus, the social costs of economic development in other regions has resulted in acceptance that the creation of social safety nets is a necessity in Eastern Europe. There are two further aspects which have influenced the actions of the agencies in Eastern Europe. The first is that it was widely accepted that the economic effects of transformation on populations accustomed to security of jobs and income security, combined with significant welfare provision, could lead to breakdowns of social peace. Consequently, as explained below, the significance of securing consent through consultations with trade unions and the use of tripartite institutions has had a greater importance than in some other regions.

TRANSFERENCE OF THE NEO-LIBERAL MODEL

At one level the process of transference of the neo-liberal model can be seen in terms of the specific instruments and mechanisms used by the IFI. However, research on the process, especially in the Latin American countries, has led to the formulation that transference (and dependence) is the outcome of three main factors: markets, linkages, and leverage (Stallings 1992). In the case of the Third World, international financial and commodity markets have had considerable positive (greater availability of resources) or negative (constricting resources and options) effects on economic developments and market conditions may make leverage more significant. In Eastern Europe it can be argued that in the first stage of the transition the anticipated influx of Western capital did not materialize and it was the end of the CMEA (with the collapse of traditional markets) that shaped conditions rather than the international markets.

Linkages are defined as 'the tendency of certain groups to identify with the interests and outlook of international actors and to support coalitions and policies reflecting them' (Stallings 1992: 52) and there are many clear examples of this in Eastern Europe. Leverage is the most direct form of international influence and centres on the IFI, although the concept is broader than the 'conditionality' of the IFI. Thus, countries without the ability to design an economic programme are at the 'mercy of the Bank and the Fund to act as substitute ministries of finance' (Stallings 1992: 58). Stallings also notes that international influence varies according to the stage of policy-making. In a simple three-stage model there is decision-making, policy implementation, and outcomes. International influence is greatest at the first and last stages and is less effective in policy implementation: 'powerful political opposition forces can undermine policies they disagreed with in the first place. Perhaps more important, lack of state capacity can severely limit the ability to implement a program, especially one involving major structural change as opposed to less fundamental demand management policies' (Stallings 1992: 85). Stallings further argues that international influence varies with issues and over time.

The Agencies' Instruments/Mechanisms

The major instruments of the neo-liberal model, designed and tested for a quarter of century, are the structural adjustment programmes, standby loans, and the targets/conditionalities negotiated with governments. Systemic transformation facilities are an innovation specifically created to maintain the balance of payments in the transitional economies of Eastern Europe. Structural adjustment programmes, a category originally applied in the First World, are designed to balance and restructure the national economies and financial systems with the aim of achieving stable and non-inflationary growth. They are, however, multifunctional and involve:

programmes of policy and institutional change necessary to modify the structure of the economy so that it can maintain both its growth rate and the viability of its balance of payments in the medium term. Several objectives are seen as implicit in this World Bank definition of structural adjustment lending, namely: (i) stabilizing the macro economic environment (ii) promoting economic growth and alleviating poverty (iii) promoting the openness of the economy (iv) improving transparency in the incentive system (v) improving efficiency in resource allocation (vi) improving scope for private sector development and (vii) strengthening institutions and capacity for policy analysis.   (Plant 1994: 6–7)

Structural adjustment is therefore a 'portmanteau phrase. Not only does it comprehend the policies themselves but it also covers the consistency, credibility, and sequencing of their implementation' (Toye 1995: 1). Structural adjustment programmes are, therefore, detailed and specific, but political responsibility rests with the national governments with whom they are negotiated. The IMF position on responsibility was elaborated in 1995:

First, what is a Fund program? There is no such thing. There are country policy programs, some of which are supported by the Fund and the others not. This does not mean (as you all well know) that we are passive. In deciding whether to support a program with its financial resources or not, the Fund (i.e. the Executive Board, but in the first instance the management and staff of the Fund) must satisfy itself that the key requirement is met that the country's policies are geared towards improving its external payments position on a sustained basis. This requirement, popularly (or unpopularly) [is] known as conditionality.   (Berlanger 1995)

The performance criteria are specific; they

typically cover the budget deficit, credit growth, external borrowing, and when appropriate the external reserve position—monitor that the underlying policies are being implemented and are having the intended effect. The underlying policies themselves include, obviously, fiscal, monetary and exchange rate policies; but also . . . a broad range of policies . . . which may [include] enterprise subsidies, restructuring or incomes policies in transitional economies.   (Berlanger 1995)

The lack of accountability has been criticized; as Raffer (1993: 152) has argued, a fundamental feature of a market system is a degree of risk; decision-makers cannot be guaranteed an outcome. However, the IFI seek to ensure that their involvement is cushioned from risk by insisting on full repayment: 'This kind of riskless decision making is certainly not a sound incentive system and is absolutely at odds with Western market systems' (Raffer 1993: 152).

The political difficulties of the process of conditionality and the importance of prior action have been recognized in recent years. Polak (quoted in Raffer 1993: 153) (a senior official) has suggested that this can be used to a country's advantage 'to minimize the policy commitments it must make in its letter of intent and thus to present itself as opting for adjustment on its own terms rather than under pressure from the Fund'. Raffer (1993: 153) comments that 'In plain English: a distressed country may choose whether to accept the IMF's conditions openly or by "cleverly" disguising them as its own free choice.' The process through which conditionality operates in practice is that there are a series of negotiations between a government and representatives of the IMF who set out the conditions for a loan. The government then submits a Letter of Intent to the IMF setting out the steps it proposes to take, which is submitted to the board of the IMF for approval. Although the government and the IMF are formally parties, there is in fact no agreement/contract between them. There is only a statement of the unilateral obligations accepted by the national government. The loans are usually disbursed in a series of tranches linked to the implementation of the programmes. There are clear examples from Eastern Europe of payments postponed for this reason. The Russian case from 1992 to 1995 is a notable example of non-disbursement (Lavigne 1995: 237).

THE STRATEGIC CHOICES OF GOVERNMENTS: IFI AS THE
SHADOW PARTNER

There is strong evidence to support Stallings's emphasis on the importance of
linkages in the process of transference. Thus, Chapter 2 explained the initial
processes of strategic choice in relation to economic reform in the different
countries. It showed how the Balcerowicz group in Poland and Gaidar and
his associates in Russia made strategic political choices for shock therapy,
and that support from international agencies was rapidly forthcoming (the
Paris Club for Poland). In these cases the evidence suggests that, although
there were no other external sources of finance, there were internal political
choices which were at least as important as the imposed external influences.
Portes (1994) emphasizes the extent to which key decision-makers in Central
and Eastern Europe were ready to endorse neo-liberal approaches, which is a
clear indication of a hegemonic process. The persistence of economic and
social crises in Eastern Europe has given the international agencies a continuing role in relation to economic reforms and thus, to the role of national
governments. In these conditions the international agencies have extensive
leverage to impose the terms of structural adjustment programmes, as
explained above.

There are two levels of strategic choice/decision-making: the international
and the national. The first is of decisive importance because the international
agencies select the economic measures from those in the framework of the
neo-liberal reform model. They transfer resources in the form of funds and
know-how, and mediate in the settlement of foreign debts, while their assess-
ments influence the decisions of other foreign lenders and investors (Lavigne
1995: 235). In 1995–6 Bulgaria relied on IMF loans to cover the internal public debt arising from the indebtedness of enterprises and thus to pay the wages
of those employed in the budget sector. The IFI therefore constitute an external strategic centre. However, it is essential to recognize that the shareholders
of the IFI may have a significant influence on their lending decisions. Thus,
different Western countries may act as sponsors for recipient countries in
Eastern Europe and the absence of such sponsorship may adversely affect the
scope, timing, and terms of loans from the IFI.

At the national level, governments formally make the decisions on the basis
of what is recommended externally. Their choice, however, is an operational
rather than a strategic one. Governments assume the obligation to secure
political assent from the parliament and then to prepare programmes of
implementation. This relates particularly to monetary and fiscal policies.
However, in the field of structural reform and especially privatization, as
shown in Chapters 2 and 4, governments have had space to exercise strategic
choices in the timing and forms of ownership change despite the recommendations of external advisers. At the national level there are two groups of

internal agencies. The first is that of the social partners, the employers and the trade unions, who participate in negotiations with the governments and have contacts with the missions and experts of the IFI. Their role is secondary but their support for the structural adjustment programmes is sought and they act as a buffer between the governments and the public at large, with the aim of maintaining social peace. The second group consists of directors of banks, officials from state departments, some managers, and representatives of local government. There are, nevertheless, wider linkages through the lobby comprising the informal network of position-holders with pro-monetarist orientations in the key areas of finance, banking, and fiscal policy. Members of this lobby mediate or participate in the negotiations with the international agencies and new governments. Technocratically minded groups from the political élites may also be in the network. This network is especially important in securing the continuity of neo-liberal reforms in each country irrespective of changes of governments. There is some indirect confirmation of the importance of this from the Deputy Managing Director of the IMF: 'The lesson from eastern Europe is that although reform measures were hard and although the governments that implemented them often lost power, their successors have not changed those reform policies' (Fisher 1996: 22).

It is normally assumed that the details of the memorandums submitted by governments to the IMF will remain confidential. In 1991, after negotiations with the IMF, the Czechoslovak government submitted a letter of intent specifying the actions it would take in the initial period of reform. The Trade Union Confederation, however, was able to secure a copy of the memorandum and published it as a tactic in the context of its negotiations with the government. Paragraph 14 of the document stated that: 'International reserves will be carefully monitored and each week a summary will be sent to the Fund and the State Bank has always to consult the Fund in cases of unexpected deterioration of the situation. . . . If additional measures and recommendations follow from the consultation these have to be implemented immediately.' Paragraph 37 set out wage policy: 'Real wages have decreased by 6 per cent in 1990. A further decrease in 1991 is unavoidable. For this purpose the policy for wage setting has been adopted which is to limit the growth of nominal wages in 1991 to a level lower than the increase in the index of consumer prices' (document supplied by CITUB).

The Bulgarian government has on three occasions (in 1991, 1992, and in 1996) prepared programme documents arising from negotiations with the IMF but has not disclosed them to the trade-union centres. Nevertheless, in 1996 a copy of the Memorandum for Structural Reforms was obtained. The nature of conditionality is illustrated by the following extract concerned particularly with inflation and the banking crisis: 'Our programme [to restore confidence in the banking system and the currency] is formulated on the basis of conservative assumptions but if there is a negative development in the key parameters we, after consultation with the IMF, will tighten the measures

. . . in order to achieve the aims set out in this Memorandum' (document supplied by CITUB).

The IFI terms for credits have also been politically contentious in Poland. Thus, at the end of 1992 and the beginning of 1993 there was a parliamentary majority against the budget restrictions required to meet IFI loan conditions. Notwithstanding this, 'President Walesa and the persuasive efforts of his government, which clearly identified the World Bank and IMF as the key actors on the economic and political scene in this regard, enabled the budget to get a majority' (Gorniak and Jerschina 1995: 186).

The question of whether it is constitutionally feasible for programmes to be rejected emerged in Hungary in 1995. The Bokrosh programme for financial stabilization developed by the Finance Minister and submitted to the IMF was challenged by the parliamentary opposition and referred to the Supreme Court. It ruled that some of the provisions were contrary to the constitution and they were therefore abrogated. The Finance Minister resigned and subsequently joined the World Bank.

Toye (1995: 8) has noted that in the past 'there was considerable support by influential voices, associated with the World Bank for authoritarian governments to be the agents of structural adjustment'. In answer to criticisms of such preferences for authoritarian government the Deputy Director of the IMF (Fisher 1996: 22) commented that:

The policies needed to reform are frequently quite difficult and people thought you needed a Pinochet to do it. Well in the '90s we have seen country after country reform as democracies. [There is] the extraordinarily powerful example of transitional countries [in the former socialist block] where those which moved most rapidly on democracy have also moved most rapidly on the economy. I think there is a lot of evidence that, at the very least having a democratic government is not bad for reform.

ECONOMIC ALTERNATIVES TO NEO-LIBERALISM

The implementation of the neo-liberal model in Eastern Europe has drawn criticisms from international organizations as well as academic writers. The report of the Economic Commission for Europe (ECE 1992: 3) noted in 1991–2 that: 'The errors of economic analysis are having serious consequences. . . . Ample evidence exists to support the view that the inevitable costs of transition have been amplified in many cases by a combination of unfounded assumptions, wrong estimates, inconsistent policies and a simple lack of action.' There had been 'too much stabilization' (ECE 1992: 41), while 'the stabilization-cum-reform programmes failed to meet the targets set by governments or specified in agreements with the IMF' (ECE 1992: 45). The next report (ECE 1993: 7) discussed

The siren call of shock therapy: the ability of a country to change—and to adjust to change—depends crucially on the nature and strength of its economic, political and legal institutions, on its social cohesiveness and traditions, and on the conditions prevailing at the start of the process of reform. . . . These considerations tend to be swept aside by the advocates of shock therapy.

Academic critics, such as Amsden *et al.* (1994: 4), have contrasted the 'Moral Crusade of Market Fundamentalism' in Eastern Europe with the positive role played by the state in the late industrializers in east Asia. They argue that 'eastern Europe's below-potential performance (and thus political instability) has stemmed from copying the wrong capitalist model—voluntarily or otherwise'. More specifically, Myant (1993) has criticized the negative effects on output of the shock therapy in Poland and Czechoslovakia.

A central concern of the ILO has always been the development of labour standards and their implementation through various instruments. The range of these standards is considerable and the main categories are: employment policy and social protection, employment and wage regulation, general conditions of work, and industrial relations and trade-union rights. In recent years the issue of the structural adjustment programmes introduced through the IFI in different areas of the world, and the social issues arising from them, have been one of the ILO's highest concerns (Plant 1994: 54). The perspective of the World Bank on labour issues is seen as deriving especially from neo-classical economics, concerned to maximize flexibility in labour markets and to remove the institutional 'rigidities' and 'distortions' deriving from labour laws and regulations and indeed government intervention. Thus, a World Bank study concluded that: 'it is not surprising to find that the neo-classical paradigm underpins implicitly, if not explicitly, the Bank's analysis of labour market and employment issues. This paradigm leads to policy recommendations that call for reducing government interventions in labour markets and market price distortions' (quoted in Plant 1994: 64). However, Plant (1994: 68) acknowledges that there is some evidence in recent years that the World Bank has accepted some aspects of social alleviation, and the recognition of poverty.

IMPLICATIONS FOR LABOUR RELATIONS

The measures for the macro-stabilization of the economy and for structural reform are linked to the management, and restriction, of money flows and the fiscal policies which restrict labour and social protection and the value of the social safety net. A framework for the transition and for specific policy on labour and social questions is set out by specialists who have worked for the World Bank (Barr 1994). Policy design for labour markets is analysed in terms of wages and employment and unemployment, whilst for social-policy and income transfers the discussion is focused on social insurance, family support, and poverty relief. All of these issues are of direct concern to the trade unions in Central and Eastern Europe and they are discussed here in terms of their consequences: the depression of real wages, unemployment, the impoverishment of vulnerable social groups, social policy, labour standards, and labour institutions.

The restriction of wages, pensions, and social benefits is the cornerstone of monetary policy in both the first and second stages of the reform. The structural adjustment programmes are designed to cut real incomes and restrict their growth, ostensibly to control inflation and maintain equilibrium in the money supply at national level. Low wages can also be seen as an instrument for increasing exports and improving the competitiveness of the economies. Less obvious is the importance of reducing wages, pensions, and social costs as an additional source for the provision of capital, of which there is an acute shortage in Eastern Europe. Control over the growth of wages is used as the main anchor for reducing inflation and maintaining it at a low level. This policy has led to drastic falls in real wages. The most striking falls have been in Bulgaria, Albania, Russia, and the Ukraine (see Vaughan-Whitehead 1995: 22–3). A major loss in countries such as Russia and Bulgaria is the growing volume of earned but unpaid wages due to the lack of funds in enterprises (Yakovlev 1995). The tax-based incomes policies promoted by the IFI are discussed in Chapter 6.

The IFI approach to wages has been criticized by other international agencies. The ECE (1992: 41) expressed doubts about the use of nominal wage anchors except for a short time and argued that: 'the specific wage policies, actually applied in eastern Europe, which led to a substantial fall in real wages, proved economically counterproductive, socially unfair and politically dangerous. Falling real wages reduced the incentives for labour reallocation, allowed inefficient sectors to maintain employment and inhibited productivity growth' (1992: 49). An ILO Conference held in Budapest at the end of 1995 set out a series of proposals for wage and incomes policy in Central and Eastern Europe. It disputed the assumption that only wage increases cause inflation and argued that they had a very minor role now. Every effort should be made to allow real wages to rise again and to promote improved productivity. (For the conference paper, see Vaughan-Whitehead 1995.)

The minimum wage has had a particular significance in Eastern Europe because of its link to the tariff wage structures and to the social benefits for unemployment and families. Research on the gap between the minimum and the average wage has been promoted by the ILO (Vaughan-Whitehead 1995). This shows that, with the exception of Poland, the gap between minimum and average wages is widening because the revision of the minimum is delayed, and typically lags two to three years behind average wages. Jackman and Rutkowski (1994: 153) argue that the minimum wage should be modified or abolished as the economy starts to recover. It has been noted that there is a continuing and significant divergence between the IFI and the ILO on the

minimum wage (Plant 1994: 197). In Bulgaria and Russia the IFI have inter-
vened to restrict improvements in the minimum wage.

Mass impoverishment has emerged as the most acute social problem in
Eastern Europe and the poor were visible from the early years of the reform.
The poor are made up of the unemployed (especially those not covered by the
state benefits safety net), ethnic minorities, young people, women, pensioners,
and the disabled. Researchers have forecast that the process of mass impoverishment is unlikely to be reduced significantly in the short or medium term.
Six years into the reforms, the number of people unable to adapt or to cope
with the burdens imposed by the reforms is increasing and not diminishing
and income inequality is growing. Recorded unemployment has not so far
been as high as expected and has not yet reached 20 per cent. As shown in
Table 3.1, in most countries it is between 10 per cent and 16 per cent, while in
Russia and the Czech Republic it is below 5 per cent. One probable explana-
tion is that there has been a tacit understanding between the major partners
since the start of the reforms that, in return for a slower pace of retrenchment,
trade unions have restrained their claims for increases in nominal wages.
There is, therefore, a bargain of lower wages in exchange for jobs which has
had the tacit acceptance of the IFI. In the Russian case it has been argued that
the statistics of registered unemployment very seriously underestimate the
real total when compared with labour-force survey data (Standing 1995a).
However, it is obvious that in the future the phenomenon of overemployment
will become an open issue. There is an expectation that, when privatized
enterprises become subject to stronger competitive and financial pressures,
labour-force reductions will acquire a mass and cyclical character and unless
there are national or regional programmes to promote retraining and alternative employment the issue of unemployment will become sharper and more
complicated.

The three pillars of the socialist social system have been summarized as
guaranteed employment, social protection via subsidized prices, and enterprise-based social benefits mostly through the direct provision of goods and
services (Standing 1996: 230). The development of the market economy
undermines these pillars and it has been pointed out that in Central and
Eastern Europe the IFI have addressed social-policy issues in their adjustment programmes much more than in the developing countries (Plant 1994:
98). In 1994 Klaus claimed that in the Czech Republic the first, economic,
stage of the transformation had been completed and the second stage would
be the social transformation centred on reforms in social policy. Standing
(1996: 230) claims that 'it is almost true to state that the revolution that has
been taking place in central and eastern Europe is the first in history in which
social policy has been shaped and influenced by international financial agencies. This is not necessarily a criticism, merely a recognition of the realities
and pressures under which numerous governments have had to operate.'
Governments have been under international pressures to restrict unemploy-

TABLE 3.1. *Unemployment 1990–1995 (%)*

Countries	Year Ending					
	1990	1991	1992	1993	1994	1995
Bulgaria	1.7	11.1	15.3	10.4	12.4	11.1
Czech Republic	0.7	4.1	2.6	3.5	3.2	2.9
Hungary	1.7	8.5	12.3	12.1	10.4	12.0
Poland	6.3	11.8	13.6	16.4	16.0	14.9
Russia	0.0	0.0	4.7	5.5	7.4	8.3
Slovakia	0.0	6.6	11.4	12.7	13.7	13.1

Source: ILO (1996), 387–405.

ment benefits, to target social benefits, and to change the basis for pensions and other forms of social insurance. The need for reform of social provisions is not questioned by the ILO; however, its staff have argued that countries should have the space to redesign their own systems based on comprehensive reviews and with governance related to the tripartite institutions (such as the Social Security Boards in Hungary) (see Cichon and Samuel 1995). This points to the difficulties of individual countries in achieving 'autonomy of governance in the context of intense pressure from the IMF, the World Bank and others to adopt a specific model' (Standing 1995b: 37).

As explained in Chapter 2, the process of political pluralism/regime change was accompanied by legislation recognizing the right to strike, to associate in trade unions, and to establish collective bargaining. This legislation was usually prepared within the framework of international standards such as those of the ILO. Thus, the Hungarian Labour Code was submitted for comment to the ILO, which considered that it was consistent with ILO conventions. 'The Government of Hungary has made a concerted overall effort to reform its labour law and industrial relations systems in line with ILO standards' (Plant 1994: 159). The ILO has made comments to other governments about changes in labour law. In the Bulgarian case, however, some of its comments on the Labour Code of 1993 were rejected by the government. Subsequently there has been a pattern of erosion of these new provisions partly through non-enforcement (see ILO-CEET 1994: 137–140).

For the ILO, freedom of association in independent trade unions and participation in collective bargaining have always been a fundamental axiom. Tripartism has also been a basic principle for standard-setting, and the ILO has welcomed the development of tripartite consultations and negotiations at the national level in Eastern Europe (see Kyloh 1995). Historically the market-based approach of the IFI has tended to see trade unions as prone to restrict the operations of the labour market. A World Bank paper of 1991 (quoted in Plant 1994: 68) challenges some common assumptions viewing organized labour as an obstacle to labour market adjustment. It argues that union responses to adjustment range from militant opposition to explicit cooperation, depending on the strength of the labour movement, economic cycles and political institutions. The conditions needed to gain workers' cooperation are seen as analogous to those which encourage business to invest, namely: political stability, a voice in policy that affects their interests, and a confidence that current sacrifices will ultimately yield a fair share of future benefits.

In a recent global overview, the World Bank (1995: 81) acknowledged the possibility of trade unions contributing to improving the competitiveness of the economy, especially at company level, but emphasized their potentially negative effects deriving from 'monopolistic behaviour' and 'opposition to reforms'. In contrast to the ILO, there was no reference to the positive advantages of national tripartite dialogue, although Fretwell and Jackman (1994: 166) recognize its importance in Eastern Europe. However, the IMF sponsored a tripartite conference for the Transition Economies of Central and Eastern Europe in 1995. Fund representatives are now required to consult representatives of the social partners in the countries where they operate. Thus, in Bulgaria, for example, trade-union centres are consulted on the distribution of the budget but not on its global size. Camdessus (1996), Managing Director of the IMF, recognized 'the social costs of adjustment' and the need for trade unions to 'try to help design social safety nets that are well targeted and cost effective' in a speech to the ETUC. Nevertheless, there is as yet no official indication of any departure from the fundamentals of the neo-liberal model.

CONCLUSIONS

The discussion in this chapter suggests that, despite its critics and doubts about its efficacy, the neo-liberal model of transition has been dominant in Russia and Eastern Europe. The hegemonic nature of the model deserves some comment. In the 1980s the populations, and finally the governments, accepted that the socialist system had failed to meet their economic expectations, especially in terms of the consumer goods which the market economy was seen to have delivered in the West. Some form of market economy was widely considered as necessary and desirable; there was considerable doubt about the socialist state as an effective agency for economic reform. The key issue is why the IMF model was bought at the expense of other roads to the market economy. Following Stallings's (1992) model of transference, the evidence in the early stages was that hegemony was based on linkages with key groups of academics and policy advisers in the different countries whose acceptance of the neo-liberal model was ideological. Chapter 2 showed how the alliance between external and internal liberals was constructed in specific countries, although other economists in these countries were more cautious about rapid economic transformation. The role of the IFI was very often combined with leverage based initially on debt, but the linkages were more decisive overall. A few years into the process of transformation the actual results of the neo-liberal model were criticized by outsiders, and the appropriateness of this model was contrasted with alternative models of development, such as the different institutional structures in east Asia, where the state has been a very proactive agent for economic development. However, given the ideological commitment of key position-holders to the neo-liberal model, there is little evidence to support the argument that alternatives were politically possible in the specific context of economic crisis. Strategic choices for key decision-makers in governments were, therefore, mainly shaped by their perceptions of popular responses within their countries. At this stage the IFI had great initial leverage in their ability to resolve the problems of external debt. Stabilization through liberalization of prices was, therefore, accepted as a bitter necessity. However, it is important to remember the counter-case of Czechoslovakia, which did not have a debt problem but has still been resolutely neo-liberal in its reform strategy.

Subsequent criticisms of the neo-liberal model derive from the unexpected depth of the transformational recessions and from the failure to revise significantly the application of the monetary mechanisms. Arguably, the continuing focus on stabilization has postponed the task of industrial restructuring. This chapter has shown the mechanisms by which the IFI have continued to impose their model, but especially in the context of continuing needs for macro-stabilization. This has provided the leverage, supported by the linkages with growing internal lobbies, for the transference and imposition of the neo-liberal model. The space for strategic choice by governments in the field of macroeconomic policy has been foreclosed by these weaknesses. Nevertheless, as shown in Chapter 2 and to be developed in the following chapter, governments did exercise strategic choice at specific points in the timing, sequence, and methods of privatization, although, once again, foreign specialists sponsored specific models.

In respect of labour relations, the IFI formally accepted a role for tripartism and trade unions especially as a bulwark against the potential social disruption of the stabilization period. Tripartism is seen, however, as a means of consultation about implementation of policies derived from the neo-liberal model. On the other hand, the ILO was able to articulate a considerable range of alternatives to the neo-liberal model, but their leverage was relatively small, except in the transformation of the trade unions. It is with regards to the substantive consequences of wage reduction, unemployment, and impoverishment that the measures derived from the neo-liberal model have had the greatest effect on labour relations. It is here that the outside criticisms from other agencies have been most trenchant but ignored by the IFI. The possible exception is that of the, perhaps tacit, acceptance of postponed unemployment.

It is possible to contrast the 'transitional' approach of the IFI with the more 'transformational' approach of many of their critics. For the former, the starting point is an end state—a market-based economy—to which all mechanisms are related and a key imperative is to achieve a sharp discontinuity from the planned economy. In contrast, a transformational orientation would set the major parameters of economic reform but allow incremental implementation on the basis of trial and error (testing and review) and take more account of country specificities.

Although the neo-liberal model has hegemonic status in Russia and much of Eastern Europe, it cannot claim unhindered success. There have been unintended consequences of the neo-liberal model which can be considered along three interrelated dimensions—the appropriateness of the theory, the efficacy of the implementation process, and the nature of the response. The first question is the extent to which the neo-liberal blueprint for transition adequately theorized the task ahead. In August 1989 the distinguished economist Kornai (1990) presented his proposals for a transition to market economy. In it he anticipated a number of difficulties—for example, wage inflation—but there was no indication of what he was later to term the 'the transformational recession' (Kornai 1994). He acknowledged (1994: 58) that: 'Neither the political statements and government programs nor the writings of economists included as urgent priorities the need to guard against recession or, later, the need to halt or combat the recession.' The depth of the depression was unexpected (Ellman 1994: 13). There is considerable debate amongst economists as to why the stabilization packages appear not to have worked as intended. For writers such as Aslund (1994: 26) from the neo-liberal wing, the problems arise from the unreconstructed behaviour of 'an old rent-seeking élite', and the solution is to persist with the bitter medicine. Others point to the institutional vacuum created by the dismantling of the command economy; Ellman (1994: 2) refers to the IMF representative in Poland who acknowledged that 'it had been a mistake to assume that state enterprises and banks would behave according to market principles', and a former head of the World Bank's East European department (Ellman 1994: 3) has concluded that 'eastern Europe is not well served by textbook advice'. Everywhere the implementation of the neo-liberal model has met with problems.

Although the IFI have been aware of the potential costs of transition on the populations of Russia and Eastern Europe, as Ellman (1994: 13–14) argues, the people themselves were largely unprepared for the social effects. The impoverishment of large sections of the populations has acted as a political constraint on the neo-liberal strategy. Although social unrest has been less than might have been predicted, the threat of what Kornai (1994: 60) refers to as a 'Weimarization of the post-socialist region' has contributed to government instability in countries such as Bulgaria and has constrained government action even in the most apparently stable countries such as Hungary and the Czech Republic.

In essence these points demonstrate the importance of the legacy of institutional and behavioural patterns and the inappropriateness of transferred mechanisms. Governments have been profoundly hampered in the implementation of neo-liberal policies, even when they have had the will to push them through. Perhaps the biggest contradiction of the neo-liberal blueprint has been its ignorance or denial of the role of the state. The weakness of states in eastern Europe and Russia is a constant feature of post-communist development. This weakness is not, as Aslund (1994: 28–9) assumes, because of their capture by the old corrupt communist élite, although this indeed can be a factor, but rather a structural feature of an institution in transition. The need for a growth strategy in which the state plays an important role is increasingly advocated (e.g., Ellman 1994; Kornai 1994). However, the hegemony of the neo-liberal model serves to characterize any argument for more state intervention in the economy as a step back to the Communist past.

The shadow partners—the IFI—have played and continue to play a key role in Eastern Europe and Russia, although criticisms of the neo-liberal strategy become increasingly vociferous. The impact of the neo-liberal strategy of stabilization has arguably led to a delay in restructuring, whilst having profound consequences on the terrain of labour relations. The next stage of the neo-liberal package—privatization—was expected to complete the fundamental basis for a market economy. The practice of privatization and its implications for labour relations are the subjects of the next chapter.

4

Privatization, Ownership Change, and Labour Relations

There has been a widespread expectation that privatization of large state enterprises, and the resulting weakening in centralized control of the economy, would radically alter the context for labour relations in Russia and Eastern Europe and, in particular, would greatly enhance the opportunities for strategy formulation at enterprise level. This chapter looks at the processes of ownership change and privatization, as a broad category of developments, and as a strategic issue at enterprise level. It is not the task here to debate the need for privatization but rather to interrogate the assumptions made about its impact upon labour relations. The discussion is organized around three themes. First, it considers the theoretical and ideological significance of privatization as a driving force for transformation in these societies. Secondly, it argues for the concept of ownership change as a contested process in preference to 'privatization' as a better means for uncovering the role of the enterprise in transformation. Finally, it explores the considerable variations in privatization processes and methods adopted in the different countries and endeavours to explain their significance for labour-relations issues. Thus, the chapter provides a bridge from the macroeconomic and political context of the earlier chapters to the enterprise-case-study focus of later chapters. In so doing it seeks to stress the interaction between the national and enterprise levels and to counter the assumption that labour relations are merely derived from the macroeconomic and political context.

THE SIGNIFICANCE OF PRIVATIZATION

In order to explore the impacts of privatization on labour relations it is necessary to unpack the notions of privatization and ownership change and look at the economic and political imperatives behind reform. In the early days of the post-communist regimes the desire to move rapidly to a market-, rather than a state-, driven system gave an enormous ideological significance to ownership changes and the assumption that privatization was the chief mechanism for industrial and economic reform. As Przeworski (1993: 141–2) has commented about Poland, this was often presented as the need to return to a 'normal economy' (see also Dabrowski *et al.* 1991; Aslund 1992). The advice and commentary of many Western economists who counselled the need for a rapid transformation of the economy reinforced such views (Kiss 1992: 1015;

see also Chapter 2 above). This has led Murrell (1992: 45), amongst others, to worry that 'too many hopes have been invested in privatization'.

This poses the question of what privatization is hoped to achieve, and here one finds a number of different answers. Estrin (1994*a*: 13–19) has demonstrated that both economic and political arguments have been used to show why privatization is necessary (see also Lavigne 1995: 158*a*). In much of the literature advocating rapid privatization it is deduced that the prerequisite for changing the behaviour of enterprises and the managers and employees who work in them is ownership change (see, e.g. Aslund 1992; and the discussion in Major 1993: 51). The only way to overcome the deficiencies of central planning and its consequences at the level of the individual firm is to restructure property relations. It is expected that the discipline of the market will restructure the actions of both managers and workers; this is sometimes referred to as the problem of agency (McFaul 1995: 39–56; see also Nuti and Portes 1993; Ernst *et al.* 1996: 93). Thus, the pattern of managerial incentives will be changed by creating real owners who will exert pressure on managers to behave in a profit-maximizing manner. In time this will give managers the incentive to restructure industry, as 'owners' seek to move out of unprofitable and into profitable areas. In the field of labour relations this is likely to require managers to restrain wage demands, shed excess labour, divest the enterprise of its social assets, and generally seek ways of improving labour productivity and product quality. Hence, the assumption is that to achieve economic renewal the behaviour of management has to be restructured by providing incentives to manage in a 'capitalist way' and that the behaviour of workers has to be changed by providing a capitalist system of discipline over labour. Similar arguments were made about the impact of privatization on labour relations in the British case—namely, that by introducing the discipline of the market and giving managers the 'freedom to manage', control would be reasserted over the workforce (see, e.g., O'Connell Davidson 1993). Foreign direct investment in Eastern Europe was thought by some to be the quickest and only guaranteed way of introducing such discipline into managerial behaviour (Stark 1990: 357–9).

This view of privatization suggests that only ownership change will produce the necessary enterprise-restructuring for company competitiveness. As the ECE (1994: 200) commented: 'the notions of privatization and restructuring have been used by the Polish authorities virtually as synonymous' (see also Amsden *et al.* 1994: 10). East European governments have been wary of industrial policy and there has been a general desire for privatization to be seen as *the* instrument of change and painful restructuring rather than state-directed policy and planning. This is hardly surprising, given the initial lack of public support for continued state interference in the economy, privatization is assumed to usher in the 'neutral logic of the market' (Rutland 1997: 280). In addition to this lack of legitimacy, a number of states also, arguably, lacked the capability to engage in sophisticated policies of

industrial restructuring. The exception to this has been the east German economy, where the agency established to manage the privatization of the economy, the Treuhandanstalt, with both the political legitimacy and the
economic means, adopted a managed approach involving some restructuring
prior to privatization (Simoneti 1993: 95–9; Carlin 1994: 137; Grabher 1995:
42–4; von Hirschhausen 1995: 65–7; Hyman 1996: 603). More cynically, one
could argue that it appealed to governments in Russia and Eastern Europe to
try and shift the social and political burdens of restructuring onto the invis-
ible hand of market forces. (It is not by accident that Mrs Thatcher's similar
project in Britain was seen by some as a prototype.)

With the exception of eastern Germany, in the rest of Eastern Europe establishing property rights was seen as the key not only to transforming corporate
governance and encouraging restructuring but also to the political project of
creating a bourgeois class who would resist attempts to roll back the reform
agenda. The 'property-owning-democracy' idea gained favour in Russia for
these reasons. Thus, the political imperative for privatization pushed for a radical transformation of the economy in order to 'secure the irreversibility of the
reform process' and create a property-owning class to underpin and legitimate
change (Estrin 1994a: 18). The political significance of restitution, as a subcat-
egory of privatization, was both its apparent ideological or moral justification,
but also its potential for diffusing capital assets and creating a group with both
the interests and material means to support the reform process. As Offe (1996:
115) has commented, 'a case-by-case approach to privatization gives the government much more scope for discretionary action and thereby increases the
probability that the government will accommodate rising anti-reformist pressures by slowing down the process. Hence restitution can be seen to have the
virtue of credibility-enhancing irreversibility.'

These arguments are reinforced by those commentators who point to the
imperative for rapid privatization in terms of the parallel need to wrest control over enterprises from the ministries and to compensate for the weak
capacity of the state to manage the transition effectively (van Brabant 1990:
125; Aslund 1992: 18–22; Perotti 1994: 55). Other arguments for privatization
stress the beneficial impact on state revenues of a sell-off of state enterprises
(see, e.g., Kiss 1992: 1017; Major 1993: 54–5; Schwartz 1995: 31). In addition
it was hoped that privatization would attract foreign investors and the
approval and support of international agencies (Kilminster 1995: 90).

This mixture of economic and political goals for the privatization process
is not necessarily compatible and has certainly not been uniformly achieved.
The speed and form of the required changes necessarily remain highly contested subjects. Some theorists cast doubt on the potential for privatization to
herald the dawn of new private market economies, arguing instead that the
best hope for a transformation of the economy comes from entrepreneurial
activity, foreign direct investment, and the establishment of new private
enterprises (see, e.g., Murrell 1992: 43–4; Kornai 1995; Kogut 1996).

At an abstract level the justifications for privatization as a means of restructuring managerial incentives is clear enough. However, this line of reasoning suggests that the main effects on labour relations will emerge only after privatization: that privatization is a precondition of labour-relations reform. As Kabalina *et al.* (1994) have commented, 'in the West restructuring is a condition of privatization, while in Russia it is the anticipated result'. The basic assumption or hypothesis is that, as privatization proceeds, the autonomy of the enterprise will increase and management will be free of 'political interference'—free to act like a manager in a capitalist enterprise. In Aslund's (1992: 70) phrase, privatization 'helps create a boundary between economics and politics'.

Given the integration of the Communist Party structures and the enterprise in the former regimes, it is easy to understand the rhetorical appeal of the notion of separating politics from the enterprise or for the creation of 'autonomous industrial relations' (Deppe and Tatur 1995: 4). The problem with such assertions, however, is their oversimplification of the processes of transformation. Much of the discussion of property rights assumes that it is possible to delineate clearly between a private market sector and a public bureaucratic sector, and that privatization can simply shift the bulk of East European economies from the latter to the former. In reality, the processes of ownership change have presented not clear choices between 'private' and 'public' control, but rather a whole series of intermediate forms of ownership. Nor is it a simple matter to identify 'owners' or infer what their strategies in relation to labour relations might be. In this context the logic of rational choice arguments about property rights begins to weaken. It is necessary to explore the issue of corporate governance and the processes of ownership change in concrete terms. In practice there is no such thing as *the* 'capitalist manager' but rather a myriad of different ways by which property rights are translated into managerial strategy. As Cooter (1992: 94) has asked, 'which capitalism' is Eastern Europe supposed to strive towards? If, indeed, any of them.

Contrasting the Anglo-American with the German or Japanese models of corporate governance, it becomes clear that the relationships between shareholders (private and institutional), managers, and the workforce can vary substantially. In the Anglo-American case, or the 'outsider model', discipline over managers is typically maintained by external owners via the stock exchange and the financial institutions; whereas in the 'insider model', characteristic of Japan, internal stakeholders are far more influential (Cooter 1992: 94; Schwartz 1995: 39–40; Ernst *et al.* 1996: 193–6). The impact of these on corporate performance and managerial strategy *vis-à-vis* human resources is much debated. Thus, there is only so far that one can go at an abstract level in predicting the likely impact of different patterns of ownership on labour relations. In reality, as Vickers and Yarrow (1988: 44) comment, 'managerial incentive structures are determined via a complex set of interactions among

factors that include the type of ownership, the degree of product market competition, and the effectiveness of regulation . . .'.

This is reminiscent of ideological debate surrounding the British privatization programmes of the 1980s and 1990s. Here, too, the assumption (and aim)
of conservative politicians was that privatization would strengthen management's hand against the trade unions and workforce. However, as research
has indicated, although labour relations have changed in the privatized companies, they have not altered uniformly. As Ferner and Collins (1991: 404)
conclude, 'patterns of industrial relations need to be explained by the interaction between the broad "logic" of privatization and the structural peculiarities of the industry concerned' (see also Fairbrother 1994). Further, as
O'Connell Davidson's (1993: 213) study of privatization in the water industry
illustrates, the capitalist employment relation is very variable:

> The point is that decisions over where to locate the employment relation are set in a
> particular legal and institutional context; they are influenced by wider economic con-
> ditions, and by the particular competitive pressures and labour market conditions in
> any given sector; they are affected by shifts to the balance of class forces, and are also
> the terrain of narrower contests between particular groups of workers and employers.

Thus, it cannot be assumed that privatization will have uniform effects on
labour relations either from country to country or from organization to organization within a country. Nor is it safe to assume, as many of the economic
models of privatization tend to, that privatization is in some sense a technical
issue and that labour-relations questions lie dormant until ownership has
been changed. In order, therefore, to look more meaningfully at the impact of
privatization on labour relations in Eastern Europe and Russia, it is necessary
to consider the unfolding of ownership change as a diverse and contested
process.

OWNERSHIP CHANGE AS A CONTESTED PROCESS

During the first six years of reform the privatization project continued to
change and develop in response to political pressures and conflicts. In none of
the countries under consideration here has privatization proceeded as quickly
or smoothly as initially hoped, nor has there been the dramatic and immediate impact on labour relations that was expected. The shake-out of labour
from the old state enterprises was initially less painful than predicted, and
researchers continue to find many examples of what appears to be a persistence of old managerial habits, whether defined as paternalism or political
exigency (e.g. Clarke and Fairbrother 1993a; Amsden *et al.* 1994: 59). As
Ernst *et al.* (1996: 3–4) remind us, the large state-owned enterprises typical of
these countries functioned not merely as economic institutions but also as
social institutions and not infrequently the major organization of a given

town or local area (see also Hill *et al.* 1997: 242–3). The implications of restructuring or privatization are therefore often considerably more visible and problematic than the simple transfer of productive assets to private owners.

Commentators are right to point out that in the British case public enterprises have been prepared for privatization by extensive restructuring, reductions in the workforce, and commercialization and that in a sense the purpose of privatization in Eastern Europe is to create the conditions in which such restructuring will be possible. However, this underplays the contested character of privatization and the fact that it is a process not a single event. The approach adopted here hypothesizes that the relationship between ownership change, enterprise behaviour, and labour relations is much more complex in reality. Privatization and ownership change are not necessarily synonymous; ownership change cannot be treated as an undifferentiated category. In practice the process of ownership transformation has proved to be complex and in some countries slow. As Clague (1992: 18) has commented, the use of the term privatization serves to obscure many important differences between recent sales of public enterprises in Western economies and the project facing East European governments. In an earlier analysis of enterprise change, the concept of marketization was found to be more useful for unpacking the impact of ownership changes on labour relations (see Thirkell *et al.* 1995*a*: 11–14).

The concept of marketization allows one to capture the means by which enterprises were progressively freed from centralized administrative control. Marketization is defined as involving five main stages: the exposure of state-owned companies to market forces by the reduction (though not necessarily the abolition) of state subsidies and state orders, and, with it, a reduction in the allocative function of ministries; the deregulation of prices and wages giving enterprises more autonomy in these areas; the loss of markets in the CMEA trade area and increasing competition in product markets and suppliers; organizational restructuring sometimes involving the break-up of large firms and typically comprising degrees of decentralization and divisionalization; and changes in ownership (Thirkell *et al.* 1995*a*: 11). Some of these processes were already under way prior to the political changes.

Through these stages of transformation, enterprises are variously opened up to the development of greater managerial autonomy and discretion to develop business strategies and reorient labour policies. Managers may also begin to mobilize within the enterprise to secure a preferred ownership change outcome or be involved in more or less legal attempts to break up the enterprise into saleable parts. Equally, the lessening of central control expands the space in which trade unions or other mechanisms of worker involvement can organize to encourage or limit change. Thus, patterns of labour relations begin to change at enterprise level which may place constraints or conditions upon the further progress of transformation. In addition to the impact of legacies from the past, ownership change is shaped by the simultaneous effects of broader processes of marketization. Hence, it has been argued that the collapse of output which characterized all the countries in the early 1990s, in the face of the loss of traditional CMEA trade, and the difficulties of finding new markets, along with structural features of the economies, were the real causes of rising unemployment, rather than the anticipated effects of privatization (ETUI 1995: 29)—a set of circumstances which in turn served to temper some earlier popular enthusiasm for rapid privatization of these economies.

The progress of ownership reforms has been dependent upon not only political consent and mobilization and administrative capability at national level, but also the availability of capital and enterprise level capabilities. Thus, there is a whole range of intermediate forms of ownership change such as corporatization, commercialization, leasing, and liquidation which do not equate to the straightforward notion of 'privatization'. The process of ownership change is also constrained at enterprise level by the market position of the organization, ambiguities in the implementation of new legislation, the competences and abilities of managers, and the potential for emerging interests to press for particular outcomes. The attempt to transform the property structure and the relations of production is constrained by the interests of management and workers at enterprise level. The strength and persistence of enterprise-based habits and customs vary from country to country and may be strengthened or reduced by different reform strategies—for example, by whether, and in what form, workers have access to shares or not. Nevertheless, in all cases the dynamics of labour relations at enterprise level remain of crucial significance for the possible success of different reform strategies.

Thus, to assess the impacts of ownership change on labour relations requires consideration of the formal and informal interaction of competing groups: old and new élites in state agencies, pressures from international agencies and foreign investors, trade-union organizations and other institutions of worker representation, enterprise management, domestic investors, and other local interests. Management at enterprise level seeks to organize its autonomy in the face of constraints from both outside and within the organization. At the heart, therefore, of any attempt to uncover emerging patterns in labour-relations changes lies a consideration of the contested nature of ownership changes.

The significance of the enterprise level has been systematically underplayed in many discussions of the transformations in Eastern Europe. This is not surprising, but equally not defensible. Much of the economic literature on privatization in Eastern Europe and Russia has failed to focus on the complexities of ownership change and has ignored the enterprise level, because real changes at this level are thought to be contingent upon ownership change. For example, van Brabant (1990: 129–31), in a list of difficulties facing the privatizing of state assets, mentions the following: the absence of capital markets, the absence of a capitalist class, the issue of foreign ownership, weak entrepreneurship, the problems with accounting rules, and the legal environment. This list gives little sense of the enterprise as an agent in privatization struggles. Thus, it is a valuable corrective to evaluate the extent to which the freeing-up of interests at enterprise levels does or does not constrain reform processes. It is the contention here that, in order to understand the changing role of the enterprise in post-communist societies, it is necessary to investigate the freeing-up of interests at this level. In particular, it is important to examine the changing role of management, and especially the shifting functions of middle management, and the scope for institutions, especially trade unions and other worker organizations, to mobilize to promote their interests. These developments are also critical to an understanding of the wider processes of transformation in these societies. In Chapters 7 and 8 full consideration is given to this level by reference to the case studies of enterprises and the impact of labour relations on ownership change and restructuring.

The next concern here is to consider the different empirical approaches to ownership change. The key issues in relation to labour relations are to what degree have laws and decrees on privatization allowed trade unions and/or workers to influence the pace and character of privatization and to what extent have the actual forms of ownership change served to restructure managerial expectations and actions and encourage or inhibit employee involvement. It is important to interrogate the extent to which the actual forms of privatization have led to new patterns of corporate governance and the next section looks at the different paths to privatization from country to country.

VARIATIONS IN 'PRIVATIZATION' PROCESSES

In practice there have been a wide variety of different forms of ownership change appearing in Eastern Europe and Russia. The processes of privatization can be more or less regulated or more or less spontaneous, but in neither case have they proved to be unproblematic. As many have remarked, the scale of the projected privatization in these countries is far in excess of even the most energetic privatization projects in the Western economies. It is also proposed against the backdrop of weak or non-existent capital markets and a shortage of domestic savings. The hoped-for inflow of foreign capital has not materialized on anything like the anticipated scale. Thus, in practice attempts to privatize these economies have faced significant and ongoing political, economic, and administrative constraints, leading to a much more contingent process than might have been assumed in the heady days immediately after the collapse of the Communist regimes.

This discussion is concerned with the projects to privatize medium and large-scale state enterprises. The policies and experience of privatizing small-scale enterprises, especially in the service sector, and the particular features of the agriculture and housing sectors are beyond the scope of this research. It will also not consider the role of restitution or policies designed to encourage the establishment of new private enterprises. (For a summary discussion of the progress of restitution and privatization of small-scale enterprises, see Cook and Kirkpatrick 1995; Schwartz 1995.)

As discussed in Chapter 2, governments in the different countries have wrestled with a number of ongoing dilemmas around both the pace and the form of privatization. The approaches adopted owe much to the specific economic and political legacy of the Communist regime as manifested in the different countries and the strength of the government to push through its preferred approach. It is generally agreed that the form of privatization has been conditioned by three broad choices. First, between commercial or mass privatization—that is, whether enterprises should be valued and sold at something approaching market price or whether shares should be distributed free or at a nominal price. Secondly, the choice between selling to outsiders and/or to insiders—that is, to existing to shareholders, e.g. manager and workers (Estrin 1994*a*; Kilminster 1995: 92; Earle and Estrin 1996; Ernst *et al.* 1996: 48–62). As Offe (1996: 108) comments, there are tensions between 'resource-based' and 'rights-based' approaches. Thirdly, the choice between the centralized (top-down) or decentralized (bottom-up) process of ownership change—that is, whether the process is state directed or management led and whether there are formal mechanisms for worker influence over the nature of change. Is it a top-down or a bottom-up procedure? From these three dimensions it is possible to construct a series of ideal typical outcomes. An example would be commercial privatization with shares sold to outsiders, which could be state or enterprise led; foreign direct investment would be the obvious example. Alternatively, there could be mass privatization, with shares going to outsiders as in the Czech Republic's centrally directed, voucher method, or with shares going to insiders under one of the more decentralized Russian methods.

These dimensions raise the question of who has formal influence over the privatization project. In other words, to what extent is the actual process of privatization a negotiated one. These issues have been ignored, largely, by the mainstream macroeconomic analyses, with some honourable exceptions (Rausser and Simon 1992; Schleifer and Vishny 1994; Frydman *et al.* 1996*b*). The actual process of privatization in each case will be the negotiated outcome of the relevant actors in the specific context of prevailing rules and regulations. Hence, the formal role accorded to different actors in the process may be very significant. The privatization project in any particular case is mediated by the role of management and the trade unions/labour collective in the organization. Thus, the enterprise level is a constituent part of the change process, not merely an outcome. It can be expected that there will be considerable variation within a country from one privatization to another. The range of outcomes can be depicted with reference to a series of strategic choice continua (see Fig. 4.1).

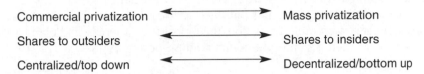

Commercial privatization ⟷ Mass privatization

Shares to outsiders ⟷ Shares to insiders

Centralized/top down ⟷ Decentralized/bottom up

FIG. 4.1. Strategic choices of privatization

The first continuum represents tensions between the aim to go for Western-style privatization to the highest bidder and the potential unpopularity of foreign direct investment, acquisition of enterprises by previous economic élites, or mafia groups, thought to have obtained their money by dubious means. It also contains a dilemma over the pace of reform; in the absence of sufficient private capital willing to invest, mass privatization offers a rapid route for privatization. The second continuum reflects the relative strengths of insider groups and the extent to which government can override insider interests or not. To a degree, the final continuum also represents the strength of government but also includes the use of different mechanisms to manage the privatization process and struggles between special privatization agencies, other government ministries, local authorities, and enterprise management to define the methods of privatization.

Allied to these issues is the question of the pace of reforms, another dimension along which countries have differed, often discussed in terms of shock therapy versus gradualism. This places the privatization projects in a broader context of other macro-economic stabilization policies (see Chapter 2). However, the speed of progress on privatization is not necessarily a reflection of whether governments have favoured shock therapy over a slower approach. We need also to consider the pace with which ownership changes have been accomplished and this is closely tied to the choice of methods.

A key factor which divides the countries considered here is the degree of centralized control over the process of privatization and this is clearly related to the specific historical legacy in each case. All the countries had centrally planned economies prior to regime collapse; however, in reality there was considerable difference in the mechanisms of enterprise management. In Hungary from the 1960s and in Poland from the early 1980s the enterprise had gained more autonomy. The assumption that property rights resided unequivocally in the state requires scrutiny. Processes of decentralization had created what Earle *et al.* (1993: 2) describe as 'property-like entitlements' at enterprise level, although this is not to go so far as to argue that a degree of operational autonomy confers explicit property rights. Nevertheless, in these cases, the state was potentially weakened in its ability to manage the subsequent move towards privatization. As Dabrowski *et al.* (1991: 404–5) comment about Poland, 'the postcommunist state did not inherit either *de facto* or *de jure* title to its enterprises, and the problem of "privatization" is thus not about the simple transfer of state assets into private hands'.

However, the Hungarian and Polish cases are not identical: in the former case managers were able to exploit their position, whereas in Poland the workers presented a significant countervailing power. As Szomburg (1993: 78) has commented:

In sum, the privatization process began in Poland in a situation characterized by the following elements: the extreme decentralization and dispersion of rights of ownership and control, second, the strong political and psychological attachment of employees to the idea of self management, employees who shared a general feeling that the 'firms are ours', and third, the extremely weak capacity of the state to supervise and monitor the behaviour of firms.

The legacy of worker struggles from the 1980s and the specific mechanism of Employees' Councils constrained the process of privatization in Poland from the start (see the discussion in Dabrowski *et al.* 1991; Gomulka and Jasinki 1994)—a fact lamented by some (Aslund 1992: 87). On the other hand, the legacy of a more decentralized economy and the experience of the VGMKs in Hungary meant that managers were better prepared initially for operating in a more market-like context, and in some instances were in a position to proceed with ownership change without much state involvement. This, coupled with relatively weak worker organizations and constantly changing procedures for privatization, has put management in Hungary in a strong position to take the initiative in plans for ownership change.

Decentralization has also characterized the Russian experience but for completely different reasons. Schleifer and Vishny (1994: 138–40) and Ericson (1995: 62) argue that property rights were also poorly defined in Russia, with at least four stakeholders in a position to lay a claim: the workers, the managers, local government, and the branch ministries. In Russia the collapse of central administrative control ('destatization') opened the way for competing interests to contest the privatization process, contributing to the delay in the process. In the early phase of economic change, before the regulations on privatization had begun to be clarified, many senior managers and enterprise directors were able to take control over the enterprise and then effectively be in a position to structure the process of ownership change. As case studies suggest, it is managers who have primarily benefited from this process in Russia (Gerchikov 1995; see also Clarke 1993; Schleifer and Vasiliev 1996).

In these three countries the weakness of central control over enterprises and the contested nature of property rights led to considerable spontaneous or 'nomenklatura' privatization in the early days after regime change (Stark 1990: 362–6; Clarke 1993: 213–15; Frydman *et al.* 1993*a*: 75; 1993*b*: 132–3; 183; Voszka 1993; Berg 1994: 170 1; Schleifer and Vishny 1994: 146 8). (In the socialist system the nomenklatura was technically the list of positions requiring political approval by the communist party, and specified the organizational level at which this was required. Hence, at enterprises the nomenklatura were the holders of such positions. In a looser sense, the term was used to denote the leading stratum (Kornai 1992: 37).) This 'profiteering', as it was often judged to be by the general public, threatened to discredit the privatization policies. It was in this context that governments had to try and reassert control over the process and privatization has tended to proceed on a case-by-case basis (Earle and Estrin 1996: 51). In Hungary, the State Property Agency was established, as the major institution to oversee privatization, in an attempt to reassert centralized control. However, as Kiss (1992: 1021–3) demonstrates, by the summer of 1991 the progress of the agency was thought to be too slow and pressure to decentralize privatization had built up again (see also Canning and Hare 1994: 186–96). In Hungary there has been a constant tension between pressures to centralize or decentralize (Canning and Hare 1994).

As research has indicated, there has been considerable competition over who controls the privatization process. This is manifested both within the state, as different ministries and agencies vie for control, as in Poland (Simoneti 1993: 85; von Hirschhausen 1995: 69), and between the state and different social groups, or what Cox has described as competition between old and new political élites (Cox 1994: 406–9; see also Henderson *et al.* 1995). Added to this are the considerable problems of institutional capacity, or rather incapacity, of the state administrative apparatuses. The complexity of privatization measures, the speed with which they were expected to be executed, and the tendency for skilled administrators to have drained away from public service have everywhere conspired to complicate the state's role in change (Barr and Harbison 1994: 22–3; Crawford and Thompson 1994: 334–6). It is in this context of debate and delay that groups will seek to mobilize resources and that legacies from the past will continue to exert an influence on outcomes.

In the Czech Republic, Slovakia, and Bulgaria the situation has been very different. In these countries there had been little decentralization of economic control prior to the 1990s and the privatization process has remained a more centrally directed process. In the Czech Republic and Slovakia governments have found it relatively easy to maintain political support for its privatization policies; facing little challenge from organized workers, the government was able to speed ahead with privatization, arguably before potential opposition groups cohered. In Bulgaria privatization has been repeatedly interrupted by the instability of governments fuelled by the unfavourable economic conditions (Jones and Rock 1994: 312). Here, organized labour has been able to champion ideas about employee share ownership, but the generally weak economic situation has forestalled genuine agreement on how to proceed.

This dynamic of decentralized versus centralized control has also conditioned the form of privatization projects. In both Poland and Hungary there have been a variety of methods reflecting the bargained nature of the process. Hungary initially eschewed a mass-privatization programme in favour of more commercial, market-based processes. Thus, privatization proceeded by sale of shares both to outsiders (foreign investment and domestic investors) and to insiders, largely managers. Employees have no formal rights of co-decision about ownership changes; there are provisions for shares for workers, but no requirements for a specific proportion to be allocated to them. As Voszka (1993) has commented, one can interpret this as a continuation of processes which pre-date the collapse of Communism. In Poland, privatization has been a more insider-dominated process, although there are a considerable variety of different privatization processes (Frydman *et al.* 1993*b*: 181–203; Simoneti 1993: 84–90; Gomulka and Jasinki 1994; Kozek *et al.* 1995: 109–16; Earle and Estrin 1996: 36–8; Vaughan-Whitehead 1997). The formal co-decision rights of Employees' Councils and the prevailing ideological support for employee ownership amongst workers has served to slow down the privatization process (Aslund 1992: 87; Cox 1994: 398; Schleifer and Vishny 1994: 138). One result is that many former state enterprises are left in an intermediate stage of ownership change, no longer state owned but commercialized as leased enterprises or state treasury companies (Kozek *et al.* 1995: 109–16).

In the Czech Republic and Slovakia the maintenance of a more centralized control facilitated a mass-privatization programme. The distribution of shares via a voucher method, at a nominal price, to all citizens results in an outsider-dominated process of ownership change in which employees have no privileged membership rights. This method has sought to sustain public support by the almost free distribution of shares and has resulted in a more rapid privatization (Aslund 1992: 83–6; Myant 1993: 234–42). Both Poland and Bulgaria have added voucher privatization to their menu of ownership change methods but have failed to use the method effectively as yet, either to achieve widespread privatization or to sustain unquestioning public support (Aslund 1992: 83–7; Schleifer and Vishny 1994: 157; Nelson and Kuzes 1994: 147).

Russia also adopted this method and has reportedly effected ownership change in many thousands of enterprises; however, critics argue that this has simply transferred ownership into the hands of the managers (Buketov 1995: 26–7; McFaul 1995: 39–47; Schleifer and Vasiliev 1996). As one commentator put it, 'The Russian ideology of mass privatization values speed of privatization over quality of individual projects . . .' (Radygin 1995: 5). In Russia as in the Czech Republic and Slovakia voucher privatization proves a politically popular method for dispersing shares (Ericson 1995: 59). In Russia a number of other different routes to privatization of medium and large-scale enterprises are possible; the most popular has involved workers and managers being able to buy up to 51 per cent of shares (Bim *et al.* 1994: 263–6). A limitation of 10 per cent on the shareholding of outside investors serves to reinforce the dominance of insider control (Frydman *et al.* 1993*a*: 42–3; Rutland 1994; Schleifer and Vishny 1994; Kilminster 1995: 97; McFaul 1995: 39–47; Ernst *et al.* 1996: 223–7). As in Poland, the endorsement of the employees or their representatives is necessary for a privatization project to go ahead, and the consent of the Council of the Labour Collective in the enterprise is required (Gerchikov 1995: 140–2). However, as case-study research indicates, ownership change in both Russia and Poland may give management the opportunity to dismantle mechanisms of worker influence (Gerchikov 1995; Kozek *et al.* 1995; Mason 1995: 356–8).

In Bulgaria tensions between governments' desire for a centralized approach and considerable popular support for employee share ownership has contributed to the generally unstable political situation, which has fore-stalled progress towards privatization (Frydman *et al.* 1993*b*: 24–7; Jones and Rock 1994). The 1992 law envisages a highly centralized policy following the Hungarian approach of commercial sales. However, the worsening position of the economy and the absence of either substantial foreign or domestic capital willing to invest has meant that the policy has moved progressively towards a mass-privatization approach (see *Bulgarian State Gazette* 1994). As Peev (1995: 859) has commented, 'the withdrawal of the state from enterprise control and the lack of new owners generate conditions for strong political influence on the managers. This is the problem of *unproductive outsider control by interest groups*' (emphasis in original).

Reviewing these various methods of privatization in the light of the earlier discussion about property rights and the need to restructure management incentives, it becomes apparent that the outcome of ownership change is much more complex than the abstract models suggest. In Russia, the result of a mixture of spontaneous privatization and free distribution of shares has arguably resulted in no real external owners to discipline management and therefore the possible persistence of labour-relations problems from the past, although senior management has typically increased its power. Schleifer and Vishny (1994: 155) argue that commentators have been overly pessimistic about the quality of Russian managers and their potential to adjust to new economic realities. They conclude in relation to Anglo-American or Japanese styles of corporate governance that: 'The emergence of these active governance structures is unlikely in Russia in the near future. Moreover, the gains from these structures are much smaller than the gains from replacing worker or government control with managerial control.'

However, not everyone shares this view, fearing instead that without 'real owners' the incentive for managers is less to make a profit and more simply to survive by postponing restructuring and radical change (see, e.g., McFaul

1995: 44–7; Frydman *et al.* 1996: 239–40). This debate reinforces the point that the nature of managerial strategies is ultimately an empirical question and cannot be simply 'read off' from the prevailing structure of property rights or mechanisms of corporate governance. (For a discussion of the theoretical and empirical effects of 'insider-dominated' privatization, see Earle and Estrin 1996; Vaughan-Whitehead 1997.)

In the Czech Republic and Slovakia the dispersion of shares via the voucher method and their effective management by a limited number of investment funds has concentrated control to a greater extent. However, behind most of these funds is the state-owned banking system (Grime and Duke 1992: 755; Takla 1994: 172–3). In practice it is not clear that the main incentive for fund managers is to force enterprise directors to take a tough line on restructuring (Takla 1994: 164–6; Kilminster 1995: 96; Coffee 1996). It is, therefore, not guaranteed that this change of ownership will rapidly lead to dramatic changes in enterprise behaviour. Indeed, the remarkably low rate of unemployment, especially in the Czech Republic, would suggest considerable resistance on the part of politicians and enterprise managements to a speedy restructuring of labour relations. Myant (1993: 243) argues that the privatization process itself encouraged managers to follow self-interest and attempt to secure their own positions whilst postponing consideration of longer-term strategies for the enterprises indefinitely.

In Hungary, the greater degree of outside ownership, foreign investment, and the longer tradition of managing in a market context more nearly create patterns of corporate governance akin to those in the Western models. However, the constant changes in privatization procedures and the slowing-down of direct foreign investment is resulting in a much more mixed picture, with managerial strategies varying along with the pattern of ownership from one case to the next (Mako and Novoszath 1995). The Hungarian approach can be characterized as essentially pragmatic, allowing for a diverse range of privatization methods as circumstances require (Simoneti 1993: 79–84; Canning and Hare 1994).

In Poland, the relatively slow pace of privatization of major companies and the development of a series of intermediate forms of ownership put some of these questions on hold. The legacy of a powerful and organized working class has meant that neither governments nor most enterprise managers are in a position to ignore the need to mobilize consent for privatization strategies. However, with one of the most buoyant private economies in terms of new enterprises, increasing numbers of people work outside the old state enterprise sector. Again it is impossible to talk about consistent effects of ownership changes.

In Bulgaria the largely stalled move towards privatization has meant that most enterprises are still locked into a basic struggle for survival. The government intervenes in major industrial disputes and is reluctant to enforce hard budget constraints on large state-owned enterprises. In this vacuum, managing directors of enterprises, local authorities, so-called 'dirty money' (the Mafia), and employee organizations all vie to be in a position to benefit from ownership change when, or if, it comes. This results in a highly politicized process in which political concerns can easily dominate economic considerations, as Peev (1995: 860) comments: 'The distribution of power among these forces, and not social efficiency considerations, is the starting point of real enterprise transformation.' As Jones and Rock (1994) conclude, it is unlikely that enterprise actors will be subject rapidly to 'outsider control' as envisaged in Western models of corporate governance.

This inevitably brief discussion of the processes of ownership change leads to the conclusion that it cannot easily be assumed that 'privatization' denotes the same methods of ownership change or will have immediate or uniform effects on labour relations at enterprise level from one case to the next. The reality of ownership change has been far from the technical process outlined by some economists. In all cases there is the attempt to create a 'political capitalism', in the sense of a new market economy established largely from above. It is also clear that former power élites attempt to use their resources and networks in order to accrue influence and wealth in the new circumstances. In the absence of considerable private domestic capital or foreign investment the Russian and East European states have been forced to develop a whole range of property transformations that lie somewhere between state and private ownership. This has led commentators such as Stark (1993) to refer to 'recombinant property'. Just as these change processes have been conditioned by institutional and political legacies from the past, they will in themselves bequeath a legacy to the continuing programmes of transformation. It may be, as Earle and Estrin (1996: 24) have argued, that the dominance of insider-dominated forms of ownership change will foreclose upon future forms of outsider privatization.

Arguably, the results of ownership change and privatization so far have been more political rather than economic. Old and new élites have jostled for advantage in the redesignation of state property. In addition to this political and legal context of ownership change, it is necessary also to build into the analysis an understanding of the impact of the enterprise on the process of change. The enterprise is not merely a passive recipient of privatization strategies but a constituent agency of the contested process, especially where employees have formal rights of consultation over privatization projects, or where organized labour is strong. With reference to the case-study enterprises discussed below, it can be seen that, even in the absence of ownership change in some cases, most enterprises have begun to restructure in the face of changing markets for their products and/or in preparation for privatization. This reinforces the point that ownership change has not been completed and will be an ongoing process.

The implications of these conclusions for labour relations are that the rapid consolidation of new stable models or patterns of interaction between management and workforces should not be expected. A comprehensive shift towards Western patterns of corporate governance remains unlikely in the short term. The strategies of owners, managers, trade unions, and employees may become increasingly disaggregated, reflecting the growing mixture of ownership forms. The task at this stage is to try and uncover the dynamics of these processes by looking at the interaction of the enterprise with its environment.

5

Trade-Union Strategies

It has been clear from the earliest moments of transformation that the trade-union movements in the five countries discussed here play a more complex role in political and economic change than their earlier history in the planned economies might have suggested. The aim of the analysis in this chapter is to uncover the processes of strategy formulation and strategic choice in the trade unions, both in the wider context of the political transition as well as in the transformation of industrial relations. A fundamental question is to what extent the new patterns of unionism are dependent on the past or are creatures of the current situation. To what degree is there national and regional specificity and are there conditions for the repetition of the historic experience and the models of behaviour of the Western trade unions from the periods of large-scale societal changes? The discussion is organized in four main sections. The first is the legacy of the previous Soviet system and its transmission-belt model of trade unionism. Secondly, there are the alternative models of trade unionism which emerged in Eastern Europe, in particular the prototype of Solidarity. Thirdly, trade unions' organizational strategies in the context of transformation are examined. Finally, there is the question of the political choices of trade unions towards economic reform. The operation of trade unions in collective bargaining and at enterprise level is fully considered in Chapters 6, 7 and 8.

THE LEGACY OF THE SOVIET SYSTEM: THE TRANSMISSION BELT

The concept of legacy offers considerable analytical potential for explaining the transitory and mixed nature of social and structural changes, such as the those in the field of trade unions and industrial relations in Eastern Europe. Three aspects of that legacy can be differentiated: the first relates to the structure of interests and authority, the second concerns the structure of organizations, and the third is behavioural. It is the interaction between these different aspects that generates the sustainability of certain structures and the undertow of conservatism amongst certain groups and individuals. In order to assess the significance and the limits of this legacy, it is worth briefly reviewing the key elements of trade-union organization in the past.

The transitional trade-union movements emerge from a relatively long history in the framework of one universal model—the transmission-belt model. The term is taken from the metaphor used by Lenin in the debate of 1920–1 about the role of the trade unions in the transition to socialism and the management of industry. Lenin challenged the thesis of the workers' opposition, on the one hand, and the theory of Trotsky, which placed the management of the enterprises in the hands of the unions (which means the workers), on the other (Lenin 1970). According to Lenin, the political organization (the Bolshevik Party) controls production whilst the unions have to serve as a transmission belt—that is, as the connection between the governing political party and the governed, i.e. the working people employed in production. The conditions for the practical implementation of the model were realized at the end of the 1920s when Soviet Russia started the transition to accelerated industrialization and a centralized, planned system. Although Lenin's principal concept of the trade unions as a transmission mechanism remained intact, their structures and functions passed through certain stages until the traditional model of developed socialism was consolidated. At the end of the 1920s and the beginning of the 1930s, after the suppression of the trade-union opposition (Cohen 1973: 300–1), the framework of the transmission belt was erected with the structures in the enterprises, in the districts, and in the industrial branches, as well as in their links with the political and operational lines of management on each hierarchical level. After the Second World War the opportunity occurred to transfer the Soviet model to the countries constituting the socialist camp. This was accomplished mainly in the period 1948–51 when the model of the socialist trade unions developed a universal character. The last significant step in the evolution of the concept of the transmission belt was the transfer of certain state functions to the unions (in line with the thesis of Khrushchev's on the enlargement of public involvement in administration and the gradual withering-away of the state) (Ruble 1981: 33–5). This involved trade unions in welfare functions: the management of social security, the organization of rest and recreation activities for the working people, and regulation of working conditions and health and safety at work.

In its complete version the transmission-belt model combined four dimensions. First, the political role in which trade unions were part of the governing bloc of the political system but were without autonomous functions—that is, without the right to generate initiatives and strategies of their own. The strategic goals and decisions in politics and the economy were defined by the Communist Party, and the role of the unions was to communicate these central directives to the working people. Secondly, there were managerial functions. There were two clearly defined hierarchical lines in the management system of industry: the political and the operational (or administrative). On each management level parallel Party bodies had been created, with trade-union bodies corresponding to them. The task of the Party was to control, and of the union to assist in the fulfilment of the production plans. The operational line was represented by the traditional management structures, as known in the West, but with the difference that the pressure on management did came not from the market but from the centrally devised plan and from the bodies for political control. The third dimension was organizational. To fulfil their function as a transmission mechanism, socialist trade unions needed a specific structure, constructed from the top down. This was achieved by following two principles: the first was symmetry (on each managerial level trade unions create units corresponding to those of the political and administrative structures); the second was the priority of the district over the industrial (branch) structures. Unlike many Western unions, built on the basis of occupations or industries, the district principle was assigned to socialist trade unions. This principle was implemented through the network of district bodies created in every municipality. Although the central plan was transferred down and disaggregated according to branches and individual enterprises, control over its fulfilment and over the activity of the workplace trade-union organizations was strongest (and possibly most efficient) through the district bodies. Finally, there was a functional dimension to the transmission-belt model. Historically, the first and basic function of trade unions is the protection and representation of interests. In the conditions of state socialism and the planned economy this role was declared unnecessary. Instead, the emphasis was placed on the positive, constructive functions: the economic, that is the prominence of production; the social, involving the distribution of social benefits, such as holiday vouchers, social assistance, and the organization of a network of social services in the enterprise; the ideological, directed towards socialization and the formation of a value system following the doctrine of 'developed' socialism; the regulatory, involving working conditions and health and safety; and social security, involving insurance in relation to pensions and health.

One of the most important differences between the transmission-belt and the classical models of trade unions (as protective organizations) was in the mechanisms of action. The unions with a protective orientation use two characteristic methods—negotiation and mobilization. These assume a developed and legally regulated system of collective bargaining, the right to strike, and the right to use other forms of pressure in the course of negotiations. For socialist trade unions the characteristic methods were: first, the transmission of directives from the centre; and, secondly, the mobilization of the base (the working people) for their fulfilment. For this purpose a wide range of mechanisms was utilized, such as socialist emulation, counterplanning, front-rank experience, the brigade organization of work, etc. (Petkov and Thirkell 1991).

This description of the evolution of the transmission-belt model and its characteristic features is necessary in order to evaluate the linkage between this legacy and the current, transitional forms of trade unionism in Eastern Europe. This is important in order to prevent the assumption that the history of socialist trade unionism has ended and that developments will start from a new beginning. As McShane (1994: 340) has put it, 'It is not accurate to depict the entire trade union movement in central Europe as having been born or reborn in 1989.' In fact, the enduring significance of the legacy outlined here can be identified along a number of dimensions. The central planning model denied and sought to suppress differences of interest amongst workers; as the model was dismantled, it was typically white-collar workers, professionals, other groups with bargaining power, and employees in the 'budget' sector, whose wages suffered as the result of the value attached to physical work, who broke away to form new unions and/or press for their sectional interests. A continuing question will therefore be the success of the post-1989 unions in responding to this fragmentation of interests. It is also clear that some past functions of trade unions have not been so easily abandoned. One example is the pressure of union members on union centres to continue to operate their social-welfare function. In Russia, many traditional trade unions have not given up their property and the management of the enormous material base of rest and recreation facilities, social and cultural clubs, which has helped them to hold on to their memberships. This shows that, from the viewpoint of the immediate interests of the rank-and-file members, the old functions should not be completely rejected. This is not because of any theoretical conviction, but for the purely pragmatic reason that the burden of the neo-liberal reform forces working people to look for opportunities to maintain the social achievements, characteristic of state socialism. What has been rejected generally both as theory and as practice is the former socialist trade unions' functions in the management of production and their abstention from the classical protective function.

At the level of behaviour, the legacy is the phenomenon in Eastern Europe of egalitarianism in the social expectations and behaviour of individuals. The ideology of 'egalitarianism' developed in the era of state socialism, when it was encouraged in all possible ways through the system of wage payment, in the distribution of welfare, in career patterns, and in the visions of everyday life provided by the media. Thus, the outburst of nostalgia in the 1990s for the equality of the socialist past is a logical offspring of that social legacy.

The impact of these patterns from the past vary from country to country and do not determine the path that the unions follow. However, they do form the base from which new strategies have been developed. It also needs to be remembered that change was under way prior to 1989 and that alternatives to the transmission belt have a history inside the countries of East and Central Europe.

THE ALTERNATIVES: SOLIDARITY AS A PROTOTYPE

Accounts of the history of the new trade unionism in Eastern Europe typically start with the birth and development of Solidarity in Poland (see, e.g., McShane 1981; Touraine and Geisicka 1983; Mason, 1995: 351). This is correct, because the founders, the leaders, and the members of Solidarity were able to demonstrate the effectiveness of an internal alternative to the state-run trade unions and in this way revived interest in the classical, protective organizations of wage labour. An equally important argument for the unique role of Solidarity was its development as a social movement that undermined the system of state socialism from within and challenged the leading role of the Communist Party. Solidarity was the only completed and successful alternative to the Leninist transmission-belt model of trade unions, which operated only in one direction—from the centre to the base with the objective of mobilizing support for fulfilling plan targets. In contrast, Solidarity was created from the base and from the start developed mechanisms for the articulation upwards of the demands of workers to the economic and political centres. It was an autonomous organization and subsequently challenged the leading role of the Party, which was the core of the Stalinist model. However, Solidarity had its prehistory, starting from the 1950s. In Poland itself, and in some other countries and periods, there were attempts (although unsuccessful) to create an alternative to the Soviet model of management and the use of the unions as a transmission belt (see, e.g., McShane 1994: 337–8). The most protracted attempt to create an alternative to the Soviet model of labour relations was in Yugoslavia, where the model of workers' self-management was initiated by the Yugoslav leadership after the rift between Belgrade and Moscow in 1948. The appearance of the Workers' Council created a new party in the system of management and labour relations at enterprise level. The self-management bodies took over managerial functions from the trade unions, such as the social policy of the enterprise. This model thus significantly expanded the field of labour relations at the level of the enterprise, and reduced the space for trade unions and management. The trade unions retained their previous function of social protection and took on the new one of organizing and supporting self-management, especially that of elections to the self-management bodies.

The other alternatives to the Soviet model were the numerous attempts to create (or use) workers' movements as an opposition to the power monopoly of the Communist parties. The base of these movements was typically the shop floor, enterprises, and industry, but the aim was political. Often the motivation for the appearance of such opposition was provided by spontaneous discontent with economic and social policy, expressed in public protests, unexpected work stoppages, or the organization of parallel worker structures. The movements and resistance organized in Hungary in 1956, Czechoslovakia in 1968, and Poland after 1956 and 1970 were of this type. However, there is an aspect of these internal alternatives that has been left out of the discussion—namely, that these unsuccessful attempts and patterns, or more generally the legacy of such opposition, continue to exert their influence after the changes in 1989, but they have not served as prototypes in the transformation of the industrial and political relations, although notable individuals from past struggles re-emerged in the post-1989 developments (on this last point see, e.g., McShane 1994: 340). In Hungary, a National Association of Workers' Councils was set up in 1989 which has attempted to draw on the tradition of the workers' councils from 1956.

The oppositional worker movements and the new structures which emerged from the middle of the 1950s often involved representatives of the intelligentsia: the workers and their immediate leaders provided the social base and the intellectuals articulated the ideas of resistance and the internal alternatives. It is an issue as to why attempts before Solidarity were never successful in creating a symbiosis between the efforts of the intelligentsia and the aspirations of the working class. One important reason for this was the structure of remuneration in the Soviet period. The salaries of the intelligentsia and administrative employees were kept intentionally at a lower level than the remuneration of the representatives of physical labour (here the ideology of the leading role of the working class and of material production was in full force). It is also part of the truth that the governing Communist parties exerted influence on, and enjoyed the support of, a considerable part of the intelligentsia, including the cultural élite, which in their turn enjoyed preferential treatment by the authorities.

TRADE UNION ORGANIZATIONAL STRATEGIES

Trade-union movements inherited from the past have had different fates. Some remained conservative even in conditions of radical changes (for example, in Russia at the time of *perestroika*). Others have been dissolved with the aim of creating new organizations in their place (the case of OPZZ, the Association of Polish Trade Unions), whilst others have undertaken a process of transformation and adaptation to the political and economic changes in the region after 1989. Following the collapse of the transmission-belt model, many Western trade unions and international trade-union confederations raced to provide help and ideas to the new and reformed unions (McShane 1994: 339, 345–6).

In the immediate period of transition in 1989 there were two groups of trade-union centres. The first were made up of the alternatives—that is, of Solidarity and the newly created movements such as *Podkrepa* in Bulgaria, the unions connected to the *Liga* (Democratic League of Independent Trade Unions) in Hungary, and *Fratia* ('Brotherhood' National Free Trade Union Confederation of Romania) in Romania. New unions of the same type appeared in the Baltic States and Albania, and in Belarus and Russia. International trade-union organizations openly promoted these new unions. The second group consisted of the established trade unions subordinate to the Party state. Political pluralism and the ending of the Communist Party monopoly opened the space for trade-union pluralism, with the development of new trade-union centres, and challenged the established trade unions to undertake reform. Three features of the transformation created the context for trade-union development: political changes legitimized the existence of the new alternative trade unions; the Communist Party was forced to with-

draw from its base in the enterprise, and in some countries legislative innovations prefigured the establishment of labour-market institutions. (Thus, the
removal of the Party organization from enterprises occurred in Hungary in
the autumn of 1989; in Czechoslovakia in early 1990; in Bulgaria in March
1990; and in Russia in November 1991.) For the former Communist trade
unions, the first strategic choice they faced was whether, or how, to reform.
For individual members, there was now a choice to leave the old trade unions,
to join the alternatives, or to participate in the reform process.

In the period 1989–92 the new alternative unions were dynamic organiza-
tions and were able to increase their membership substantially. Thus,
Podkrepa grew from 20,000 in 1989 to 500,000 in 1991 and the *Liga* in
Hungary claimed more than 200,000 in 1991 (Hethy 1992: 45). However,
Solidarity's membership declined rapidly and by 1993 it had only 1.7 million
members compared with more than four million in 1981 (Gortat 1994: 117).
Although the successor union centres lost members, their total remained
larger. The dichotomy between the new and the reformed trade unions generated tension, competition, and struggle between the national trade-union
centres as well as in the field of labour relations. The negative effect of this
competition was that in some cases it became a struggle which diverted attention from the real interests of the members at the base and confused them, as
well as absorbing the energy of the rival organizations.

The new unions embodied different models of organizational development
and operation from the reformed ones, combining elements of both organization and movement. The unions which operated this model with some success are Solidarity and *Podkrepa*. Both unions began with a group (core) of
individuals, located in enterprises or in a particular district. Sometimes the
groups were initiated and designed from outside as well as from inside the
enterprise. Having developed an embryo organization and a programme,
they developed parallel organizational structures: in the enterprise and in the
district. Dual membership in the plant and in the local organization is oblig-
atory. This model facilitates and accelerates the diffusion of the groups
(cores) to other enterprises and territorial units, and in a short time the
formation of a national structure for the organization/movement.

From the standpoint of history, this combination of characteristics of organization and movement is not confined to Eastern European trade unions. It
has been typical in Western industrial relations to make a distinction (often
too baldly) between the economic or industrial and the political or social
movement functions of trade unions (Hyman 1994*b*: 135). Back in 1970
Flanders had written that 'Trade unions are a mixture of movement and
organization and the relationship between the two is the way to an understanding of the dynamics of their growth' (Flanders 1975: 43). Flanders identified the characteristics of movements and was particularly concerned with
the issue of converting the emerging temporary movements into a permanent
(trade-union) organization. The history of Western trade unions offers other

patterns of interaction with existing movements, such as the peace movement in the 1960s or ecological movements in the 1980s.

Solidarity's organizational innovation of combining movement and organization created a nucleus which became central to its dynamics and growth. Expansion took place not through the incorporation of existing units, but through the reproduction of the nucleus elsewhere. The orientation of the new unions was not primarily to the enterprise, but to the external political environment which they aimed to reshape and not to adapt to. As McShane (1981: 67–8) explains, the key structure of Solidarity was at the territorial level of the region, where considerable economic and political power was vested so that it mirrored the actual power structure. In periods of social change and transformation on the societal level the combination of organization and movement provides a strategic advantage in the political arena. The second advantage in these conditions is the possibility to transpose functions and to alter or redefine the aims of the newly created structures.

The organizational aspect is more appropriate to the field of labour relations, where there are existing structures which the new organization has to take into account. This also relates to legislation, as well as established procedures. Labour relations are an institutionalized reality and highly organized agencies have an advantage in it. However, in the political arena as well as in civil society movements are more effective in times of change, as shown by the activity of Solidarity in the 1980s and *Podkrepa* in the period 1990–2. In these times the unions created external networks and civil-society structures which functioned as pressure groups and when necessary as *electoral organizations*. When political and societal aims replace the union ones, the organization functions as a structural base and the movement becomes the leading agency. In this way the union imitates the behaviour and tactics of political parties. This can be shown with the development of Solidarity, which shows a number of turning points—that is, the times when it altered its strategy, priorities, and major field of activity. This has happened several times with Solidarity as shown by the periodization in Table 5.1; in this case, all the turning points are associated with elections.

This chronology can be compared with the turning points in the development of *Podkrepa* in Bulgaria to bring out the remarkable resemblance in the strategies of these two similar structures. In *Podkrepa*, from 1989 to 1992, activity was predominantly political, the difference being that the opposition which *Podkrepa* had supported had lost the elections in 1990, although industrial action initiated by *Podkrepa* was the primary cause of the fall of the Lukhanov government in November 1990. The neo-liberal reform of 1991 received some partial support (under the coalition government) and in 1992 from the UDF government which had come to power with the assistance of *Podkrepa*. The subsequent actions were not different in principle from those of Solidarity, including the prospect for the revival of political activity following the return to power of the Socialist Party in December 1994.

TABLE 5.1. *Strategies and turning points of the Solidarity trade union, 1989–1995*

Date	Strategy
1989–90	Organizing a civil movement, winning the election, and participating in parliament and government.
1990–3	Supporting the neo-liberal reform and shock therapy, but conflicts emerge between Solidarity and the government and with the political organizations separating from Solidarity.
1993–5	Securing some alleviation of the neo-liberal reform from the left socialist government. Developing measures to protect membership.
1995–	Increasing political activity. After the defeat of Walesa in the presidential election, Solidarity attempts to create a new political bloc.

Note: This account of the strategies and turning points is based on information from non-standard interviews with officials of Solidarity and industrial-relations experts in Poland.

In summary, the phenomenon organization-movement which was born at the time of late socialism, and played a key role in the initial period in the transitions in Poland and Bulgaria, has three main characteristics: duality of structure—that is, of movement and organization; duality of purpose—that is, political and industrial; and the transposition of functions between the two wings. The nature of the phenomenon makes it complicated to manage. Maintaining cohesion becomes difficult because at intervals structures separate from them and operate autonomously in the trade-union and political arenas. Solidarity hived off a number of union organizations, and acted as the base for the development of several political organizations which at times were in conflict with that base (Gortat 1994: 19–20). *Podkrepa* separated from the political union (UDF) of which it had been a founding organization and entered into a long-term conflict with the government of the UDF (1991–2) and with the coalition as a whole.

In Czechoslovakia independent strike committees organized a national strike in November 1989 and called for the abolition of the official trade union. In the two republics, independent trade-union confederations were created early in 1990, and at a congress in March the official trade union was disbanded and replaced by the federal organization CSKOZ (the Czech and Slovak Trade Union Confederation). The confederations in the two republics provided broad support for Civic Forum (in the Czech Republic) and Public Against Violence (in Slovakia) and were politically committed to the removal of former communists from their key state and trade-union positions. Thus, there was some similarity with the political roles of Solidarity and *Podkrepa*, but CSKOZ preserved the inherited trade-union structures, with the exception of the district ones. With the partition of Czechoslovakia, CSKOZ ceased to function, and trade-union activities in the two republics were carried out by the republican confederations. Thus, the pattern of trade-union development in the former Czechoslovakia was very specific. Subsequently, however, the trade unions in the Czech Republic and Slovakia did not have any direct presence in the political arena even after the division of the country until 1996, when the Czech Confederation of trade unions (CMKOZ) participated actively in the parliamentary elections in support of the social democratic party and managed to have some of its representatives elected. So although, as Mason (1995: 367) claims, the Czech unions have retained greater political legitimacy than some of their other Eastern European counterparts, this has been a consequence of their lack of power rather than an indication of it. It is useful to compare what happened in Hungary, where the first independent trade union was set up in May 1988 and the *Liga* was established as federation of new unions. Although politically the *Liga* was formally independent, it had a close relationship with the Free Democrats (Fagan 1991: 31). Like *Podkrepa*, it was strongly opposed to the Kadar regime and to the established trade unions. However, the nature of the political transformation crisis in Hungary (see Chapter 2) was such that the *Liga*'s political significance was not equivalent to that of *Podkrepa*.

The Reform of Established Trade Unions

The first strategic choice made by the established trade unions in Eastern Europe at the beginning of the transition was which of the two trajectories to follow: to build up new alternative structures or to reform the inherited structures. There were sufficient conditions for such a choice, since, along with the proclaimed principle of pluralism in all countries, the basis of trade union membership imposed under the state socialism was abolished.

MSzOSz in Hungary and CITUB in Bulgaria are typical examples of the reformed trade unions. In contrast to the new trade unions, they did not have a prototype and their development was incremental in character. The start of internal reform was, first, the public rejection of the transmission model and, second, the declaration of independence from any party and especially from the Communist Party. This was accompanied by acceptance of the European social-democratic tradition of combining negotiations and mobilization as major elements of trade-union tactics. Restructuring came third, with the aim of clearing some space for the development of branch and occupational organizations. Branch federations organized from the base upward became the main structure of the reformed trade-union centres and these federations combined to form the national confederation. Thus, the former centralized trade-union structure with its power concentrated at the top and with the domination of regional over branch structures was abandoned. The confederal structure of the reformed trade union allows branch organizations to enjoy sufficient autonomy to make them attractive and to facilitate mass involvement. However, they are not so flexible and effective in undertaking joint actions of solidarity when necessary.

The reform of the established unions in Poland and Russia followed different sequences. In Poland, OPZZ had adopted the classical protective function in the 1980s in response to the challenge from Solidarity, though it retained political links with the Communist (later reformed Social Democratic) Party, so that trade-union reform preceded political change. In Russia, the process of reform which had been identified by Gorbachev was delayed. He appealed directly to the trade unions to stop their 'dancing' with enterprise managers and to focus their efforts on social protection at the enterprises (Gorbachev 1987: 114). However, the trade-union leadership at that time failed to seize the opportunity, remaining passive and opposed to market reforms. Subsequently, the issue of FITUR's endorsement of, or opposition to, market reform and the ambiguity of its positions in relation to the political crises of August 1991 and September 1993 reflected leadership uncertainty and the weakness of general membership support. Reform was, therefore, a protracted process.

The pluralization of the trade union movement in Eastern Europe has gone through two phases, the first from 1989 to 1991–2, and the second from 1992 onwards. The division during the first phase was along the new/old line and its outcome was the shaping of the three major trends: new (alternative) trade unions, reforming (established) unions, and unreformed unions. As the dichotomy 'new/old' receded into the background, the trade-union arena acquired a more differentiated character which complicates the typology and renders it conditional. As shown in Table 5.2, one of the lines of demarcation is between dependent (on parties, religious organizations) and independent trade unions. Another is between organizations adhering to the 'classical' model and mixed organizations such as cooperative structures (Cooperative Forum, SOTSPROF (Association of Socialist Trade Unions)) or club-type forms such as *Edinstvo* ('Unity'), which has district, not workplace membership (see also McShane 1994: 342–3; Mason 1995: 349).

TABLE 5.2. *Typology of Eastern European trade unions*

Phase of differentiation	Nature of trade union
First	New alternative (Solidarity, *Podkrepa*, *Liga*, *Fratia*)
	Old, reformed (CSKOZ, MSzOSz, and CITUB)
	Old, delayed reformed (FITUR)
Second	Party or government oriented (OPZZ, *Edinstvo*, and CFTUOB)
	Branch autonomous
	Other (Worker Councils, Cooperative Forum, SOTSPROF, Christian trade unions)

After 1992–3 the development of the trade-union movement in Eastern Europe entered a new stage. On the one side, the neo-liberal reform and tripartism encountered serious obstacles and faced a crisis. On the other, the dichotomy between new and old unions began to dissolve and the union movements grew more diverse. According to information from the ILO East European Office (Budapest), in 1995 there were eighty trade-union confederations and national federations in the ex-socialist countries. ETUC had admitted ten centres with 11 million members from those countries which had signed association agreements with the EU. That shows that since 1993 the East European trade-union movement underwent an intensive process of restructuring and quantitative change bringing it closer to the Western realities of pluralism. As for the level of unionization, it comes close to the standards of the Scandinavian and north European countries (Table 5.3).

TABLE 5.3. *National trade-union organizations and membership in six countries in Central and Eastern Europe, 1991 and 1995*

Countries	Trade-union density (%)	Trade-union centres	Trade-union membership	
			1991 (000s)	1995 (000s)
Bulgaria	60	CITUB	2,370	1,060
		Podkrepa		350
		CFTUOB		240
		TOTAL		1,650
Czechoslovakia		CSKOZ	6,098	
Czech Republic	45	CMKOZ		2,500
		Christian trade union		50
		Cultural Federation		100
		TOTAL		2,650
Hungary	45	MSzOSz		600
		Liga		60
		Autonomous trade unions		100
		Worker councils		100
		Cooperative Forum		250
		TOTAL		1,110
Poland	40	Solidarity	5,000	2,000
		OPZZ		4,000
		TOTAL		6,000
Russia	75	FITUR		55,000
		SOTSPROF		400
		Independent Federations		—
		TOTAL		60,000
Slovakia		KOZ		1,200

The Institutionalization of Trade Unions: Quantitative Decline and Qualitative Development

The process of institutionalization of East European trade unions was relatively rapid. It was facilitated by the revision of the existing laws and the introduction of new legislation settling the rights of association, strike, trade-union functionaries' protection, etc. (see Chapter 2). However, institutionalization received its strongest impetus with the legal regulation of tripartism and of collective bargaining at enterprise and branch level. In Hungary and Bulgaria these are regulated by the Labour Code, while special laws or government acts are passed in the other countries. The new legislation is predominantly facilitative in character, which assists the search for the most appropriate national patterns and regulation through supportive legislation or special agreements between the partners. This largely explains the differences in the construction of the tripartite structures in the individual countries. Characteristically, in the first years after the political change the trade unions in certain countries appeared as the active agency in the search for the legislative and institutional solutions for establishing social partnership. That is understandable, because the organizational restructuring and training in the trade unions for the needs of the nascent tripartism developed faster than the corresponding changes in the employers' structures and even in the state bodies. It is relevant to emphasize that these processes were encouraged by the ILO, the European Trade Union Confederation (ETUC), the International Confederation of Free Trade Unions (ICFTU), and other international agencies supporting social partnership and dialogue with the trade unions. Within a relatively short period of time (1990–3) the overall framework of social partnership consisting of the national tripartite institutions and its subdivisions, the regulatory system, and the products—accords—and other instruments of tripartism was completed in the whole of Eastern Europe. It is necessary to note that the last element of institutionalization— i.e. the traditions, models, and habits of partnership—is not yet completed and is likely to require a long period of time and sufficient experience. Whether the expansion of the membership base beyond the boundaries of labour and the orientation towards non-traditional forms of membership can be a successful strategy for East European trade unionism is an open question.

Since the very beginning of their transformation, the trade unions in Eastern Europe have been faced with the dilemma whether to follow a path of reintegration of different factions leading to a higher level of trade-union membership, yet having a harmful effect upon the emerging pluralism, or whether to tolerate increasing differentiation, which brings the danger of fragmentation. A brief survey of the national situations reveals that the second trend is gaining ground and fragmentation is already a fact in most countries. Thus, for example, owing to the peculiarities of the law in Poland and Romania, the trade-union structures with national claims are exceeding the

number of 200. There are over ninety trade unions in Russia; nine union centres in Hungary claim participation in the national tripartite body and in
Bulgaria their number is eleven. Fragmentation results in a numerical decline
depriving some union centres of the critical mass of members needed for
mobilization and pressure through branch and national actions. The Czech
and Slovak trade unions are the least fragmented (Mason 1995: 350). The
other factors generating a loss of trade-union membership in the region are
privatization, the effect of shock therapy, and mass unemployment. Thus
Solidarity, which initially backed shock therapy, lost four million members in
three years. There was a large drop in membership in *Podkrepa* and CITUB
in Bulgaria in 1991–2.

Trade Union Organization and Internal Dynamics

The trade unions are organized at three levels: top, middle, and base. The base
consists of primary units (organizations), which are established at the enterprises, offices, and institutions and are united into federations or other branch
formations—miners, metalworkers, railway workers, employees within the
medical sphere, etc. (Some trade unions admit individual membership of the
federations and of the national organizations.) This vertical line is combined
with a horizontal one which unites them into territorial structures for towns,
villages, and regions. In the traditional trade unions, the territorial structures
prevail over the branch ones. Other combinations are also possible—for
example, when professional groups combine at regional level and afterwards
affiliate to the national organization. The different organizational structures
of unions reflect their origins. The new trade unions such as Solidarity,
Podkrepa, Liga, etc. were founded as unions of territorial structures and there
was a delay before branch structures were established. Reform of the established trade unions started with the restructuring of the existing federations
or with the establishment of new ones 'from the base'. However, the organizational power of the territorial structures is weakened or eliminated completely, as happened in Czechoslovakia. In Russia the regional structures of
the established trade unions have been preserved, and some of them have
gained considerable autonomy—for example, in Saint Petersburg and
Moscow.

   The research project in the six countries showed that, at the beginning of
the changes, the centres and the base organizations were the most active,
while the middle level had the intermediary function or was inclined to resist
the increasing power of the centre. In all countries, except the former
Czechoslovakia, separation of the branch trade unions from the centre
occurred because of interorganizational controversies and conflicts. Most
often, the separatist tendencies occur in the chemical industries, culture and
energy, and specific professional groups such as air-traffic controllers and
customs officers. Gradually, the initial pressure from the base organizations

on the centres and governments for the resolution of local problems (wages, change of managers, social allowances, etc.) has weakened. In 1993–4 the researchers noted a general decrease in the militancy of enterprise organizations, while the middle level of the federations gained considerable importance.

The issue of centralization versus decentralization in trade unions is a long-standing one. Observations show that the decentralized model of trade-union organization dominates in East European countries. Irrespective of whether they are traditional, reformed, or new, all national organizations experience some centrifugal pressures and, as a result, provide considerable autonomy for the branch structures. Though this preserves unity within a loose and flexible national trade-union structure, experience has shown that solidarity during common actions is difficult to achieve because of the branch controversies and expressions of sectional interests. Decentralization and the intensification of inter-branch separatism has been welcomed and encouraged by governments. In most countries there have been attempts to eliminate national negotiations or to reduce their importance, favouring bilateral negotiations at branch level. The governments' arguments are of two kinds: first, that, if tripartite commissions have too much influence, they diminish the role of parliament; secondly, that, in a deregulated market economy, branches and employers should operate independently.

POLITICAL CHOICES AND ECONOMIC REFORM

Do trade unions in Eastern Europe have a strategy in the field of economic reforms? The answer ought to be in the affirmative in terms of the general attitude towards the changes aimed at transforming the planned command economy into a market one. For both pragmatic and political considerations, most trade unions expressed their support from the inception of the most difficult period of macroeconomic stabilization. This support enabled them to participate in negotiation of the terms of price liberalization and anti-inflationary policy which marked the start of the monetary reform. This participation in turn stimulated the development of mechanisms for the representation of the interests of different branches and occupational groups generating the organizational dynamics and established the trade unions as a major strategic agency on the national level. Refusal to give support would have been vulnerable from a political point of view at the outset of transition, as there was an accepted parallel between the economic reform and the democratization of the societies in the East. For this reason, organized acts of opposition were rare and without any particular effect.

The East European trade unions seem to have made their choice of strategy on economic reform and most of them have preferred dialogue to confrontation. This has been a strategic choice in the post-socialist evolution. It is true that the tactics of support were different. Solidarity and *Podkrepa* entered the legislative and executive power and became jointly responsible both for the new economic and labour legislation and for decision-making in the operational management of the reform. Later on, after successful participation in the elections, FITUR (Russia), the independent trade unions in Hungary, and the revived trade unions in Poland also sent their representatives to the parliaments and in Hungary and Poland even joined the government. KOZ and CITUB have so far refrained from direct participation in the institutions of political power, but they are active partners in tripartite negotiations.

Irrespective of whether the option chosen is participative or negotiative, it does not alter the basic fact that the East European trade unions have accepted the concept of shared responsibility. It was this concept that dictated their behaviour in the first, monetary phase of the economic transformations. Yet how far was shared responsibility the result of real strategic choice? Choice implies the presence of several alternatives and available space to manœuvre. In the case of the economic reforms, the trade unions did not have either. The neo-liberal model is a fact, as shown in Chapter 3. It was imposed by the international financial institutions and accepted by the national governments. Under these circumstances the trade unions had no choice; they simply participated in a strategy chosen and imposed in advance, and so were driven into the confines of the monetary reform. Their acceptance was based on the assumption that, although there were severe difficulties in the short term, the medium term would see gains and improvements.

However, there are indications that the model of social transformation in the social sphere may generate conflicts in the tripartite process and lead to a revision of the general position of the trade unions on the economic reform. The trade unions in the Czech Republic, Hungary, and Slovakia have publicly confronted the governments on strategic, and not particular, issues, such as social payments. In December 1994 in the Czech Republic, and in February 1995 in Hungary, the work of the national tripartite bodies was interrupted for months on end because of a trade-union refusal to endorse the government's projects. Mass demonstrations were organized in the Czech Republic and Slovakia and there was a general strike of the railway workers in Hungary in 1995. There were interruptions in the tripartite negotiations in Bulgaria (in 1992, 1994 and 1996), in Poland, and in Russia; strikes were conducted in all three countries against wage cuts or non-payment in the industrial and public sectors.

In Eastern Europe, the social-contract concept was launched for the first time by the Minister of Labour and Social Welfare in Poland, Kuron. Solidarity was very active in the development of the pact, but it became known as the Kuron Pact. Its specific feature is that, in addition to wages, the trade-union and worker participation in privatization became subject to agreement. After taking power in 1994, the socialist government in Hungary launched the idea of a social pact. Although the trade unions had publicly expressed their readiness to negotiate on this issue, no agreement was reached, owing to the existing differences on social expenditures. In Bulgaria, the idea of a social pact was not developed, owing to the differences arising in the field of incomes policy as a matter of principle between the trade unions and the socialist government from the very beginning of its taking office.

The refusal on the part of the East European trade unions to give their support to the neo-liberal social reform and their reluctance to be committed in long-term social contracts reflect the pressure of their members for a stronger position. Having dominated in the ideology and practice of the Eastern societies in the initial period of transformation, neo-corporativism cannot easily find new stimuli. The trade unions can be expected to become the first institutional partner attempting to edge out of the trap of tripartism. However, that does not imply that they are ready to propose a new reform strategy. Whether in the medium and longer term they have a strategy to secure and preserve their role as an active partner in the transformation of industrial and economic relations is a question discussed in the final conclusions to this book.

6

Distribution and Collective Bargaining

The distribution of rewards, their structure, and the mechanisms for implementing them reflect both the economic development of a society and its political and economic values. In the socialist societies the structures and mechanisms of distribution were determined and maintained by conscious political choices and politically expressed values; these included the leading role of the working class, a greater value for physical than mental labour, and a relatively egalitarian structure of differentials. The marketization of the economy in the countries of Eastern Europe and Russia means substantial changes both in the institutions of distribution, and of the values shaping the structures of rewards. A common assumption about the likely trajectory of development in these countries was that the depoliticization of labour relations brought about by privatization would lead to the establishment of 'normal' labour relations, which meant, in effect, collective bargaining between independent employers and trade unions and a structure of differentials dictated by the market.

The first aim of this chapter is to explain the structures and mechanisms shaping distribution and the nature of agreements under the socialist system. Chapter 2 explored the political and economic changes underpinning labour-relations developments and showed that, in the countries studied, political transformation was soon followed by laws on trade unions and collective bargaining similar to those found in industrialized market economies. The independence accorded to trade unions and the possibilities for the creation of alternatives to the established unions were seen as examples of the process of democratization involving the representation of interests in a form not permissible under the socialist system. Collective bargaining in Western countries is the product of a long process of institutionalization. In Eastern Europe this foreign import has occurred with only an indirect legacy and no tradition on which to build, and this necessarily raises questions about the speed and extent to which institutionalization can proceed. A common feature of Western market economies is the apparent separation of politics and economics. This contrasts sharply with the legacy of the integration of politics and economics in the Party state and raises questions about the pace and process of separation in Eastern Europe. The first section of the chapter reviews the nature of this legacy.

The second aim of the chapter is to discuss the mechanisms for the implementation of wage policies and the development of collective agreements since the collapse of the Soviet system. The transference of collective-bargaining models took place in the context of economic crisis and the macroeconomic stabilization policies promoted by the IFI, as explained in Chapter 3. These conditions had major implications for policies on income distribution and wages and for the functioning of tripartite and collective-bargaining institutions. These developments are discussed in the next four sections of the chapter: the pattern of distribution and agreements under central planning; the transformation of distribution mechanisms at national level; the regulation of terms and conditions at lower levels; and the exploration of a number of the country cases in greater detail to investigate the similarities and differences in the patterns of development. A final section summarizes trends and issues in collective bargaining.

DISTRIBUTION AND AGREEMENTS UNDER CENTRAL PLANNING

Before discussing the process of transformation of income distribution and wage determination developing with the marketization of the economy, it is necessary to examine the structures and mechanisms of distribution (and appropriation) which operated in the centrally planned economy. This approach facilitates the recognition of the nature of the institutional legacy and poses the question of which features have changed and which have persisted.

The process of central planning was designed to integrate and control the development of the economy as a whole. The basic structure was that of the branch, controlled by a ministry, to which every enterprise (and other organizations) were allocated and which was the agency for planning and control. As Domànski and Heynes (1995: 326) point out, 'Sectoral differences in wages were a major determinant of income inequality under socialism, and much more important than in western countries.' Bargaining between branches rather than within, was the most significant determinant of distribution (Domànski and Heynes 1995: 327). Each enterprise had a wage fund which was formed on the basis of central rules and which was tightly controlled: 'In a socialist economy the analysis of wages has to start from central wage policy because the latter is actually enforced. Hardly any indicator in the economy wide plan is fulfilled more precisely or with smaller relative deviations than the targets for wages' (Kornai 1980: 377). Control over wages was significant, of course, for the growth of incomes provided in the national plan and for the control of inflation. It was, however, also important in the appropriation of funds for investment from enterprises which were allocated centrally.

There were four main instruments for control of enterprise income and the payment of individuals, the first three being imposed from above. The first was the manual of grades and wage rates which set out as state standards the specification for all the jobs in each branch, the skills required by the worker to undertake a given job, and the requirements for upgrading. This was known as the tariff and was prepared for each branch. The second was the manual of salary scales for specialists and white-collar workers which was used to fix the complements and salary scales for every position. The third was the general standards for remuneration contained in the Labour Code such as for overtime, shiftwork, and the minimum wage. The fourth was the internal enterprise regulations on the formation of the wage fund and the individual payment of manual and non-manual workers. Quarterly and annual bonuses (premia) were related to plan fulfilment. The tautness of the plan, and therefore the potential for bonuses, depended on the success of the director in negotiations with the higher ministry authorities. In the process of plan bargaining, the director represented the interests of the work-force (the collective) and the trade union was not directly involved. Inside the enterprise the process of informal bargaining was primarily between supervisors and work groups within the shop. In the Soviet Union and Bulgaria, the brigade organization of work, with elected brigade leaders, promoted the brigade leader as the representative of the interests of the work group in relation to internal, informal, bargaining with enterprise management. It partly paralleled, therefore, the role of the director in external bargaining. (See Ashwin 1997, for example, on the representative role of the brigade leader in a Russian mine.)

However, a significant aspect of distribution came from the social funds of the enterprise, from which were derived various social-welfare benefits—such as the provision of housing, holiday accommodation, kindergartens, canteens, and other social benefits, as well as expenditure on health and safety and the number of training places (the latter was significant as training led to upgrading and hence affected the wage rate). The size of the social fund was related to plan fulfilment and its provisions were set out in the annual collective agreement signed by the director and trade union. The agreement did not include wages, because distribution was related to plan fulfilment. Like the plan, fulfilment of the agreement was a state duty. There was a lot of detail in the collective agreement because it was derived from tasks specified in the plan, and its preparation and signature coincided with that of the planning cycle. Clarke and Fairbrother (1994*a*: 17) summarize the process in the Soviet Union, and Lado (1994) does the same for Hungary, where she suggests that it was the practice to consult with work groups. A major restriction on the coverage of collective agreements was that they were confined to enterprises in production so that employees in health, education, public administration, and culture were outside this mechanism. (The development of laws and regulations on collective agreements in different socialist countries is discussed by Nagy (1984).) The classical payment system was strongly individualized, but during the 1980s collective forms of work organization, especially brigades, were developed to promote group identity. However, the cult of the individual worker was fostered through the mechanisms of socialist emulation organized by the trade union and intended to improve production motivation. Pictures of individual leading workers were commonly displayed in factories in a way rarely found in capitalist forms of organization.

The socialist system of distribution was the product of the specific system of economic organization and changes in this had implications for the system of distribution. However, the institutional structures were related to the political system, especially the trade unions. During the 1980s, attempts at economic reform included effects on the mechanisms of wage determination. Thus, an early manifestation of *perestroika* in the Soviet Union was the wage reform of 1986 (Filtzer 1994) and the attempt, by extending *khozrachet* (internal self-accounting), to link wages to the economic performance of the enterprise. Such limited decentralization was also apparent in Bulgaria through applying the policy of residual income to the distribution of enterprise funds in the period 1982–8 (Petkov and Thirkell 1991: 108–11). In Hungary, wage decentralization as an aspect of economic reform was a continuing issue.

TRANSFORMATION OF DISTRIBUTION MECHANISMS AT NATIONAL LEVEL

The essence of distribution and of the mechanisms associated with the past was that they were mediated by the institutions of the state and it was the branch structures which determined the main relativities in the distribution of incomes. In principle, transformation towards a market economy implies much greater autonomy for enterprises and other employing organizations, greater decentralization of the mechanisms of income and wage distribution, and a greater role for market forces in influencing the price of labour. It implies autonomous employers and independent trade unions. As shown in Chapter 2, the legislation enabling the autonomy of trade unions, with the right to negotiate on wages and other issues, has been passed in all of the countries. However, as shown in Chapter 3, the need to rebalance the economies and the macro-stabilization parameters imposed by the IFI as a condition of support have been designed to impose the general depression of real wages, which depends on action by the state and its agencies. At the same time, the disengagement by the state from micro-level involvement in enterprises has been slower than some anticipated. Despite ownership change and other measures to reduce its role, the state has remained the leading agency in the operation of the economy. In relation to distribution, the nature of national wage policy has focused, first, on the extent to which states have sought directly to depress real wages and, secondly, on the mechanisms they have employed and the processes by which they have been implemented. Within the parameters set by the IFI, governments have a choice of imposing a centralized tax-based wage policy on wage increases at the place of employment, with or without tripartite consent, or of seeking to negotiate a national tripartite wage policy, as was done in Hungary from 1992 to 1995. In practice the scope of the wage tax has varied in relation to economic conditions and political circumstances. The expectation has been that, when sufficient control over inflation has been achieved, the tax-based policy becomes unnecessary. The degree to which an effective system of personal income tax has been established is also relevant to the control of wages.

The issue of wage policy and the control of inflation had been identified by Kornai (1990: 13) (in proposals presented in Hungarian in August 1989), where decentralization of control over wages had already been on the political agenda for some time. Kornai articulated what was to become the orthodoxy for wage policy. In his view, whereas under the central planning, wages were tightly controlled, the transition to a market economy would lead to the loss of these control mechanisms and to wage inflation, because of the continuation of soft budget constraints on state enterprises. In the transition stage, wage discipline was essential: 'The further reform goes towards liberalization of wage administration, the more quickly wages start to escalate. Bureaucratic compulsion is no longer enforced, but the counter interest created by private ownership has not replaced it' (Kornai 1990: 98). He did not, however, at that time discuss any need to depress real wages. Thus, in the Soviet Union *perestroika* saw attempts to decentralize the system of wage determination and the enterprise wage fund. The shift from direct to indirect wage control was considered to require the introduction of a tax on increases in the wage fund above specific limits (the Abalkin tax of 1989) in order to relate it to production and to restrict income differentials (Yakovlev 1995: 304).

Tax-based incomes policies have been operated in all the countries as a feature of their stabilization strategies and the wage fund has been used as the unit of assessment (details are summarized in Vaughan-Whitehead 1995: 17). Thus, state control of the parameters of income distribution and therefore of collective bargaining on wages has been a major condition of the transformation. As discussed in Chapter 3, the effectiveness of tax-based policies in controlling inflation has been questioned in papers published by the ILO. The specific negative consequences are that it inhibits the development of decentralized payment systems related to enterprise performance and productivity and prevents wages from acting to improve motivation and efficiency (Vaughan-Whitehead 1995: 16, 18). It encourages payment by non-monetary forms, the use of casual labour, and the concealment of wages. (Under the previous system a worker criterion for a director was his success in negotiating a good plan; this becomes his success in avoiding the wage tax.) The policy issues (strategic choices) have been of two kinds: the first is the nature of the process—that is, whether the decisions have been by the state alone or whether the settlements have derived from discussions with the trade unions and employers at the national level; the second is whether and when such policies can be suspended, reducing central control and allowing more scope for market forces and space for negotiations.

The process in Poland shows how implementation was initiated, altered, and finally abandoned in 1995. It was originally part of the package negotiated in 1989 with Solidarity and OPZZ to reduce inflation and implemented in 1990; foreign advisers were involved (Kabaj 1995: 221–4). The *popiwek*, as it was termed, was modified in 1992, when private employers were exempted. Its further revision was a key issue of continuing negotiations between successive governments and the Polish trade unions until it was finally abolished in 1994. The National Tripartite Commission was then authorized to set target maxima for wage increases in the public and private sectors for all enterprises employing more than fifty people. This was a 'turning point' in relations between government, employers, and trade unions (Kabaj 1995: 225).

At the same time, as noted in Chapter 3, the level of the minimum wage determined at national level has been a major concern in the discussions about the growth of poverty and inequality which are beyond the scope of this book. In a narrower sense, increases in the national minimum wage, whether or not as the result of tripartite discussions, have been a significant revision mechanism for collective agreements at the lower levels of the branch and the enterprise. A major question is how far tripartite national minimum increases are the mechanism for modifying enterprise agreements—that is, the degree of articulation downwards and whether it is transmitted via branch agreements. Before considering the degree of articulation of national agreements at lower levels it is important to consider the role of employers in these processes.

The role and organization of employers have been a continuing concern among writers and researchers in Eastern Europe (see, e.g., Kyloh 1995; Mason 1995). Thus, national tripartite social dialogue of the kind favoured by the ILO requires 'peak' level organizations of employers as well as trade unions. It has been noted that

in general employer organizations are in a much less consolidated state than trade unions. Their constituency has been subject to constant change due to the collapse of state industry and the emphasis on privatization, as well as the development of small and medium-sized enterprises. Consequently employer organizations are extremely heterogeneous and the status of their membership is often unclear. (Hethy and Kyloh 1995: 15)

At the level of the branch there are clearly major variations depending particularly on the extent of state involvement.

Thus, in the budget sector and public transport (especially railways) the state is still the main employer. In some other sectors, such as mining, energy, and the military industrial complex, employers combine to lobby the state for subsidies and other concessions and there is evidence, for example, from the Czech Republic and Bulgaria that trade unions operate in coalition with employers for this purpose. Sectoral, industrial (and regional) groups of employers are very significant in Russia, as interest groups, but it is doubtful if the trade unions are significant partners in the lobbying process. Where subsidies are involved, the consequences for employment and wages and therefore labour relations may be direct. Otherwise, the basis for negotiation on wages and other social benefits is limited. Lado (1994: 10) points out that at branch level employers' organizations were 'much more professional chambers (or business organizations) than distinct interest groups that represent employers' interests towards worker representatives'. Thus, the available evidence does not provide much support for a common approach to labour relations and branch agreements where the state is not a major controller of workplaces. Independent owners do not associate, as employers, in order to establish or maintain a common price for labour in their sector. There does not appear to be any prospect for the German, Dutch, or Scandinavian type of private-sector employer organization and collective bargaining, at least in the short-to-medium term.

THE REGULATION OF TERMS AND CONDITIONS OF EMPLOYMENT AT LOWER LEVELS

The next issue to consider is how terms and conditions of employment below the national level are regulated, given the existence of some national standards in the form of labour codes and associated regulations. In principle there are three main methods of regulation: collective bargaining involving negotiation/consultation with one or more trade unions; negotiation/consultation with a works council; and unilateral determination by the employer taking account of the supply of labour needed. A major empirical question is the extent to which these different methods apply—especially the coverage of employees by collective agreements. At the same time there are a number of levels at which regulation may take place: national, branch, company/enterprise, plant, and also occasionally regional. The relationship between levels and the linking mechanisms is important. A more particular question is the range of issues covered by collective agreements and whether the items of the traditional socialist collective agreement survive. All these questions involve trends in the processes of institutionalization. This means shifts from hegemonic state institutionalization to institutionalization with a plurality of agencies. There are now more autonomous owners with some space to develop strategies and autonomous, and to some extent competing, trade unions (see Chapter 5).

Evidence of the extent to which employees in the economies of the six countries are now covered by the terms of collective agreements is necessarily very limited. A common conclusion by specialists, for example, from Bulgaria, Hungary, Poland, and Slovakia is that in newly created private enterprises there is little formal institutionalization of labour relations in the form of trade-union recognition and therefore of collective agreements (Thirkell *et al.* 1995*b*). The principal quantitative source of data is the Report of the ILO Survey in Bulgaria, Czech Republic, Hungary, Poland and Slovakia (ILO-CEET 1996). This is based on 3,200 questionnaires completed by trade-union representatives who were members of teams who negotiated collective agreements in a range of sectors. The survey was able to obtain factual details on the bargaining process and the perceptions of trade-union participants for a population in each country. The report data show that in all the countries covered there were a significant number of collective agreements negotiated by trade-union representatives drawn from a spectrum of employing organizations in terms of sector: production, services, and from what is conventionally termed the budget sector, which is predominantly health and education. The report suggests that the primary frame of reference for the interpretation of the results has to be the national context, since there are significant variations by the size, sector, property form, ownership, and market of the bargaining unit—the nature of the data does not allow precise comparisons between the countries. The principal general finding was that collective bargaining took place mainly at the local level and that most of the wage issues were settled at that level, though the terms in local agreements were often supplementary to higher level agreements at the sector or national level—for example, provisions set out in labour codes. In all the countries trade-union membership of bargaining units had declined more often than it had risen, but generally all employees in the unit were covered by the terms of the collective agreement. In all countries budget sector units differed most from other unit groups—union membership was lower, local agreements were less common, and the range of issues in the agreements was the smallest.

The data on the scope of collective agreements is interesting because of the question of old and new items—that is, the extent to which issues that were included in the socialist agreements have persisted. Clearly the inclusion of wages and the changes in the functions of trade unions shift the dynamics of the agreement. Another new issue is that of trade-union facilities. A majority, usually a large one, of agreements in all the countries included provisions on this and this can be interpreted as indicative of a measure of trade-union institutionalization. An indicator of the institutionalization of collective bargaining is the inclusion of a disputes procedure. This ranged from 55 per cent of agreements in Hungary to 82 per cent in Slovakia. However, the inclusion of a peace clause was significantly less common. There is also the question of provisions which can be seen as legacies from socialist collective agreements. The survey showed that traditional subjects of health and safety, vocational training, housing, and health care were still common and continued alongside wage and other provisions such as part-time contracts. This suggests that the substantive content of collective agreements has shifted from the traditional topics to include wage issues, but that they still incorporate a range of social-expenditure topics familiar from the past.

COUNTRY CASES

This section deals with the trajectory of wage determination, collective agreements, and the bargaining process in the Czech Republic, Hungary, Bulgaria, and Russia. The aim of these cases is to explain the development of the processes of wage determination and the articulation of collective relationships between the different levels—national, often mediated through tripartism, branch, and enterprise. Although there are general similarities, there have been significant differences between countries resulting originally from varying political and economic conditions.

In the Czech Republic political stability and the programmatic development of the economic reform under governments led by Klaus since 1990 have been critical conditions shaping the issues of wage distribution and collective agreements. The initial legislation on collective bargaining, of December 1990, gave important rights to trade unions and provided for branch level, as well as enterprise level, agreements. However, the initial collective agreements did not cover wages which were still governed by the central tariff scales (Rusnok and Fassman 1995: 134). This law, 'largely inspired by similar German law' (Rusnok and Fassman 1995: 139), reflected the social-democratic approach of one wing of Civic Forum and not the neo-liberal approach of Klaus, who had not yet divided the party. This act was followed by the establishment of the tripartite institutions, which in January 1991 produced the General Agreement as the framework to facilitate social and economic reform and specifically minimum wages, indexation in relation to prices, and regulations for wage payments according to economic performance. In practice, as elsewhere, tripartism has functioned as a process to legitimate the reduction of real wages. In exchange for giving the unions a formally strong role in collective bargaining and with an important consultative role on social policy, the government has aimed to marginalize their influence on other issues of substance.

The tripartite agreements were accompanied by the government decree that, if the tripartite guidelines were exceeded, then there would be punitive taxation on the employers who were, however, free to pay less. In 1991 the minimum wage was the most important issue and functioned as a revision mechanism transmitted through industry agreements to enterprises. In 1992 wage levels were outside the general agreement and the government imposed rules which allowed some flexibility—for example, bonuses from profits were fully liberalized. Since 1992 it has been the government which has made the rules and set the norms on wage regulation with the nominal agreement of the tripartite council. The rules have become more liberal and in 1995 centralized wage regulation was abandoned, with only the minimum wage fixed centrally. The trade unions' main aim has been to press for improvements in the minimum wage.

Branch-level collective agreements were negotiated for the first time in 1993 but government policy is that there should be collective agreements only at the level of the enterprise and the number and coverage of branch agreements has decreased. The thirty branch agreements in 1995 covered only 20 per cent of workers and did not always include wages. In line with government policy, the Ministry of Labour has not exercised its option to extend the coverage of agreements within a branch. On the other hand, 50 per cent of workplaces have collective agreements (Kubinkova 1996) and where collective agreements continue they cover all workers in the bargaining unit including lower management. The government intention has been to increase the number of individual contracts, as permitted by the law. Many employers wished to move in this direction, which is facilitated by the absence of any legal backing for the traditional tariff scales. Pollert and Hradecka (1994: 58) cite a case of individualization at Czech Electric: 'individual pay contracts [were] agreed entirely between the mistr (foreman) and the individual employee', but this took place in the context of general restructuring involving the ending of the piece-rate system.

In Hungary, issues of national wage policy, and especially of decentralization of control, emerged strongly during the 1980s. Pressure for the relaxation of central control underlay the introduction of the new collective forms of work organization such as enterprise work partnerships which, like the cooperatives in the Soviet Union, were outside the normal central wage controls. The prototype of national tripartite discussions in 1988 was centrally concerned with wage policy and aimed at combining some control, along with decentralization, by fixing the minimum wage and setting the parameters for wage increases at lower levels. This was a landmark in shifting direct control from the government/state to representative tripartite bodies. The concept of implementing national wage policy on the basis of tripartite negotiations, as opposed to an imposed tax-based one, was also a distinctive Hungarian innovation. The development of a strict and progressive personal income tax from 1988 was considered to facilitate control over wages and inflation better than administrative measures. In 1992 direct central control of wages was suspended and abolished a year later, although there were tripartite recommendations for average, minimum and maximum, wage increases. However, as a result of the deterioration in the economic situation and the measures for macroeconomic stabilization required by government economists and the IFI, central control was reinstated for 1995.

The main focus in Hungary for the four years from 1988 was on the development of institutionalization at the national level. The legal regulation of the institutions and mechanisms of collective bargaining and collective agreement was deferred until the passing of the Labour Code in 1992. This was a turning point in the development of the industrial-relations system and the agencies for collective bargaining. The government tried to make works councils rather than trade unions the bargaining agent at the level of the enterprise but were unsuccessful. Trade-union success in the works-councils elections of 1993 legitimated their role as bargaining agents and the mechanisms for collective bargaining. This development and the suspension of central wage controls raised the question of the constitution of the structures of collective bargaining at both the branch and enterprise levels, and there were expectations about an increase in the extension of collective agreements at these levels. The NCRI 'decided (in Autumn 1991) to work out an institutional framework for sectoral (industry) level collective bargaining and agreements by which the remaining administrative barriers on wage determination by the Government could be eliminated in 1992' (Hethy 1992: 40).

In Hungary intermediate level agreements for the branch or region were identified as the 'missing middle level of collective bargaining' (Hethy and Csuhaj 1990: 39–40). It was envisaged that they would be an integral element of bargaining serving to articulate national agreements downwards to enterprise level. However, as Berki and Lado (1995: 208) indicate, there was a decline in the number of intermediate-level wage agreements and a very substantial fall in coverage between 1992 and 1994. As Berki and Lado (1995: 209–10) explain, these agreements covered only a small part of the employers and employees in the branch and were concluded by *ad hoc* groupings of employers, not by associations, so that it is more accurate to class them as 'multi-employer collective agreements'. They are found in pharmaceuticals, furniture, printing, textiles, baking, and chemicals. Wages are not always part of these agreements. Hungarian trade unions regard the extension of branch agreements as a mechanism for securing minimum social benefits and reducing wage differentials, but this has been hindered by the absence of employers organized at this level and by the legal regulations in the Labour Code which limit extension from enterprise to branch.

Berki and Lado (1995: 217) suggest that the 'future of the intermediate level is a crucial issue' for a stable bargaining system. This could develop organically as the result of market forces on employers or through an interventionist approach for a number of economic and social reasons. In a considerable part of the economy there is no possibility of workplace collective agreements: 'If the social partners wish to have greater control over labour market processes and if they want to avoid significant differentiation of wages and working conditions, the conclusion of intermediate level agreements and their extension to entire branches/sectors seems a realistic option' (Berki and Lado 1995: 217). The number of workplace agreements registered increased from 391 in 1992 to 816 in 1995, but the coverage of employees declined from 566,777 to 490,905. The decline in coverage has been strongly influenced by the organizational restructuring of the large, multi-plant enterprises with large numbers of employees, characteristic of the socialist economy. Many of these have been reorganized into much smaller companies and many new organizations have been established, so that at the end of 1995 there were more than 100,000 employing organizations.

The potential for negotiating a collective agreement is mainly for enterprises employing more than fifty persons, but this depends on the functioning of a trade union within the enterprise, and in some 30 per cent of enterprises employing more than fifty persons there was no trade union (Voros 1996). The Promed case (with 190 employees) discussed in Chapter 8 illustrates the process of organizational restructuring, the disintegration of collective labour relations, and the unilateral determination of wages by management, although formally there was a trade-union presence. The ILO survey (ILO-CEET 1996) showed that in 16 per cent of the Hungarian units the basic salary was agreed individually between the employee and the employer—the highest proportion in the six countries.

In Bulgaria, as explained in Chapter 2, the process of economic reform has been influenced by the instability of governments and by recurring economic crises (there were seven governments between 1989 and 1997). The crisis of 1989 and the interval to the end of April saw the formal creation of a national tripartite structure, a General Agreement and Guidelines on Collective Bargaining, albeit voluntary. This process of institutional change was a direct response to the threat to social peace generated by the strike waves which began at the end of 1989. A tax-based wage policy on wage increases above a centrally determined norm had been established in 1989 before the political changes.

Progress on collective agreements in 1990 was patchy and initially drew on the guidelines and standards set out in the Labour Code; but there was no other attempt to reform the system of wage determination until 1991. This was in the context of price liberalization and other aspects of the shock-therapy package introduced by the Popov coalition. Trade-union consent to maintain social peace was a central feature of the General Agreement in 1991 and underlay the tripartite decision to enhance the institutionalization of collective bargaining in July–September. The Decree on Wages and Collective Bargaining of July 1991 established a legal basis for collective agreements which were to be negotiated by the beginning of September. This was a major attempt to decentralize wage-fixing and wage-bargaining. The national minimum wage agreed by the Tripartite Commission was to form the basis for wage negotiations at enterprise level. Details of later changes in national wage policy from 1991 to 1993 are set out in an ILO-CEET report (1994: 42). Thus, the implementation of collective bargaining was closely linked to national tripartite decisions.

Evidence on the coverage of collective agreements in 1991 suggested that about 74 per cent of the workforce were covered by collective agreements on wages (Thirkell and Tseneva 1992: 365). The initial agreements of 1990 were primarily procedural or incorporated provisions from the Labour Code—in some cases reflecting the desire of local union representatives to secure management commitment to these and other established standards. Notable topics showing continuity from the earlier form of collective agreement were those linked to the enterprise social fund, such as housing, transport, and kindergartens, which were now the subject of collective bargaining. However, by September 1991 the inclusion of wages had become the norm.

The period 1991–5 has seen a series of regulations and revisions (listed in Tzanov 1995). These have reflected the continuing economic problems and pressures. A major consequence of the lingering crisis has been the continuation, in differing forms, of a tax-based incomes policy with the wage funds as the basis of assessment. Economic difficulties were accompanied by industrial conflicts: 'strikes had become a regular feature of the Bulgarian labour market [from 1991 to 1993] and were primarily over wages' (ILO-CEET 1994: 53). Political conflicts reduced the scope of tripartite agreement and the UDF government of 1991–2 attempted to reduce the power of the national trade-union confederations in two ways: first, to decentralize negotiations from the national tripartite level to the level of the branch; and, secondly, as in Hungary, to make works councils instead of trade unions the bargaining agent at the level of the enterprise. The trade-union confederations were successful in resisting these proposals. The replacement of the UDF government by the Berov coalition government of technocrats in 1993 opened the way for a wider range of tripartite negotiations and the full legal regulation of tripartism and collective bargaining in the Labour Code of January 1993.

The ILO survey (ILO-CEET 1996) data for Bulgaria show that the proportion of units where the basic wage was determined by national sectoral agreements (51 per cent) was significantly higher than in the other countries. The main reason for this was the delay in privatization, which meant that decentralization of ownership was delayed and relatively little restructuring of enterprises has occurred. For CITUB, a major issue was the problems associated with securing the involvement of ministry representatives in sector negotiations (Neikova 1996). Other distinguishing features from Bulgaria are that trade-union membership declines less than in other countries, and that the terms of collective agreement are confined to trade-union members but other workers can join the contract by applying to both employers and trade unions who are parties to the agreement. In such cases, these workers are often pressured to pay affiliation fees to the contracting union (Aro *et al.* 1996). Hill, Martin, and Vidinova (1997: 240) analyse the breadth and downward articulation of collective bargaining through tripartism and sectoral agreements to the enterprise and find 'that the scope of enterprise wage determination is . . . highly circumscribed'. The persistence of centralization (including the salience of labour-code provisions which embrace social funds) is attributed to tax policy and the postponement of privatization, as well as the success of the trade unions in establishing a system of peak level concentration: 'partly as a result of the political power of trade unions and partly under the guidance of international organizations, especially the ILO . . .' (Hill *et al.* 1997: 236).

In Russia collective agreements are made at four levels—national, branch, regional, and enterprise—and the first three are tripartite, including representatives of the state as well as trade unions and employers. Yakovlev (1995: 316) suggests that 'In practice, however, this system is implemented in an extremely formal manner, the process of bargaining being very complicated and uncoordinated.' The importance of branch and regional agreements is a significant feature of labour relations in Russia. At the end of 1995 there were fifty-eight industrial tariff agreements covering particularly the production branches, and the key provision was that of the minimum rate to operate in that branch. Regional agreements (of which there were forty-two) included provisions on the development of the regional economy and the issues of social protection and unemployment. For example, agreements contained provisions on the socially acceptable level of unemployment which, when reached, triggered a six-month delay in the implementation of mass redundancies by an employer. The Law on Collective Agreements specifies the subjects which may be included in enterprise-level agreements:

method system and rate of payment; compensation and additional payments; the mechanism for the revision of pay taking account of increases in prices, the level of inflation and the meeting of targets defined by a collective agreement; employment retraining and conditions for layoffs; length of working time, rest periods and leave; improvement of working conditions and protection of labour, including women and youth; ecological security; observance of the interests of workers in connection with the privatization of their enterprise; control over meeting targets in a collective agreement, responsibility of the sides, social partnership ensuring normal functioning of a trade union; no strike in relation to terms of a collective agreement which is fully implemented and in time.   (FITUR 1996)

In 1995 the coverage of enterprises and other organizations was about 70 per cent (data from FITUR 1996).

In conditions of continuing economic crisis, however, the implementation of agreements is a major question. The FITUR Report identified the non-payment of wages and other benefits as the central issue. It commented that implementation of the commitments in the federal general agreements was the core issue and suggested that generally about 25 per cent of them were not enacted. At enterprise level the wage tax (and other new forms of taxation) and the resultant lack of funds are regularly cited as the principal constraint on both production and wage payment. (This information was gained from research visits to enterprises (see Appendix B).)

The 1992 law on collective agreements specifies that wages should be included but this is not always the case so that there are some similarities with the traditional collective agreement (Tchetvernina, interviews, see Appendix B). There are significant variations between sectors. Thus, in mining and some parts of transport, worker mobilization has transformed trade-union representation and wage negotiations have become important. The evidence from Novosibirsk is that there the agreements generally do include wages and the national increases in the minimum wage functions as the main revision mechanism at enterprise level (Gerchikov, interview, see Appendix B). However, in some Russian enterprises the trade-union organization has ceased to exist and in such situations there are examples of the collective agreement being signed by the director and the chairperson of the council of the labour collective. Yakovlev (1995: 316) suggests that there are often no collective agreements in privatized enterprises, 'since the trade unions themselves pretend that all the workers have become owners'.

The extent to which there is a significant process of negotiation between management and the trade union is questioned. Clarke and Fairbrother argue that welfare and distribution remain a primary trade-union function at the enterprise and that the trade union frequently functions as a part of the administration: 'most union officials we have interviewed continue to regard pay as a matter for the administration' (Clarke and Fairbrother 1993*d*: 193). A 1995 survey confirmed that workers mainly appeal to the trade union for goods and social benefits—for example, buying places in sanatoria and rest houses (Centre for Labour Market Studies 1995: 13–14). Worker responses to the question of who defended their interests showed that 41 per cent considered that the director or management was their real defender, while only 13 per cent saw the trade union in this role (Centre for Labour Market Studies 1995: 20). This illustrates the persistence of the traditional pattern of relationships. An account of the relationships between enterprise managements and trade unions, within the different levels of union organization, and between enterprise trade unions and workers in the Novosibirsk region is provided by Gerchikov (1995: 152–8). Another example of the survival of a traditional mechanism is the display in enterprises of portraits of leading workers. This was originally linked to the socialist emulation competitions, which were centrally abandoned under *perestroika*. Visits to enterprises in Nizhni Novgorod and Tver in 1994 and 1996 produced examples of the continuation of this practice (see Appendix B).

TRENDS AND ISSUES IN DISTRIBUTION AND COLLECTIVE BARGAINING

The starting point for this chapter was the socialist system of centralized control over distribution and wages through state structures and mechanisms. Although in all the countries there has been a significant element of dismantling state structures and the promotion of ownership change, states still are, in varying degrees, the main economic agents through their operation of macroeconomic stabilization measures and through their role as direct employers. Thus, the relative depoliticization of labour relations characteristic of developed market economies has not so far occurred.

Throughout the period of macro-stabilization the state has been an active agent in setting and controlling national wage policy influenced by international agencies and fears of inflation. The reliance on tax-based incomes policies can be seen as a legacy, as this was the mechanism used in the past for restraining wage increases. However, the effectiveness of tax-based policies in controlling inflation has been significantly questioned by the ILO and there have been continuous pressures from trade unions (and also from employers). By 1995 the Czech Republic, Poland, and Slovakia had abolished such controls, while in Russia the Federal Assembly declared an intention to do so in 1996; Bulgaria remained the exception. However, the dramatic reversal of the pioneering attempt in Hungary to substitute a negotiated wage policy suggests that reversions could occur elsewhere. The Hungarian experience of recentralization is important in showing how national wage policy is dependent on economic circumstances and the perceptions of IFI, which may change quite rapidly.

These changes in the form of state control over wages combined with the economic crises and the emergence of some aspects of market forces have shifted/undermined the socialist patterns of differentials. This process influences the differentials between branches, within branches, and within enterprises. Thus, the relative economic success of some branches, often related to market position and/or bargaining power, has significantly altered their place in the structure of branch differentials. (For data on trends in branch differentials for Bulgaria, the Czech Republic, Hungary, and Slovakia, see Vaughan-Whitehead 1995.) Formerly the horizontal differentials between enterprises in the same branch were usually narrow but economic changes have now altered the traditional relationships and differentials are often substantial and determined primarily by the economic situation of the enterprise. Within enterprises the vertical differentials between the lowest grades and senior managers were relatively narrow in the past compared with capitalist countries. The evidence from the researchers involved in the ESRC research project (see Appendix A) was that these differentials had become much wider.

Wage policies and the establishment of collective bargaining for the budget sector have been a contentious issue in all of the countries. The sector comprises, in particular, health, education, culture, and science, but also the civil and local-government services and housing. Generally all remain employees of the state and are therefore paid from the state budget. A general tendency has been for the relative wage of employees in this sector to suffer in comparison with those in other sectors. (The ILO talks about the 'fragmentation of the labour force', of which this is one example (Vaughan-Whitehead 1995: 69).) A major cause of this is that the wages of the budgetary sector have been linked to multiples of the national minimum wage in most countries (but not Hungary). As set out at length by Standing and Vaughan-Whitehead (1995), the restricted and irregular revisions of the minimum wage have had severe effects for the increase in poverty, and in Russia, for example, have been below the subsistence minimum.

A common trend has been to create national grading structures to cover employees in the budget sector—for example, in Russia and the Czech Republic in 1992 and in Bulgaria in 1995. Vaughan-Whitehead (1995: 62) noted that the tight control over the minimum wage 'is partly to control wages in the budgetary sector according to the policy advised by International Organizations such as the IMF'. The direct connection between international loans and the budgetary sector is illustrated by the Bulgarian case, where enterprise debts absorbed most of the state budget so that the international loans were used to pay employees in the budget sector.

In relation to collective bargaining, the ILO survey (ILO-CEET 1996: 125) concluded that, in all countries, budget-sector units differed most from other unit groups—union membership was lower, local agreements were less common, and the range of issues in the agreements was the smallest. However, an indication of the tensions created by wage policy in some parts of this sector is the incidence of strikes over wages. For the actions of doctors and teachers in Russia in 1992, see Connor (1996: 78–81). There were teachers' strikes in Bulgaria in 1992, 1993, 1994, and 1996 and in Hungary in 1995. The groups in the budget sector were traditionally disadvantaged in the centrally planned economy and many of these workers were active in new trade unions in the period of regime change. However, their position relative to other sectors has worsened in the early post-Soviet years.

The ambiguity of the role or place of the branch in the new conditions is a further legacy from the past. This issue varies according to the development of economic reform. The continuing importance of the branch level in Bulgaria is linked to the postponement of privatization. Privatization of state enterprises is expected to take bargaining to the enterprise level. In Russia it is a combination of inertia, institutional recombination at intermediate levels, and scale. In the Czech Republic government policy and the pattern of decentralization are likely to continue. The very limited results of the national policy to promote intermediate-level bargaining in Hungary indicate the difficulties for this level except in the budget sector.

A principal finding of the ILO survey (ILO-CEET 1996) was that local, normally enterprise, collective agreements are a common form of regulation with extensive coverage, which is also true of Russia. In terms of the substantive content of collective agreements, the inclusion of wages has been a major change from the past, but this has been added to more traditional concerns about social-fund items. A more open question is the extent to which collective agreements at any level will be enforced. As Hethy (1994: 321–2) has commented, 'Doubts also persist about the representativeness and organizational effectiveness of both unions and employers at enterprise, sectoral and national levels, and in the emerging public and private sectors.' In addition the capacity of the state, through inspectors, labour courts, or other mechanisms of enforcement, to guarantee conditions established in labour codes or other labour legislation must be doubted. The anticipatory or pre-emptive nature of much legislation in the field of labour relations that is establishing standards designed for a market economy which does not yet exist is clearly one factor mitigating against effective implementation (Thirkell *et al.* 1995: 25–9).

Future prospects for the institutionalization and coverage of collective bargaining will be shaped by two main structural trends in the context of governments' economic policy. First, the extent to which trade unions are able to retain their memberships; and, secondly, the related factor of enterprise size. The creation of new small enterprises is strongly correlated with the absence of trade-union recognition and membership and this is coupled with the effects of the organizational restructuring of larger enterprises leading to a multiplicity of employing organizations which has occurred in Hungary with negative effects on membership and collective bargaining. In larger enterprises the prospects are, of course, better.

7

Inside the Enterprise

The previous chapters have discussed the processes of reform primarily at the national level. Here the focus is on the enterprise as the unit of analysis, the processes of change within it, and, especially, the interaction between what happens in the external environment and developments within the enterprise. In the centrally planned economy the significance of the enterprise had two main dimensions. First, the focus of management 'was mainly related to the macro level' and changes within the enterprise 'reflected the external requirements of the administrative-cum-political system rather than the problems associated with the functioning of the enterprise itself' (Federowicz 1994: 95). Secondly, in the one-party state the enterprise was the 'constitutive institution of the new socialist society' (Szczpanski, quoted in Federowicz 1994: 124). It provided the full employment which was the essence of socialist society together with rewards through a whole range of social and welfare services as well as earnings. The enterprise was the base of the party organization with its membership founded on the workplace and not on the locality.

Under the system of central planning the relationship of enterprises to their customers and suppliers was determined mainly by ministries and there was substantial central control over prices and wages. There was significant central influence over the design of the internal structures of the enterprise, as, for example, in the brigade system of work which was widespread in the Soviet Union, Bulgaria, and Czechoslovakia (Petkov and Thirkell 1991). Although there were repeated attempts to reform the Soviet model and develop new mechanisms for the management of enterprises, these strategies came from above rather than from enterprise management. Significantly, in the 1980s it was wage reform in Hungary associated with the VGMKs and the law on cooperatives in the Soviet Union which provided new opportunities for enterprise autonomy in which management could alter internal organizational structures and labour relations. In the traditional 'Soviet' environment the most important activity of enterprise directors was bargaining over plan targets and seeking additional resources from central branch authorities (Burawoy and Lukacs 1992; Myant 1993). Thus, as Markoczy (1993: 286) comments, 'these companies did not make strategic decisions in terms of economic rationality'. The constraints on enterprise autonomy in the planned economy meant that the scope for enterprise strategy in the choice of markets, in the design of enterprise structures, and in labour relations was very limited. The development of a market economy in theory enlarges the scope for enterprise strategy and frees up interests within the enterprise. In the process of transition from a centrally planned economy, 'the anticipation that interests will take shape from below, to be followed by action is of central importance in the construction of a market economy and democratic political system' (Federowicz 1994: 123). In this context the enterprise can be seen as one arena in which the interests of different strata and occupations are structured, restructured, and perhaps articulated.

However, the problems of macroeconomic stabilization have created major issues for enterprise managements. Thus, market failure, inflation, and financial crisis put pressures on enterprise managements to which they may respond as a challenge but also as a constraint. In addition, laws on ownership change and privatization may create other opportunities or threats. Laws and developments in political organizations and trade unions may also affect what happens within the enterprise. Consequently, external agencies such as ministries, political parties, or trade unions may be in interaction with top management and other groups inside the enterprise.

In Chapter 4 the contested nature of ownership change and privatization was discussed. It was argued that labour relations at enterprise level are of crucial significance for the possible success of different reform strategies. As will be seen in the cases examined in this chapter, the process of ownership change is constrained at enterprise level by the market position of the organization, ambiguities in the implementation of new legislation, the competences and abilities of managers, and the potential for emerging interests within the enterprise to press for particular outcomes.

In this chapter the primary aims are to use the case-study evidence to show, first, the process of change and, second, the current outcomes of the change process in terms of labour relations. With respect to the change process, the aim is to show the participation or otherwise of holders of positions inside and outside the enterprise and of agencies such as trade unions or employee councils on the succession of events such as restructuring, ownership change, the replacement of directors, and so on. With regard to the labour-relations outcomes, it is necessary to specify the different aspects of labour relations with which this chapter is concerned. It is suggested that there are four main aspects of importance. First, there is the question of employment and the employment relationship. The most significant part of this is the legacy of surplus employment, which is widely seen as a fundamental characteristic of socialist enterprises. It is derived from the fact that reduction of the workforce to increase efficiency was neither politically acceptable nor encouraged by the mechanisms of central planning, which generally defined enterprise importance according to the number of employees. The second aspect is the role of internal representative institutions within the enterprise and how they operate and whether they develop or decline. The third consideration is the restructuring of the internal organization of the enterprise. This concerns, especially in larger enterprises, the relations between two levels: between the top and the middle; and between the middle and the base. A fourth aspect is changes in the structure of rewards and in systems of payment and the mechanisms of agreement. Here the question is of whether there have been significant changes in differentials, the introduction of new criteria such as wage increases related to ability to pay or earnings linked to sales, and the relative importance of external criteria such as the results of tripartism (minimum wages).

This chapter draws on eight cases, three Russian, three Polish, and one each from Bulgaria and Slovakia (see Fig. 7.1). The initial discussion is of four cases (one from each of the four countries) in which the number of employees was initially more than 2,000 and internal restructuring was a significant issue. The Russian and Slovak enterprises were privatized but by the end of 1996 the Bulgarian and Polish cases had not been. The second group comprises four enterprises, two Polish and two Russian, initially with less than 1,000 employees. All of these are now privatized, but the process of ownership change was completed much more rapidly in the Russian than in the Polish cases.

Bulgaria	FLEXTOOLS Hand tools and motors		
Poland	POLTOOLS Industrial tools	MEDEX Medical equipment	COLDCUTS Food
Russia	SIBERTURB Large electrical turbines	MATOOLS Machine tools	LEBAGS Leather haberdashery
Slovakia	SPRINGS Mechanical springs		

FIG. 7.1. Case study enterprises

Note: See Appendix A for the details of the research undertaken.

PROTOTYPE RESTRUCTURING IN ENGINEERING

The two enterprises discussed in this section come from the engineering sector. They are both examples of prototype restructuring, in that management in both enterprises was experimenting with new managerial structures in the late 1980s before the leval changes on ownership.

Springs

At the Slovak enterprise Springs, a large engineering firm which had a workforce of 2,000 employees in 1990, organizational restructuring began in 1989 before the political changes later that year. Springs is an example of prototype restructuring in which the process has been characterized as 'centralized decentralization'; in certain enterprises the process of structural divisionalization was promoted or facilitated by the central authorities as an experiment in organizational design. Of particular interest is the impact of restructuring and ownership change on the different groups within the enterprise.

The election of a new Director in August 1989 was the critical event which led to major organizational restructuring in advance of wider political change and economic reform. The idea was to emulate an enterprise structure more similar to that of Western enterprises than that of most Czechoslovak enterprises. In essence, this was defined as involving the divisionalization of the different sections of the enterprise and the increasing autonomy of the divisions. It was developed by a group of consultants in conjunction with the candidate (from outside the enterprise) who won the election as Director. The State Enterprise Law of 1987, which required the election of directors organized by the Council of the Labour Collective, provided the opportunity for mobilizing interests behind the change. The regional Communist Party committee opposed the proposal on the grounds that it was a new and Western concept of management structure, involving decentralization, rather than a soviet-inspired model. However, the internal enterprise coalition, including the enterprise party committee, was in favour and the wider political changes in November removed all remaining political obstacles. The programme for divisionalization was put to the general assembly of employees by the external candidate and he secured 97 per cent of the votes.

It was recognized that, despite the consent of the workforce to the principle, implementation of the programme would require further internal mobilization for a period of six months, in order to prepare and to explain it fully to the employees. The central aim of the restructuring was to decentralize operational control to divisions which were given more financial independence. The size of the headquarters would be reduced and it would function primarily for strategy formulation. There was opposition from some headquarters staff, so that cooperation was lost and the units of the chief engineer and the legal adviser were closed down. However, there was no opposition from the workforce. It is significant that the concept of the restructuring was essentially managerial. It was designed to give some authority to operational managers but also to provide accounting information by which the costs of operations in relation to products could be assessed and inefficiencies could be identified. Although the consent of employees was needed, there was no conception of new approaches to the motivation of the workforce; it was assumed that increased efficiency was to come through changes in managerial structures and mechanisms.

The political changes of November 1989 coincided with the development of the divisional structure. The appointment of divisional heads was done by competition in order to avoid political influence on selection. Seven divisions

were established in January 1990 and they came into operation in July, with
an internal market and internal prices which were fixed by the centre. Each
division was a profit centre and had its own account at the enterprise bank,
which operated like a commercial bank charging interest on loans to
divisions. However, although the corporate centre controlled 80 per cent of
investments, 20 per cent remained with the divisions.

The process of restructuring (and political changes) led to a reorganization
and separation of interests both vertically and horizontally. Thus, the trade-
union representatives ceased to be part of the management team and managers joined a separate association, while there was a change in trade-union
office-holders at the time of the political changes. In each division trade-
union sections were established and the mechanisms of collective agreements
were negotiated at both enterprise and divisional level. One of the aims of
divisionalization was to relate bonuses to economic performance in order to
foster employee identification with the division. The members of less prosperous divisions in particular expressed dissatisfaction with the transfer of
administrative and accounting staff from the centre to the divisional level.
First-line supervisors, on the other hand, were dissatisfied that divisions were
not as fully independent as they had anticipated.

In 1991, in conditions of market crisis, the enterprise was successful in sub-
stituting its own distribution network for that of the established trade organization and in developing direct export links so that the value of exports in
that year was almost four times as much as in 1989. Also in 1991 there was a
reduction of one-third in the number of employees, from 2,100 to 1,400. This,
however, was mainly the result of divestment of activities and employees to
private firms and other companies rather than redundancy leading to loss of
employment. This restructuring of activities through leasing of services and
non-core activities was the first stage of privatization in 1991. Arising from
the 1991 Privatization Act, management prepared a project approved by the
ministry. By creating an external fund which they controlled and selling assets
to a foreign joint venture they were able to achieve a controlling interest in the
company's share for a group of twenty-four managers—in effect it became a
management buyout with the support of the divisions. The constitution of the
joint stock company at the end of 1992 did not provoke competing interests.
Decentralization in this context was set in the framework of business plans.
The divisions had operational responsibility for implementing these plans,
but quality control, the wage system, the management of human resources,
and investment were centrally controlled. The formal institutions and mechanisms of labour relations have changed very little since 1991. There was an
enterprise trade-union committee composed of representatives from the divisions which met top management to negotiate the collective agreement within
the framework of the branch agreement.

Between 1993 and 1995 there was a further process of internal restructuring and ownership change. Several divisions were merged and replaced by

four joint stock companies wholly owned by the holding company but which now became legally the employers of the workers—a process which initially provoked mistrust among the workers. However, the structure of trade-union representation has not been altered by this change and the tariff scales remain the basis for grading. Actual earnings have, however, increased more than the general trend. The changes in the structures and strategies of the management have gradually resulted in increases in labour productivity and an intensification of the labour process.

The case of Springs is remarkable for the continuing, uninterrupted, succession of managerially led changes. The enterprise has been reshaped according to the criteria selected by managers rather than externally driven. There were two main occasions when management had to cope with external constraints: the first was in securing political acceptance of the restructuring in 1989; the second was when a top-management group achieved a controlling shareholding in 1991, when the national political strategy for privatization was designed to establish a preponderance of external governance. In Springs restructuring and ownership change has involved a series of stages: initial divisionalization, divestment of activities, formal ownership change, and further internal restructuring changing divisions into companies. The initial restructuring required mobilization from the top to secure the consent of the workforce and the only opposition came from within groups of managers. The subsequent changes in internal structure evoked concern from sections of the workforce, but management was able to secure consent through negotiations with their representatives.

Clarke *et al.* (1994) have argued in respect of Russian enterprises that restructuring is predominantly at the top of the enterprises and that the reorganization of the labour process itself remains unattempted, in part because management fears the conflicts that this might involve. In Springs the reorganization of the labour process has been gradual and the most significant changes have occurred recently resulting in improvements in labour productivity. What is striking about the case is the continuity of change from before 1989 and the enterprise-led nature of the ownership-change processes.

Siberturb

This enterprise makes turbines and equipment used in hydroelectric plants, which have been marketed abroad as well as in the domestic market, and engines for washing machines. Experience of foreign markets and the economic changes promoted under *perestroika* stimulated top management to develop a strategy for increasing enterprise autonomy, to diversify its products, and to improve quality. As early as 1988 management used product diversification as a means of getting some freedom from ministry control over product prices. The political environment of *perestroika* enabled pressures for enterprise autonomy to grow and coincided with the decline of party influence in enterprise management. The development of enterprise strategy was seen to require internal decentralization to increase production flexibility and to provide more incentives directly related to results for middle management and for workers. The Director, who took up the post at the end of 1989, had previously had some training in Germany and this influenced his ideas of the model of organizational restructuring which should be followed. The first stage in the drive to organize autonomy came with the negotiation of a leasing arrangement with the ministry in August 1990. The enterprise trade union was the agency by which the consent to the change was secured from the labour collective. The essential features of the leasing agreement were that the enterprise could use its assets as it chose, while profits could be used to buy new assets which could be sold. The original assets could not be sold and rent for them was paid to the ministry, but the enterprise had the option of buying them over a period of fifteen years. The change in legal status made it possible to restructure the enterprise internally and to create internal divisions and units with greater autonomy. Leasehold status permitted economic autonomy to be given to the research institute which developed new products and to the consumer-goods department which sold products and services both inside the enterprise and outside from 1991.

The process of organizational restructuring developed in stages from 1991. The general objective was to devolve budgets to the twenty departments and the ten service sections with performance-related pay—a percentage of profits being distributed as bonuses. Restructuring led to the removal of a whole layer of middle management. The general strategy of top management in relation to departments has been as far as possible to develop them from cost centres to profit centres and, where possible, into companies with majority shareholding by the centre. Reorganization of the management structure and the development of a team of middle managers have been the most difficult tasks for top management and involved extensive retraining in the period 1991–3. The process of internal reorganization was accompanied by product diversification.

The original ownership strategy was gradually to buy the enterprise from the ministry over several years, but in 1992 the successive, and continually revised, decrees on privatization functioned as a threat and forced the management to decide on pre-emptive privatization in the summer of 1992, to avoid the upward valuation of enterprise assets. To convince the workforce, management ran a series of meetings about the opportunity for becoming a joint stock company. Mobilization for the required ballot was judged by the Director to require his presence at shop-floor meetings. The event revealed different perceptions of interest inside the enterprise: top management was strongly in favour, while middle management recognized that the change could offer an opportunity for more autonomy and rewards. Brigade leaders were sceptical about the advantages and the overwhelming majority of workers were critical about the price they would have to pay for their shares and saw it as a move imposed upon them by the state. Thus, in one department they resented the idea that they would be buying the outdated equipment used there. However, management succeeded in getting 77 per cent of the labour collective to vote for transformation into a joint stock company at the end of 1992. Although technically the organization was an 'open' shareholding company, with outside as well as inside shareholders, the great majority of shares were held by managers and employees within the enterprise. Worker share ownership was determined by length of service and average salary. Ownership change was accompanied by changes in institutions. All shareholders are invited to attend the annual general meeting and up to 200 attend. Some attend as individuals but most workers give their manager the proxy for their vote. The AGM elects the Managing Director and the Board of Directors. The latter is composed of representatives from the divisions and employees, and meets monthly. In the election the existing Director received the most votes but this was not a foregone conclusion. A manager explained: 'There was an idea to dismiss the Director. The threat of it was quite real. But he presented the situation to the people in such a way that he won it. He achieved his goal by inviting television and reporters and by his skill in conducting the negotiations' (interview, 1992). The process of developing the Board of Directors as a management agency making a series of policy and other decisions was made difficult by the legacy of the Council of the Labour Collective, which lapsed in 1990 and did not operate in this way. In theory the AGM could function as a channel for the representation of employee interests, but up to 1995 it had not functioned in this way to any significant extent beyond the election of directors. An executive board meets weekly.

The re-election of the Managing Director was contested at another large Siberian metal manufacturing enterprise. In that case the re-election of the General Manager for a further five years was contested by a departmental head. At the AGM the General Manager obtained 52 per cent of the votes and the departmental head 46 per cent. In this enterprise 50 per cent of the shares were held by outsiders and the departmental head used the trade union and the erstwhile *komsomol* as agencies in a coalition to mobilize the support of outside shareholders to demand an extraordinary meeting at which the General Manager was voted out. In this case the outcome of internal conflicts was shaped by linkages with interests in the political arena outside.

At Siberturb the initial strategy was to avoid external financial links, but the market crisis of 1991–2 led to a reversal of this, and, in order to diversify production and enter new markets, it associated with, or founded, more than thirty organizations, including banks, investment funds, and other enterprises. Survival remained the strategic issue in 1993. The question of reducing the labour force had emerged in 1990–1, when many poor performers were dismissed. There were, however, no mass lay-offs because the enterprise trade union was opposed and because the management judged that direct dismissals were not effective: 'we have tried this with the only result in many

conflicts and no positive effects. It is like when you try to drive crows away
from the roof and they fly up but they immediately settle down in the same
place so it is a futile attempt. The point is to activate the economy and real
interests of concrete people' (interview, Managing Director, 1992). However,
in the second half of 1992 nearly 400 workers left as a result of decentralizing
the decisions to units and restricting their wage funds. This measure enabled
units to keep skilled workers and increase their wages slightly. The
researchers judged that the trade union at Siberturb was the most professional of all the enterprises studied; membership was 98 per cent. The
Managing Director explained his policy: 'There is no sense in getting rid of
the trade union at the present moment. If we get rid of this one now another
one or two or three would appear; then it will be necessary to conclude collective agreements with each of them. We can't avoid the trade union's existence' (interview, 1992). (There had been attempts by groups of workers to set
up alternative trade unions in 1991.)

The trade-union leadership recognized that 'the main function of the trade
union is employee protection' but found some contradictions in ownership
because 'it is not clear who should be protected against whom because everyone is an owner and at the same time everyone is hired including the administration' (interview, Trade Union President, 1993).

Apart from the period of economic crisis from 1991 to early 1992, when there
were a number of strikes, mainly about delays in the payment of wages, labour
relations have been peaceful and the practice of demonstrations with other
workers in the city has subsided. The changes in structure affected the parties
to the collective agreement, which came to be negotiated between the trade-
union committee and the council of directors. In 1995 the main issues were
wages and detailed changes in terms and conditions. Although managers and
highly skilled specialists are paid on contract, the majority of workers continue
to be paid by the tariff system—another example of continuity derived from the
traditions of socialist emulation (competition) by which leading workers were
awarded prizes. This continued but was now termed the 'director's prize'. A
similar adaptation was found at the car plant in Nizhni Novgorod in 1996,
where 'socialist' competition had become the 'director's competition'.

The strategy for social policy in the enterprise has involved changes and
then a reversal. The financial crisis at the start of 1992 led the enterprise, like
many others, to reduce its expenditure on social facilities and benefits. This
was reversed at the end of the year, when the surplus share vouchers were used
to buy holiday homes and other recreational facilities. This combined the
aims of retaining employees and avoiding tax, as social benefits were taxed
less than wages. Maintenance of social assets in this way suggests both that
managers, trade unions, and employees still expect the enterprise to play a
substantial role in providing social assets and meeting the non-wage needs of
its employees and that there are incentives in the current situation to maintain
social spending. The persistence of this legacy has been noted in other case

study research in Russian enterprises (Mikhalev 1996; Tratch *et al.* 1996; Ashwin 1997: 118–22).

For top management the key structural issue of central and divisional control had been a continuing one of balancing organizational integration with internal autonomy and resolving the continuing conflicts of interests between departments. In other respects the conclusion of the case-study research is that the insider-dominated change in ownership had not yet changed labour relations to a great degree.

Springs and Siberturb Compared

Although there are major differences in both the products and locations of these enterprises there are a significant number of similarities. The organization of autonomy sought and promoted by the directors was an early goal. In both cases the reorganization of the management structure was identified as a key strategy and this was based on the imitation of foreign structures. The exclusion/reduction of external ownership was largely achieved in both enterprises. The actual process of mobilization of support for ownership change from the workforce was a significant one in both cases. In both enterprises internal divisionalization and the need to transform the role of middle management became the focus of internal and to some extent continuing conflicts. Such struggles were more significant than conflicts with the workforce, though in both cases there was some degree of institutionalization in terms of trade-union recognition and collective agreements. There was, however, a divergence in social policy: consistent divestment at Springs but a revival at Siberturb.

RESTRUCTURING WITHOUT OWNERSHIP CHANGE IN ENGINEERING

This pair of cases comes from the engineering sector. Both enterprises make tools, Poltools mainly for industrial uses, while Flextools is engaged in manufacture primarily for the consumer market. In 1990 they both employed about 2,000 employees. Despite some changes in the ownership relationship, neither had been privatized by the end of 1996. They are, therefore, of particular interest in terms of the extent to which processes of restructuring have proceeded in the absence of privatization.

Poltools

This enterprise was a flagship company (part of a Kombinat) in the 1980s, with good political connections through its Director which enabled it to secure improved technologies at a time when such investment was rarely available to other enterprises. The new technology enabled some production to be made at world standards. The workforce is predominantly male. Its 'political' status led to it being selected for the introduction of the brigade organization of work in the period 1986–9. (It was visited in 1988 by Gorbachev and Jaruzelski to consider the viability of the brigade model for *perestroika* reforms. Brigade organization of work was adopted only in a small number of enterprises in Poland.) This restructuring, implemented through party activists, was designed to establish the brigades as cost centres, with the brigade leaders negotiating with the departmental manager and eliminating the intervening level of management. One interpretation of this restructuring led by the Director was that it would neutralize the influence of the Employees' Council. In practice this top-down restructuring produced negative reactions among the workforce, because its operation was seen as depending on an arbitrary system of payment and on personal connections. In 1988 the company was externally proposed for prototype transformation into a so-called nomenklatura company. This process was blocked by Solidarity, which had re-established itself following the changed political climate in February 1989. Solidarity, which in this enterprise had been mainly an organization of blue-collar workers, became the leading agency in articulating worker interests in relation to the restructuring of the enterprise and the form of privatization. During the 1980s OPZZ had been dominated by middle management, but after 1989 it became less active and stood aside from the interest issues around privatization.

In 1989 conflict was centred on the form of privatization and specifically on the formation of internal companies, in which it seemed that the shares would be distributed to people, both inside and outside the company, who had connections with the Director. Following a strike organized by Solidarity, the Director resigned in 1990. His successor was appointed on the basis of a plan to restore the internal structures and end the internal companies. However, he failed to achieve the latter and the Employee Affairs Director concluded that the Director was improperly involved in these companies. With the support of Solidarity and a proposal for privatization to include employee shareholding, in 1991 the Employee Affairs Director was able to organize a successful campaign against the Director and to take over from him as an 'administrative director'. The idea of employee shareholding became popular as a form of privatization with some teams of workers, although the practicality of raising sufficient funds from them was doubtful.

In 1991 the Ministry of Property Transformation included Poltools in the list of 400 enterprises scheduled for 'commercialization' followed by 'mass privatization'. Management used all its efforts and was successful in getting it withdrawn from this list. The new Director was appointed on the basis of a 'management contract' with the Ministry signed at the beginning of 1992. The intention was to strengthen the power of the Director (the Employees' Council was dissolved at this time), and to provide a financial incentive to produce a restructuring programme. Although the support of Solidarity had been a major factor in the Director's appointment, he soon attempted to reduce the union's role. He hoped to build a strong management structure unhampered by 'social factors' and to exclude the trade unions from decisions on restructuring. This was, however, a period of extreme financial difficulty for the enterprise. The Solidarity representatives demanded to see the programme for restructuring the enterprise, but the Director refused. The issue of the programme became the main source of conflict within the enterprise. Solidarity pressed for the establishment of the management board delayed by the Director and later Solidarity complained to the Ministry of Industry. In June 1993 the Ministry ended the Director's contract and announced a competition for the position. The grounds for the action were delays in setting up a supervisory board and developing the restructuring programme and the deterioration of financial results in 1992. (Solidarity immediately negotiated an increase in wages for employees with the interim Director.) The commission for appointing his successor in 1993 consisted of five external representatives (three from the Ministry and two from banks) and four internal representatives (two from the Advisory Council and one each from Solidarity and OPZZ). There were ten candidates (four internal and six external) and they were asked to present programmes for the development of the enterprise based on study of enterprise documents. The candidate favoured by OPZZ, the former chief accountant, who was also supported by Solidarity, was successful. The researcher's judgement was that in the selection process the opinion of the employee representatives was important but not decisive and that within the commission consensus was achieved on the appointment which was on the basis of a managerial contract. The enterprise remained a state company and privatization was deferred pending stabilization of the enterprise's financial and market situation. The outcome of the selection process was the establishment, for the first time for many years, of an internal consensus around the programme of restructuring.

Flextools

This enterprise was founded in the early 1960s, but its main development dates from 1968, when it secured a licence from a foreign company to make electrical tools. This cooperation, which provided technical and managerial know-how, lasted until 1986, when Bulgarian failure to meet delivery targets led to the severance of the arrangement by the foreign partner. Production was oriented for exports—formerly to the Soviet Union and more recently towards the west.

In common with other Bulgarian enterprises, the principal change in labour relations in the 1980s was the introduction of the brigade organization of work and the increased powers given to the labour collective. Changes in trade-union organization followed the political changes at the end of 1989, when about 100 employees were laid off. *Podkrepa* was established in the enterprise and the branch trade union affiliated to CITUB was restructured. The basis of the *Podkrepa* membership was political: the initial common interest of its members, drawn from across the enterprise, was anti-communism. By 1993 its functions were primarily industrial, but its eighty or so members continued as a separate organization. The first major threat to the enterprise and its employees came with the market crisis of 1991–2. The management aimed to secure employment as far as possible and, although 150 workers were laid off, the fall in production was proportionately much greater. However, the company was able to remain solvent because it could raise prices and secure credits. Recruitment was restricted and new workers were hired on short-term contracts.

In August 1992 the replacement of the General Director was a significant event in the development of the enterprise. In this year a large number of directors were replaced in the context of policies supported by the UDF government elected in October 1991. These events revealed the roles of internal and external agencies and the perceptions of interests of different groups within the enterprise. The main driving force for change was the organization of *Podkrepa* inside the enterprise, which floated the idea early in 1992, but it was soon linked with the national organization and with the ruling coalition of the UDF in the locality. The case against the Director was nominally based on the need to secure the future of the enterprise; it was claimed that he had been responsible for earlier mistakes and the failure to move beyond a survival strategy. On the other hand, from the standpoint of employees, he had successfully reoriented the shift from the Russian to Western markets, and had maintained employment at a relatively high level and a wage level which was high for the district. Consequently, the mobilization for the change was at the top of the enterprise and not positively endorsed by the base. At this time the Ministry initiated proposals for privatization which involved negotiations with potential foreign partners. Top management saw ownership change in this form as a potential threat rather than an opportunity to operate with more freedom. The fear was that a foreign owner might buy the plant and close it to remove competition.

Changes in labour relations were strongly influenced by developments in policy at the national level. The process of collective bargaining began in the summer of 1991, stimulated externally by the national tripartite initiative (Thirkell and Teseneva 1992). In the joint negotiations the unions were the leading agency and wages were the most contentious issue. There were similar annual negotiations in 1992 and 1993. In 1993 the negotiations were set in the context of the new Labour Code, which extended the range of issues for negotiation. Commissions of management and union representatives were set up to agree issues of interpretation of the agreement and to assess the competence of those threatened with dismissal.

At the end of 1994 the enterprise was officially placed in the privatization procedure, which made it open to offers, including those from foreign investors as well as Bulgarian business groups. However, by August 1995 the Privatization Agency had made no decision about ownership. In May 1995 the General Director was dismissed, as was the Production Director with whom he had been in conflict, whilst the former Director dismissed in 1992 returned to the Board. These positional changes were the result of external events, including the sessional meeting of the regional Bulgarian Socialist Party in May which decided on the replacement of politically unacceptable directors. However, more significant in the context of prospective privatization were the internal links with competing external business groups. The General Director had connections with one of these groups, but the Production Director did not support this. A second group sought support from the trade unions in Flextools and in other enterprises in the competition for control of enterprises through privatization. CITUB finally decided in favour of the Director's dismissal. *Podkrepa*, on the other hand, had at one stage threatened a strike if the Production Director was dismissed.

There has been a significant shift in the attitude of management towards privatization. As explained above, this was formerly seen as a threat which might lead to the takeover of its markets and the closure of the enterprise by a foreign buyer. Until recently their position was that the enterprise should remain state property, but with provision for shares to be held by management, the workers, and external holders. The shift in approach has been caused by recognition that substantial investment for modern technology is essential to meet growing competition from China and that prospective Bulgarian business groups may be a source of capital to ensure a prosperous company. For the workforce, apart from the issue of managerial appointments which was mainly one for the union leadership, the main issue in privatization was the acquisition of a 20 per cent block of shares allocated for employee purchase at half price, for which 80 per cent of the workforce has applied. However, the vouchers and workers' savings will not be sufficient to buy all the block, and the trade unions will press potential buyers of the enterprise to cover the remaining part of the block as part of the deal.

Poltools and Flextools Compared

Both of these enterprises had a legacy as leading enterprises in terms of products and technology, but Solidarity, as a revived agency from the early 1980s, was a more significant institutional inheritance. Solidarity focused on the hostility to changes that had been imposed in the 1980s. Changes at this time in Flextools were not a disputed issue. At Poltools restructuring and the position of successive managing directors became the salient issue over the whole period. The constellation of internal forces was sufficient to block restructuring until 1994 and the external agencies were unsuccessful in directing the enterprise towards a viable form of privatization. The trade unions in this case seem to have developed as institutions with the support of their members, whereas management was unsuccessful in developing institutional structures and mechanisms. At Flextools the replacement of general directors was more closely related to developments in the party political arena although the internal agencies had an active part, but the issues were not primarily about enterprise restructuring.

The presence of two trade unions in both enterprises and their development make an interesting contrast, especially in the shifting balance between political and industrial functions. Thus, both Solidarity and *Podkrepa* had political functions, but these shifted to mainly industrial functions in post-socialist conditions. The reformed unions—CITUB and OPZZ—both limited their functions to those of interest representation within an employment rather than a political framework. In the Polish enterprise the range of issues which came within the field of management—union labour relations was wider than in Flextools, mainly because of the salience of restructuring as an issue at Poltools. In the Bulgarian plant external standards from the tripartite negotiations and the Labour Code were more apparent than at Poltools and the periodic process of collective bargaining was more institutionalized, including the development of commissions. Both of the cases indicate the negotiated and contingent nature of privatization; in neither enterprise was it a simple exercise for external agencies to implement their reform agendas. Employees at Poltools were attracted to employee share ownership as an aspect of privatization. This was also apparent later in Flextools.

NEW DIRECTORS AS AGENTS OF TRANSFORMATION

The next two enterprises to be discussed, producing machine tools and medical equipment respectively, provide examples where the appointment of new Managing Directors was critical for the formulation of survival strategies.

Matools

This enterprise was a main producer of machine tools originally established in 1931. It had accumulated debts in the middle 1980s but the turning point in its development was the arrival of a new Managing Director, who had trained in Germany, with his team of new managers in 1988. The initial strategy was devoted to product diversification, reducing debts, and accumulating capital as the precondition for the organization of autonomy through leasing. It also involved some internal decentralization. Some 70 per cent of existing managers were replaced in 1989. The 1987 Law of Enterprises allowed, but did not require, some independence from state/ministry control. The Managing Director foresaw that the pending economic reform would involve changes in ownership and would also require the restructuring of management and production. He defined the strategic goals for transformation as, first, to retain highly skilled workers but to 'get rid of slackers and drunkards' and, second, to strengthen the enterprise in terms of the market and of management.

There were major stages in the organization of autonomy in 1991. At the beginning of the year it became a leasehold company and in May it was established as a joint stock company, thus getting free of ministry control. Although nominally an 'open' company, with provision for outside shareholders, it was provided that for the first five years it should operate as a closed company, so that employees who left had to return their shares to the enterprise. Ownership change was accompanied by internal restructuring, initially creating internal shareholding companies. This conception derived from the work of a German consultant and was seen as imitating a Western model of organization. Originally there were four product-oriented firms (for example, 'machine tools' and 'consumer goods') and five service organizations, but later more were created which became legally independent and operated on the basis of contracts with the centre, which functioned as a type of holding company. Shares in these companies were held by managers and employees, although the controlling interest was retained by the centre.

Internal innovations in structure facilitated responses to the changes in the external environment by product diversification (and new technology) and the development of a sales culture. All managers and employees came to see selling goods as the basic task of the enterprise, and some managers and even some workers argued that employees should not be paid until their products had been sold. In the conditions of economic and financial crisis, the enterprise was successful in achieving sales as a trading organization and through barter and was able to maintain and even increase its labour force—950 in 1994 compared with 825 in 1988. Despite this direct attempt at cultural change, when the enterprise was visited in 1993 portraits of leading workers were prominently displayed, as had been the custom with 'socialist emulation'. Similar displays were found in some enterprises in Nizhni Novgorod in 1994 and in Tver, indicating that management judged the traditional strategy of seeking to combine 'moral' with material stimuli as still relevant.

There were a succession of changes in labour relations. The role of the trade union in the enterprise was marginal and it did not even sign the collective agreement. As its leader explained, the union's role had been 'to persuade employees to work overtime'—that is, the traditional function of promoting production. In October 1992 the deduction of union dues was terminated by management and the union ended. The only articulated concern of employees was about the continuation of sick pay, which had been a union function, and the workers then accepted the assurance that sick pay would continue. The trade-union chair became President of the Production Council, which replaced the union as the institution representing employee interests. (The 1991 collective agreement had been signed by the management and the

President of the Council.) There were, however, spontaneous actions by sections of the workforce which occurred without any relationship to the Council as an institution, the provisions of the collective agreement, or the President of the Council. Thus, in May 1992 workers in the assembly went on strike for a wage increase. On another occasion there was a walkout in the transport department. These were unorganized protest actions and consistent with workers' low opinion of these representative institutions. The collective agreement was revised in 1993 to include more procedural provisions, but there is no evidence that it was seen as a significant mechanism—certainly this was the view of the Managing Director when interviewed in 1995. It was, as the researchers noted, a mechanism outside 'the real life of the enterprise'. The annual shareholders' meeting was equally seen as an institution of purely formal significance; when the Director withdrew his annual written report, this action was not questioned.

Two major changes were made in the methods of payment. All jobs were evaluated by rating to establish the basic rate, and a contract system was introduced to ensure flexibility by workers agreeing to do any task they were assigned, thus avoiding the provisions of the Labour Code. Although, in the context of job insecurity, compliance was secured, both changes were resented by workers, who saw them as managerial devices representing a change in the customary values of a 'fair day's wage'. Workers were also encouraged to regard their earnings as a private matter to be concealed from their colleagues and that a breach of this could lead to dismissal. These changes reduced the former importance of highly skilled workers.

This case is distinctive, in that top management aimed to secure a shift from the traditional values of employees, but the early results of the attempts to changes values had, at most, only a qualified success. The researchers noted that the traditional, technologically based lines of division and the accompanying values persisted: administration and workers; middle and top management; production departments and auxiliary departments; production and offices. The one major change was in the enhanced self-perception of the office staff now responsible for securing the orders on which the producers depended. This inverted the traditional values, in which production had ranked highest. The extent of German imitation was also distinctive, embracing the concepts of the internal firms, the management structure, the privatization process, and the institution of the Employees' Council.

Medex

This company, which produces medical equipment, had stagnated in the 1980s and failed to develop new products and improve existing ones. Its products were bought by local-authority institutions and a third of its production went to the Soviet Union—the latter market collapsed in 1991. Many employees left voluntarily because of the low wages and the number of staff had fallen to 800 by the end of 1989. At the end of the 1970s the Director of the enterprise had unexpectedly emigrated and a party organizer had been imposed as a replacement. However, during the 1980s it was a 'quiet' company without involvement in the strikes elsewhere and Solidarity concentrated on establishing the Enterprise Council set up in 1981 in advance of the legislation. In 1988 the newly elected Employees' Council was more active than its predecessor in facing up to the problems of the enterprise (its President was active in Solidarity), and it came to the position that wages were low because the Managing Director was not effective and had no strategy for the company. In January 1989—that is, before the political changes— the council got rid of the Director and his deputy, which in the political conditions of the time was a brave decision. In this episode the council was the only independent and active agency; the party and OPZZ were passive and so was the workforce. The new Managing Director was one of seven candidates assessed by a private consultancy. The candidates made presentations to the consultancy and to the Employees' Council and the appointment was made in June 1989. This event was the turning point in the history of the organization.

The new Director's strategy was to improve the quality of management and to concentrate in himself power over the employees. He was soon involved in conflicts with the Employees' Council and its President over the restructuring of the management organization and of the marketing strategy. Restructuring involved reducing the number of departments, gradually reducing the number of middle managers, reorganizing project teams, establishing a new marketing unit, and revitalizing research and development.

The loss of the Soviet market and the Polish financial crisis of 1991 led to redundancies, while the subsidiaries became independent and owned by private capital. Further market problems led to large redundancies early in 1992 in which the trade unions played no part in the selection of workers. In 1990 the enterprise had employed 800 but this had fallen to 180 by September 1992 as a result of redundancies and reorganizations, but numbers increased slightly in 1993 and were 200 in 1994. The survival of the enterprise was the consequence of the intensive search for new customers and the reductions in jobs. There was general agreement within the enterprise about the need for privatization, but it was also realized that there would be major problems in achieving it. The prospect of a foreign link initially appeared attractive, but an Italian partner withdrew. The Director investigated different forms of privatization, including employee shareholding, but the employees did not have enough money and private investors in Poland were not interested. Job losses and the fear of them weakened the power of employees and their trade unions. Two activists of OPZZ were dismissed (illegally) without any reaction from the membership, who feared they might also be sacked, and OPZZ disintegrated as an organization. The President of Solidarity, who had leadership qualities, lacked support from his members, although a third of the employees paid union dues. An attempt by the regional official of Solidarity to negotiate with the Director was rejected and the official was sent off the premises. In these circumstances it was not surprising that it was the Director who determined the strategy of privatization through liquidation, a process in which the role of the Employees' Council was purely nominal and in which the Director secured a high proportion of the shares.

Matools and Medex Compared

In both cases the turning points in the development of the enterprises came with new Directors who acted as the agents of transformation and who identified the reorganization of management as strategic issues. There were significant differences in the outcomes of the respective survival strategies. Thus, Matools remained at a similar size while Medex was dramatically reduced in size, becoming a small enterprise with a 75 per cent reduction in employment.

At Medex the Managing Director set out, successfully, to eliminate the powers, influence, and legacy of representative institutions. The organization and maintenance of autonomy were not difficult and labour relations became individualized. At Matools, once the organization of autonomy had been achieved, a strategic issue was considered to be the motivation of both managers and employees. This underlay the internal restructuring and a series of changes in the organization of work and rewards. The expectation of major shifts in the culture of the enterprise and its employees deriving from these and from share ownership had not materialized. Ownership change at Matools was closely linked to the internal restructuring, but at Medex major restructuring was not impeded by delays in ownership change.

FACING UP TO COMPETITIVE MARKETS IN CONSUMER PRODUCTS

This section compares the processes of transformation in a Russian and a Polish enterprise which have had to shift from a pattern of administered distribution of their products to marketing their consumer products in competitive markets. Marketization has, therefore, had a direct impact on these enterprises.

Lebags

The factory, situated in Novosibirsk, employs some 800 workers, of whom 75 per cent are women, and for many years has made leather goods for the consumer market. When the Director was appointed in 1985 to head the state enterprise there were two subsidiary enterprises in other Siberian cities. Until

1990 almost all of the factory's production was determined by state contracts for wholesale deliveries. By 1992 this pattern had largely gone and the factory organized its own marketing and distribution in Siberia and other parts of the former Soviet Union, having to compete with imports from abroad.

The Managing Director, who had received some training in Germany, was personally responsible for the series of strategic choices in relation to ownership change, organizational restructuring, and changes in labour relations, all set out in the context of the evolving business strategy:

Our general strategic goal is to win a sunny place in the market. With 62 years experience in light industry and skilled manpower we want a steady position in the market from the Urals to the Far East. Then we will be able to enter foreign markets. The main thing is to do what we are now doing but in a more efficient and professional manner and to ensure decent wages and social services for the people. (interview, 1992)

The fulfilment of these goals required product diversification, the development of retail outlets, increased production specialization (each brigade to make one article), and the upgrading of worker skills.

The first stage in the transformation of the enterprise, in the middle of 1991, was the creation of an independent internal joint stock company with seven managers and thirty-five workers. This parallel structure was intended to serve several functions: as an agency for selling products at market prices (outside the prices fixed by the ministry); to earn capital towards the purchase of the enterprise and to be in a strong position in the event of competitive bidding; and to provide staff with experience of working outside the conditions of state ownership, including higher earnings.

At the end of 1991 the elimination of the enterprise trade union took place. Workers had become critical of the trade union's involvement in acquiring and distributing scarce goods. The external decision of the regional trade-union council that in future decisions on the main issues would be made without representatives from the factory made workers resent the transfer of some dues and they decided they would no longer subsidize the higher body. The principal action was the Director's decision to suspend the automatic deduction of trade-union dues from wages, in order to show workers how much they were paying for the union. Workers had always been sceptical of the value of the union, which they saw as the administration's 'tail'. Workers then signed a declaration that they did not want to pay for the union and it was then disbanded. The elimination of the trade union coincided with an extensive campaign organized by the Director, within the different parts of the factory and with work teams, to win the support of middle management and workers for the privatization programme, which was eventually approved at a conference of the whole workforce in 1992.

The purchase of shares was open to all employees, except those on probation, and about 90 per cent of employees became shareholders (those with fifteen years' service got them free of charge). Researchers noted that, at the end of 1991 and the beginning of 1992, employees were generally in favour of the joint stock company, but by the middle of the year the attitude was generally negative. As a manager put it, 'they swear out against this privatization', which they interpreted as the administration profiting and depriving them of their rights. The payment of the first dividends in March 1993 was seen as very small, especially in comparison with end-of-year bonuses, and few employees took up the option of buying additional shares. On the other hand when the management offered to buy workers' shares at an indexed price, few employees took up the offer, hoping that in time they would appreciate.

The dissolution of the trade union and the ownership change was followed by the replacement of the Council of the Labour Collective with an Enterprise Council, elected by employee shareholders. This functioned as a new institution to represent the interests of the shareholder employees. Membership is on the basis of one member for every thirty workers, together with some nominations by the Director. The original conception of the council's function was that it should make and monitor policy in the fields of production and social policy. However, in practice the council has principally discharged the functions of the former trade union, especially in the field of social provision. Its activities have included assistance to pensioners and the signing of the annual collective agreement as a modified form of the traditional 'cooperative agreement', dealing with social development, skill training, safety, and working conditions. The council does not have the function of employee representation, although there are councils at the level of the department to facilitate consultation. Employees generally judged the work of the council favourably in comparison with that of the former trade union.

Despite some changes in the organization of management, the functions of departmental managers remained principally operational and financial control was still centralized. However, the Director was the initiator of a human-resource strategy with several facets, all intended to improve workforce skills and motivation. There was steady replacement of older workers and a selection process for new recruits with better qualifications. In-house training and education were consistently promoted and there was a series of attempts by the Director to improve motivation by changing payment mechanisms and relating salaries to ratings of skill. However, the extension of piece-work was resisted by both workers and their supervisors and the researchers noted some passive resistance to the new ideas and the general transformation.

The general conclusion about this enterprise is that there was little overt articulation of interests by social groups within the enterprise and the controlling role of the Director and his associates in labour relations was unchallenged. There was, however, a significant level of unarticulated conflict. The researchers noted that share ownership was not regarded as a significant right by most employees, since top management had the main concentration of shares, and they suggested that eventually some institutional form of interest representation might have positive functions for the enterprise by reducing apathy and passive resistance. It seemed, however, unlikely that such an institution would be created autonomously by the workforce.

Coldcuts

The enterprise, which manufactures a range of meat products, including sausages and cold cuts of meat, had some 600 employees in 1991. It is located in the outskirts of a major city where its products are sold. The plant had been part of a multi-plant enterprise and a monopoly producer, with its products distributed administratively. The ending of state control over distribution had important organizational consequences. The plant separated from the enterprise in 1989 and had since operated successfully in a very competitive market. From then on management led an ongoing search for product development and improvement, introduced computerization and new technology, and restructured some departments. The enterprise has its own network of shops.

Labour relations, in terms of wages and conditions, have been regulated at the level of the internal units with the trade union, while policy issues are dealt with at company level with the involvement of the Employees' Council. The Managing Director was chosen by the Employees' Council in 1987. There are two trade-union organizations: the branch union (OPZZ), founded in 1984, had some 140 members drawn from a range of occupations including white-collar workers and managers as well as those with low qualifications; Solidarity, refounded in 1990 following the political changes, had some ninety members, including a core of highly qualified professionals, who secured by election a dominant position on the Employees' Council in 1992, which until then had been mainly composed of supporters of the Managing Director. The younger Solidarity activists campaigned against the Managing Director and his supporters.

The ongoing issue of strategic choice and the principal focus of interest articulation have been that of ownership change and privatization. Ownership change involved a competition which initially attracted bids from five organizations and was seen as a stage by which the enterprise would develop, especially through the inflow of capital. The OPZZ and its members did not oppose the form of privatization proposed, but Solidarity did, arguing that an employee share company would serve the interests of employees better. The difficulty with this was that the employees did not have sufficient money to buy the shares.

In this case the initiative in relation to strategic choice on ownership change came from the Managing Director but was effectively blocked by the Employees' Council, which had the power to demand an election for the post of Managing Director. The Solidarity representatives hoped that the value of the plant would not increase so that the prospect of employee purchase at the lowest price would be improved. In 1993 The Managing Director organized a delegation to visit an enterprise in the same branch where an employee share company had already been established. The delegation consisted of the Managing Director, the chair and vice-chair of the Employees' Council, and the leader of Solidarity in the enterprise. Following the visit the Managing Director was encouraged to support a project for an employees' share company, believing that it would be possible to concentrate shares in the hands of a small number of managerial staff. The impending Enterprise Pact in the national arena reinforced the disposition towards employee share ownership on all sides.

In the 1994 elections to the Employees' Council the Managing Director hoped that new members would be elected, but Solidarity maintained its majority. However, in 1995 after two years of conflict, the internal impasse was broken and agreement was reached on the privatization route. Despite the development of new products and the maintenance of a relatively healthy market position, the enterprise had not engaged in any major restructuring. Two explanations appear to underlie this 'organizational torpor': first, the management team was technically well educated but had little experience or sense of managing in a competitive market situation; secondly, the workforce was stable, many with long service and consisting of several family groups. In particular, the shops were run by people with family connections to key managers in the firm. As a result, management took very little initiative in respect of labour-relations issues and there was no real attempt to intensify management control. This was most clearly evidenced by the continuing high levels of theft within the plant.

Coldcuts is an example of an enterprise that almost tried to pretend that nothing had changed. Management was not prepared, or able, to try and mobilize support for major change. Management and the workforce were united in trying to preserve the enterprise for insiders.

Lebags and Coldcuts Compared

Both enterprises were successful in the transformation from administrative control of product distribution to operating effectively in competitive market environments. However, at Coldcuts this was achieved before the repeatedly postponed ownership change was agreed. This points to the importance of organizational autonomy, though the absence of ownership change may restrict access to investment. A coalition of managerial interests articulated through the Employees' Council restricted the Managing Director's choices of strategy on ownership change.

At Lebags the Managing Director was able to restructure the organization of management and to promote human-resource management (HRM) approaches in relation to the workforce without any significant constraint. Representation of employee interests is through the Employee Council, but the degree of articulation is limited and the concentration of power in the Director has not been challenged. The cases illustrate opposite ends of the scale with regard to managerial initiative and the degree of influence of mechanisms of employee representation. In Lebags management grasped the opportunities marketization provided to steer the organization in certain directions. In Coldcuts the management rested on its relatively secure market position, acted defensively, and provided the space for the Employees' Council to take a major role in mobilizing consent for an employee share ownership form of privatization.

SUMMARY OF FINDINGS

This chapter has set out to show examples of the dynamics of restructuring, ownership change, and privatization at enterprise level. These cases, drawing on the evidence available over a period of several years, dispel any assumptions that the process of enterprise transformation in Eastern Europe is a relatively straightforward one, involving one or two stages carried out over a short period of time. The reality is that there is significant diversity, not only between countries but also within them.

A central issue is the relationship between laws on ownership change, the process of marketization, and managerial strategies at the level of the enterprise. As might be expected, there are different patterns. Thus, marketization or ownership change may be seen as impending opportunities or as threats to enterprise survival. There is, however, a pattern evidenced in the three Russian cases and Springs where the organization of managerial autonomy from ministry control was a central motive of top managements, which provided the dynamics of the cases, and to a considerable extent this was achieved before ownership change occurred. In these cases a key concern of top managements became the desire to preserve their autonomy from the threat that might be posed by external owners. Thus, in these enterprises internal restructuring was consciously designed to cope with the anticipated challenges of marketization and was derived in varying degrees from the imitation of Western models of management organization. Despite the unexpected scale of the economic transformation crisis, these enterprises were able to survive rather successfully.

Ownership change has often had more than one stage—for example, 'commercialization' in Poland and 'leasing' in Russia. In respect of the process as a whole, a key labour-relations issue has been whether or not the consent of the workforce, or a representative institution, is a required feature of privatization. Workforce consent is to some extent a legacy of the general trend towards forms of worker participation which were characteristic of labour relations in the 1980s, which included workers' rights to elect directors and other managerial personnel. In the Russian cases the consent of the workforce (the labour collective) was a necessary element, whilst in Poland the representative institution of the Employees' Council has been a necessary agency for consent to ownership change.

The Russian cases show that mobilization of consent for ownership change could require campaigning by management, sometimes assisted by the trade union, but ultimately there was no significant opposition from the workforce as a whole. In the Polish cases the institutional legacy from the 1980s of Employees' Councils and trade unions made them significant agencies, whether in support of specific forms of ownership change or in opposition to them. Although the Czechoslovak form of privatization was based on citizen vouchers, in the prototype case of Springs workforce consent was needed and was obtained without difficulty. In the cases of the larger divisionalized enterprises, the role of middle management in ownership change could be significant, and interests of middle managers, sometimes redefined by divisionalization, could make them agents in the process of securing consent or opposing.

The legacy of more decentralized management in the period 1986–9 served as an important backdrop to privatization attempts in the early 1990s. In some cases, as in Springs and Siberturb, such decentralization allowed skilful directors to pre-empt national programmes of ownership change and orchestrate privatization in a form that preserved their interests and their stake in the enterprise. The legacy of self-management mechanisms created in the 1980s also served to complicate the process of ownership change. The legacy was more enduring where, as in Coldcuts, activists were able to use the mechanisms to press for their preferred ownership-change option. In other cases, such as Medex, self-management mechanisms were easily overcome by management. Hence, such legacies are not path-determining but rather shape future events depending upon the other circumstances prevailing around the enterprise; factors such as market position, the competence of managers, and the ability of the trade unions to mobilize support mediate the impact of legacies.

A common theme in the cases is the role of directors in the process of ownership change and of labour relations. In their study of enterprise transformation in three Polish cases, Konecki and Kulpinska (1995: 248) concluded that 'the turning points in the histories of these companies are connected with the appearance of new top managers, usually headed by a new organizational leader. The leader contributes or works out jointly with an initiative group created by him or her a new definition of organizational reality.' Such turning points and processes, or at least the attempts to achieve this, are clearly found in Springs, Siberturb, Matools, Medex, and Lebags. In the first four the development of managerial groups/teams was an explicit goal, irrespective of whether it was combined with internal restructuring and divisionalization. In other enterprises, such as Poltools, Flextools, and Coldcuts, the absence or inhibition of such direction is the key dynamic of these cases.

The Poltools case shows five years of mainly internal conflicts in which a succession of managing directors failed to secure consent for their restructuring proposals from the workforce, whose interests were articulated by Solidarity. The external privatization agency was continuously involved but was successfully resisted by the coalition of the Managing Director and the workforce when it included the enterprise in the list for early privatization. In Flextools the restructuring of sales has been more important than the restructuring of the enterprise.

Konecki and Kulpinska (1995: 249) go on to note that such internal changes 'seem to be as important for the organizational changes in the company as external reforms administered by the state'. It is, however, clear that awareness of impending future changes in economic reform was a significant feature of top-management perceptions in several enterprises and was a key element in their strategic choices. On the other hand, in the case of Bulgarian Flextools, where privatization was repeatedly postponed, the attitudes of top management shifted over time: initially privatization was seen as a threat which might lead to closure of the enterprise by a foreign competitor, but subsequently it was viewed as the only way of getting access to capital for technological improvement. Here the relationship to the external institutional environment was influenced more directly by the changing fortunes of the political parties, which were reflected in the changes of managing directors. The role of the trade unions as agencies in these changes was significant, although their actions cannot be seen as autonomous but rather as the result of interaction with outside organizations. As the privatization of Flextools approached in 1995 it was notable that potential owner groups from outside sought trade-union, as well as managerial, support for their strategies. The Polish cases also illustrate the shifting perceptions of the opportunities and threats related to different potential partners and different forms of ownership change.

Replacement of directors, either by internal initiative as in Poland, or by outside forces as in Bulgaria, is a recurring theme. The Employees' Council's decision to replace the Director and his deputy in 1988, was the turning point for the eventual transformation of the Medex enterprise. Conversely, the rejection of a succession of directors at Poltools constrained its transformation until the selection of a director who enjoyed the support of a broad coalition within the enterprise.

As explained in the introduction to this chapter, the previous structures, institutions, and mechanisms of labour relations were mainly imposed centrally on the enterprise by the state. The only significant exception was the changes in the structures of representation (the employees' councils and the restructured OPZZ) in Poland, which were a response to mobilization generated by Solidarity as a movement. This leads to the issue of the extent to which the new opportunities for enterprise management to make strategic choices for their enterprises have led to managerially initiated strategies in the field of labour relations. Labour relations include the institutions of employee representation—that is, trade unions and councils—and those mechanisms related to the labour process involving the organization of work and systems of payment and reward.

In terms of managerial strategies towards employee representation there are clearly a range of possibilities. These include the acceptance of existing structures, transformation of them, replacement by new or alternative structures, or their erosion and elimination. Thus, at Siberturb, Springs, and Flextools managements accepted the trade unions inherited from the past, now reformed as representatives of employee interests and as parties in collective bargaining. At Siberturb the representation of employees as shareholders was also institutionalized. Matools and Lebags are examples of a strategy found in other Russian enterprises (for example, an enterprise in Tver, visited in 1995 and 1996, see Appendix B), of the elimination of the trade union and its replacement by an employees' council. There were also institutions for the representation of employees as shareholders but there was no evidence, at least in the initial period, that they were used significantly for interest articulation. Polish Medex is the only one of the cases where the managerial strategy was to marginalize or eliminate trade unions and the employee council.

In terms of other aspects of labour relations, including the labour process, managerial strategies to increase productivity have generally derived from changes in the management structure and have often, though not necessarily, been accompanied by reductions in the number of employees. In many cases most reductions in the workforce have occurred as a result of the divestment or separation of parts of the enterprise. Changes to, or modification of, payment systems have also occurred. The most ambitious attempt to transform both management and the labour process took place at Matools and was intended to replace the prevailing values and motivation of everyone in the enterprise. However, the research concluded that the outcome fell significantly short of the Managing Director's ambitious hopes and expectations and that, if such a transformation were to occur, it would require a much longer time period.

It is clear from these cases that the speed of ownership change and the form of privatization, where it has occurred, have typically been insider-dominated processes. As a result, structures of corporate governance have not moved quickly to Western European patterns. Insiders, both management and workers, have frequently seen potential external owners as a threat. It may be that the forms of ownership that have developed will forestall, at least in the immediate future, moves towards greater external ownership and hence independent owner/shareholder control over enterprise activities. Existing forms of insider-dominated ownership may serve to perpetuate behaviour from the past, as new incentives are provided to sustain employment levels where possible, to maintain social expenditure, and to preserve the enterprise for its insiders. The extent to which foreign ownership may result in radically different orientations and policies is considered in the next chapter.

8

Foreign Ownership and its Consequences

In the period after the political changes of 1989 there were widespread expectations in Central and Eastern Europe of a substantial inwards flow of foreign investment. This was hoped to raise technological standards and improve export potential and, by implication, lead to the introduction of new management techniques and improve the quality of management. Although there has been significant foreign investment in, for example, Hungary, in general the expectations have not been fulfilled so far (ECE 1994: 159; Ernst *et al.* 1996: 19, 52; Kogut 1996). The aim of this chapter is to examine the impact of foreign ownership on labour relations. The effects of foreign direct investment may, of course, derive from various causes, depending, in part, on the nature of the changes in ownership. Bangert and Poor (1993: 820–1) have outlined the evolutionary pattern of multinational involvement in the Hungarian economy and the corresponding input to HRM policies for different stages from 'buyer–seller' to joint venture and wholly owned subsidiary. They suggest that in joint ventures there will be a large input to HRM practices while in the last the input will be total. There are choices to be made by foreign companies in respect of a range of issues linked to HRM and labour relations. Thus, the balance between expatriate and local managements is a strategic choice for HRM. In terms of labour relations there is potentially a wide range of choices. At a general level there is the possibility, first, of accepting local institutions and mechanisms of labour relations, secondly, of seeking to adapt or replace them, and, thirdly, of attempting to transfer those operating in the foreign company's home plants. In practice some combination is probable. Research in Hungary has illustrated specific consequences for labour relations in joint ventures. Thus Bangert and Poor (1993: 837) note that 93 per cent of 165 joint ventures surveyed did not have union representation. An extensive review of both HRM and labour relations at the workplaces of joint ventures is provided by Neumann (1992). From their study of multinational firms operating in Hungary, Mako and Novoszath (1994: 161) concluded that these organizations had adopted a variety of very different strategies for developing their labour relations, so that the generality was one of heterogeneity.

This chapter is based on five cases (see Fig. 8.1). The first, Slovcar, from Slovakia, shows how foreign management was able to introduce managerial practices for restructuring the organization of work which it had not yet tried in its domestic plants whilst retaining the indigenous representational structures. This is followed by the cases of the Hungarian Promed and the Bulgarian Foundry. These are treated as a pair, linked by the fact that in both a period of joint ownership led to conflicts between the internal and the external partners, the termination of the joint venture, and reversion to indigenous ownership. Finally Hungair and Bosair are considered as a matched pair, distinguished principally by the fact that so far only the first of these has experienced foreign ownership and privatization whereas in the latter privatization (and foreign partnership) has been repeatedly deferred. This permits comparison in terms of changes in the development of labour relations in the two cases on the basis of the factual and the counterfactual.

Bulgaria	FOUNDRY	BOSAIR air transport
Hungary	PROMED Protective equipment	HUNGAIR air transport
Slovakia	SLOVCAR cars	

FIG. 8.1. Foreign-ownership case studies

Note: See Appendix A for the details of the research undertaken.

A FOREIGN TAKEOVER IN THE VEHICLES INDUSTRY

Slovcar is the offspring of a multi-product Slovak engineering enterprise and a foreign multinational which in 1991 acquired a controlling shareholding for the development of operations based in one of the five plants formerly run by the Slovak enterprise, which in 1990 had 4,500 employees. Five foreign multinationals were involved in negotiations about the acquisition. The choice of the German company was based on its financial position and the proposed production programme. The enterprise trade union was consulted continuously and supported the choice in the knowledge of the favourable conditions offered in the German factories. The arrangement created an entirely new company in which the 20 per cent shareholding owned by the Slovak government was based on the value of the site and infrastructure and was planned to fall to only 3 per cent when projected foreign investment had been completed. The Slovak enterprise had many features characteristic of socialist engineering enterprises. These included a very diverse production profile made up of small batches and even single items with a multi-layer management structure and a large technical and administrative superstructure. Since 1990, however, its plants had become independent and undergone a process of delayering and rationalization, especially in reducing the number of indirect employees and specialists. In Slovcar the process of restructuring has been carried out independently, led by the management and consultants of the multinational and based on criteria and approaches from the parent company. From the start, motivation of staff and workers was identified as a key issue for the management of human resources and there was substantial investment in training. Management structure, intended as a lean organization, was built upon the principle that operational management should be decentralized as far as possible, and this was intended to foster motivation.The complex organizational structure inherited from the Slovak enterprise has been transformed into a simpler one based on German practice. The initial managerial cadre were mainly transferred from Germany, but by 1995 Slovaks held the top posts and the policy was to replace the remaining Germans through internal promotions.

In this case, the development of labour-relations institutions and of interest articulation has to be considered in the context of the development of business strategy, the restructuring of management, and a sophisticated strategy for the management of human resources. The last of these was explicitly recognized as underpinning the business strategy. The current production profile is based on the assembly of semi-finished products and components imported from other plants. Batch production of special models is highly labour intensive and requires efficient teamwork. At the operational level, the management considers that the philosophy of *kaizen* and the teamwork mechanisms derived from it have been fundamental to the motivation of employees. This restructuring of the labour process has contributed to the factory's success in scoring high on the corporation's quality criteria.

Unlike the redesign of the management structure, which was strongly influenced by the models operated in the German plants, the *kaizen* approach was derived from that adopted by Nissan in the UK and was not transferred or imposed from Germany. Textbooks on *kaizen* were translated into Slovak. Structurally the implementation of *kaizen* involved the creation of teams of 10–15 workers with responsibility for results, with flexibility and neighbour control and the system of visual management. There are daily meetings with the supervisor/team leader and more general meetings twice a week. The *kaizen* approach of continuous improvement in the quality of employees is seen to require continuing development. The productivity performance indicator of cars per employee day is in the process of being replaced by that of the costs per unit of sales.

One outcome of these changes has been that the composition of the labour force has been substantially restructured. In 1991 the total labour force was only 211. The subsequent expansion of production has resulted in increases as follows: 1993—460; 1994—817; and 1995—1,758. A major innovation has been the selection process for operatives: interviews with the potential supervisor followed by a probationary period. Criteria include a preference for the

25–35 age range and evidence indicating positive/cooperative attitudes and an ability to work in teams and to accept responsibility. Most workers can speak German as well as Slovak. These procedures were mainly developed in Slovakia rather than transferred from Germany. Employees who had previously worked for the Slovak enterprise had to go through the same procedure. By 1993 only 25 per cent of the workforce had formerly worked for the Slovak enterprise. Labour turnover has been extremely low in contrast to the very high rates characteristic of the traditional Slovak enterprise. Training has been facilitated by the quality of the Slovak education system.

The development of labour-relations institutions, especially the role of the trade unions, and the processes of participation and collective bargaining, have followed a mainly incremental path. Initially management set up a works council on the German model. This, however, lacked any foundation in Czechoslovak law after the repeal of the 1987 State Enterprise Act in 1990, although there was no formal prohibition of such institutions. After a short period the management disbanded it and decided to recognize the trade union as an agency for the representation and articulation of employee interests.

When the company was founded in 1991, employee membership of the former trade union lapsed when they ceased to pay membership subscriptions, and for a time the functions of the trade union, including those set out in labour legislation, were carried out by the Personnel Manager. After production started in 1992, some employees decided that they wished to be represented by a trade union and joined the engineering union, which was officially registered in May. The company supported and facilitated this, but its approach was to allow the trade-union organization to develop organically from the base—mobilization for the creation of a preparatory committee occurred among the workers in the assembly shop, who wanted the trade union to be built autonomously from the base up without employer involvement. The preparatory committee made proposals on the basis of representation and structure to a general meeting which elected its representatives by secret ballot in the summer of 1992. The trade-union structure operates at three levels: at the work-group or team level, each with an elected shop steward; at the level of the department, with a council of shop stewards meeting weekly intended as a structure for the transmission of information between the different levels; and at enterprise level the president, paid by the company but chosen by the committee of seven elected by the whole of the membership (about 80 per cent of the workforce). Early in 1993 economic problems in the enterprise had adverse effects on the workers which generated pressures on the union officials, and the president was dismissed by the committee on the grounds that he was unable to fulfil the requirements of the post.

In the regular meetings between the union committee and management representatives the aim has been to achieve consensus and cooperation. The union representatives early on sought to achieve participation in management decisions on, for example, future investment and the development of the enterprise. The development of the union was, however, also influenced by the external union—for example, the branch collective agreement of the engineering industry was used as a model for the initial negotiations. The first collective agreement was negotiated in the summer of 1993 and the union succeeded in getting general increases in wages and additional holidays for younger workers. In subsequent years the annual negotiations for the collective agreement have led to tough bargaining on wages and overtime payments. By the standards achieved elsewhere in the district the union is regarded as very successful in its results and a model which trade unions in other enterprises would like to follow.

This case shows a process of successful and complete organizational transformation. Although the management structures were transferred from the parent company, the *kaizen* philosophy was transferred from another company and not from the parent company. The implementation of a sophisticated HRM strategy with recruitment directly related to selection criteria and including the transformation of the labour process was judged as fundamental to the success of the company. The transfer of ownership was not contested externally or internally and was endorsed by the trade union in the expectation that it would lead to improved earnings and prospects. The management initiative in transferring a works council as the main institution for collective labour relations was later abandoned as inappropriate. The trade union organization developed autonomously from the base with the acquiescence of management and was an active agency in negotiations. Thus, the model of labour relations combined advanced human resource techniques with a significant degree of collective representation.

CONFLICTING AIMS IN JOINT VENTURES

The next two cases to be discussed involve enterprises seeking foreign partners as a means to ensure survival. Both enterprises initiated the search for joint ventures at an early stage of the wider economic transformation. In practice, the negotiation and arrangement of joint ventures proved far more precarious than was expected by the enterprises.

Promed

This plant was one of six integrated into an enterprise in the 1960s by its General Director. In the 1970s and early 1980s it functioned as a very successful flagship enterprise which enjoyed a high prestige of which its 5,000 employees were fully aware. A large proportion (80 per cent) of its production was exported and there were significant hard-currency earnings. After 1985, in common with some other Hungarian enterprises, it began to run into financial difficulties as a result of the weakening of foreign markets, although it was able in the short term to secure credits from the state banks. The issue of the corporate strategy and enterprise structure appropriate for the longer term became the focus of a power struggle between the General Director and the enterprise Party Secretary which lasted for two years. Both sought to use external networks to mobilize resources at high levels in the Party. The Party Secretary was also able to secure the internal support of the plant Directors and he became General Director. His argument was that the restructuring of the enterprise was essential for its survival and this should be based on decentralization (including the dismantling of much of the very large headquarters which was the basis of the previous General Director's control), and more autonomy for the plant Directors. The new General Director's pioneering financial solution was that the debts owed to the banks should be converted into shares which could then be traded. In January 1988 the enterprise became the first Hungarian shareholding company with shares held by the banks and the enterprise, although at this time there was not yet legal provision for this form of 'spontaneous privatization'. The change in status from that of state ownership gave the enterprise more autonomy in relation to ministries and the right to take independent action with respect to other enterprises and organizations. Within the enterprise at the headquarters the majority of the several hundred staff were dismissed and it now functioned as a holding company. The six plants and departments such as Foreign Trade and Research and Development became separate companies, although the majority of shares were owned by the holding company.

The Promed plant which is the subject of this case was constituted as a company in January 1988 with about 300 employees. Its main product was personal protective equipment, which was made principally to state orders from the Army and from the Ministry of the Interior, for the police and civil defence. These orders provided a secure market at prices which covered the costs of the reserves of labour, equipment, and supplies which were typical of enterprises operating in the socialist economy. However, from 1988 these orders and those from the agricultural and chemical industries dropped sharply—by 60 per cent in 1988 and by 30 per cent in 1989 compared with 1987. At the same time there was new competition from foreign producers. For the management of Promed the collapse of the markets posed the issue of a strategy for survival.

The initial survival strategy was to develop new products for civilian rather than defence markets and to look for new markets. It was soon apparent that the company lacked the working capital and the expertise to do this. Management therefore came to the conclusion that the most promising solution would be to establish collaboration with a foreign partner. A connection was made with a foreign-owned multinational operating with some product markets similar to those of Promed. This company was family owned and controlled by a man who had emigrated from Hungary in 1949. He saw the situation in Eastern Europe as providing an opportunity for expansion into new markets producing with cheaper labour costs and with little requirement for capital investment. Promed was soon identified as an appropriate partner and negotiations to establish a joint venture began. For the management of Promed the project appeared to offer access to know-how, capital, and other markets. The process, completed in March 1990, took ten months and the agreement had to take account of two conditions imposed by the foreign partner: that there should be only a single Hungarian shareholder and that the Managing Director should be replaced by a manager from another plant of the enterprise. The Hungarian and foreign partner each owned 50 per cent of the shares and had two members of the board. Shortly after the establishment of the joint venture the Gulf War broke out which created a boom in sales and the plant worked at full capacity for some months.

The initial response of the workforce (including middle management as well as manual workers) to the change in ownership was a negative one. They had lost 'their' company and the Director they respected to a foreign owner who was only interested in profit, and with the change went the social and other benefits (canteen, kindergarten, and holidays) that had been part of the employment package. They hoped, however, for increased wages. Their negative perception of the foreign owner was modified when they learnt that he had played a part, although a small one, in getting the Gulf War contract which had made the survival of the enterprise possible.

According to an interview with the Managing Director at the end of 1992, the biggest single internal problem had been to change the mentality of the management. There had been a shift in the criteria for assessing the operation of the factory associated with the changes in ownership. The change from state ownership in 1988 had increased the concern with the criterion of profitability but not that of productivity. Under the joint venture, Western accounting systems were used to highlight profit and return on capital employed. In addition, there was now continual emphasis from the foreign owner on productivity.

Promed was managerially a microcosm of the socialist production and management processes. Although the workforce was not large, there was an elaborate and hierarchical departmental structure with seven different levels. This was later reduced to four as part of a management reorganization. The organization of production had remained unchanged and only part of the extensive range of equipment was used and it was no longer technologically up to date. However, management has been able to secure investment for new technologies and new products and by 1994 had achieved European quality standards. The major shift has been from a production-led organization to a market-led one. In the former model there was a significant group of qualified technologists, who lost influence relative to that of the new group of staff responsible for marketing introduced by the Managing Director.

The foreign owner exercised pressure for improvements in productivity. It is estimated that labour productivity on the shop floor increased by 10–15 per cent, so that there was some intensification of the labour process as a result of workers' desire to preserve their jobs in conditions where unemployment was increasing, and the less effective workers were dismissed. By 1996 the labour force had fallen to 120 as a result of dismissals and wastage.

Formerly the plant trade union had been a unit of the enterprise trade union. The great majority of employees were members, for which they secured social benefits and some representation in wage negotiations, promotion, and awards. After the political changes the membership and influence of the union declined for three main reasons: first, the removal of the 'obligation' to belong—many employees left as a gesture of personal freedom; secondly, the new Labour Code significantly limited trade-union rights by removing the power of veto; and, thirdly, it no longer had social benefits to distribute. Membership fell to 25 per cent as voluntary and involuntary redundancies reduced the labour force. New employees in marketing did not join. The foreign owner was opposed to the trade union being a significant agency within the plant. The role of the trade-union secretary has become almost entirely formal—in 1995 she visited the Managing Director on only two occasions. In this situation the Managing Director has come to play a significant transitional role. In the previous system it was possible in some enterprises for the Director to be seen as representing the interests of the workforce against the higher authorities, usually the ministries. The new Managing Director sought to represent, where possible, the interests of the workers against the pressures from the foreign owners and thus to maintain a paternalist approach in changed conditions.

The Works Council, elected in 1993, officially represents the interests of all employees. However, the management team created and selected by the Managing Director, and including, on a personal basis, the President of the Works Council but not the Trade Union President, is the main institution. It meets regularly as a forum for participation to consider important issues and prepare proposals. Thus, on wages the management team prepares proposals and the Managing Director decides on the general increase for the company. The internal distribution between departments and grades is decided by the managers. The Presidents of the Works Council and of the Trade Union are informed of the decisions but they are not able to question them. Except in times of crisis, the wage levels for a given job have compared favourably with those in the locality.

The Managing Director's strategic aim was to preserve the company as a successful manufacturing operation, but during 1994 he began to recognize that this was different from the aim of the foreign owner, whose primary interest in Promed was as an outlet for supplies from his Western company, which were sold to Promed at high prices. The Managing Director recognized that this behaviour of the foreign owner was a threat to the future of the enterprise; he judged that there was the possibility that the foreign owner would seek to close the enterprise as a production unit. During 1994 a struggle for the control and ownership of the company emerged involving three parties: the foreign owner, the Hungarian owner, and the Managing Director and his senior managers. With declining profits the foreign owner wished to buy all the shares and realize the assets. The Hungarian owner was also prepared to sell, but not necessarily to the foreign owner. The Managing Director and his team aimed to secure the company, and the conclusion of an important contract in 1995 made possible the Hungarian purchase of the shares.

The workforce welcomed the outcome but had no involvement in it. The initial privatization and restructuring did not involve the trade union or the workforce and the establishment of the joint venture was also a closed process. In the re-establishment of Hungarian ownership only the management team was involved. There was a significant simplification of the management structure. There was pressure from the foreign owner to increase profitability and labour productivity, which led to reductions in the labour force. The foreign owner was also hostile to the trade union, but the union withered autonomously rather than through direct managerial pressure. For labour relations the significance of this case is that it shows the silent decay of the institutions of collective labour relations and their replacement by a paternalist and individualist model.

Foundry

Foundry was one plant of a state enterprise. The process by which it became involved in a joint venture with an Austrian organization began at the end of 1990, which was unusually early for this kind of connection in the manufacturing sector in Bulgaria. The initial contact was facilitated by a group from the Bulgarian political élite who had Austrian connections in their network. For the management of Foundry, faced with the collapse of sales in Bulgaria in the worsening economic crisis and the loss of Eastern markets with the end of Comecon, the possibility of securing investment (to raise the technical standards) and access to Western markets offered the possibility of survival for the plant. For the Austrians there was the possibility of access to Eastern markets when the recession lifted.

The initial contract of December 1990 between the Austrian company and the Bulgarian enterprise was for the lease of part of the plant's capacity. A few month's later, in May 1991, the remaining capacity was leased by the joint venture comprised of 40 per cent ownership by the Bulgarian enterprise and 60 per cent by two Austrian firms. The aim was to create a self-financing enterprise, with the aid of credits from both Austrian and Bulgarian banks, to re-establish its traditional markets in Bulgaria and in the former Comecon countries, and to export to new markets in the West. The joint venture was therefore seen as having a strategic potential in relation to markets and to the other producers in the industry in Bulgaria. Thus, one of the longer-term strategic possibilities was seen as extending ownership to include the purchase of shares in the main Bulgarian manufacturer of diesel engines which Foundry had previously supplied with components. Operational management was to be shared between foreigners (Austrians and Serbs) and Bulgarians.

The first change in labour relations was to cancel the contracts of all 600 employees and to re-engage 350 of them on annual contracts which provided relatively high wages for the locality. However, the Austrians did not wish to recognize the trade union, and during 1991 this became an issue which involved the district and national trade-union organizations before recognition was eventually conceded in September. This was followed by a dispute over the recognition of the Trade Union President, who was not an employee of the joint venture but had retained his office in the Bulgarian-owned part of the site. This recognition issue was resolved by a strike in October, but it was linked to the issue of managerial styles: the Bulgarian workers respected the competences and technical expertise of those managers who were Austrian but objected to the styles of both Serb and Bulgarian managers and they were able to secure the dismissal of most of them. This coincided with a change in the Austrian management team and the newcomers suspected that the Bulgarians were involved in financial irregularities.

As a means of improving relations with the workers, the Austrians appointed a worker representative to the general assembly of the joint venture and initiated internal restructuring of the organization into profit centres. The concept of worker representative was alien to Bulgarian traditions and it did not function effectively; nor did the profit centres. With the increase in sales in 1992 the number of employees was raised to 600 but in 1992 industrial-relations issues became interlinked with conflicts between the Austrian and the Bulgarian owners. The Bulgarian enterprise was liquidated by the state in March 1992 and a new Bulgarian manager was selected to represent Bulgarian interests on the Foundry site and in the joint venture, while two Bulgarian managers (of whom one was the architect of the joint venture) unexpectedly left the joint venture. Their departure was preceded by trade-union demands and pressure. The new manager judged that the terms of the lease were unsatisfactory for Foundry and found that the rent had not been received. His assessment was that there were significant market opportunities to be developed which could be exploited with partners other than the Austrians and that these could lead to higher wages for the workers. The strategy of the joint venture was to move towards a dominant market share for foundry products in Bulgaria. The goal of the new manager was to reverse this and establish market dominance for the Bulgarian company at least by securing a majority shareholding in the joint venture. Simultaneously there was pressure for wage increases from the shop floor, a campaign using the national media against the joint venture, and moves by the Bulgarian banks to block the accounts of the joint venture because of its debts. An important outcome of the conflict was that the Bulgarian company achieved its strategy of securing access to the Austrian market.

During the summer of 1992 there was continuing pressure from the workforce on a range of issues around the collective agreement which led to a strike in July (although wages were among the highest in the region), eventually resolved with the signing of the collective agreement in September 1992. There were constant tensions at this plant and pressure, partly mobilized by the Trade Union President, who fed information to some workers, who would then spread it around the factory. During the conflict the joint-venture management refused to negotiate with the trade union and took the issue of the legality of the strike to a labour court. Locally this action was seen as directed against the Trade Union President, whom the management regarded as the key actor in the strike. The court ruled, unexpectedly, that the strike was legal, which was a serious blow to the Austrians and the joint-venture management. It opened a new possibility to step up pressure by different Bulgarian groups.

In November the Austrians announced that they had no money to pay wages because they had not received money from their trading partners in Austria. A few days later angry workers surrounded a car in which the Austrian managers were travelling and bumped and shook it. Two days later the Austrians returned to Vienna. The company ceased to operate at the beginning of 1993, although attempts were made to arrange a settlement with the Austrians involving meetings with the Bulgarian banks and the Ministry of Industry coordinated by CITUB. The proposals were for a rescue operation, an increase in capital investment, and the formation of a new company partly financed by Bulgarian banks. The Ministry of Industry required a joint proposal for the continuation of Foundry signed by Foundry, the Bulgarian company, the trade union, and the banks as the condition for a ministry decision on supporting the project. However, the agreement of the banks was not forthcoming. With the end of the joint venture the plant reverted to the ownership of the Bulgarian company, which operated on a very restricted basis until it was declared bankrupt by the district court in December 1995 and it was entered on the (secret) list of enterprises to be liquidated in order to meet the criteria set by the international agencies for a loan. In 1996 the Supreme Court overruled the decision of the district court and the enterprise was removed from the liquidation list.

This case shows the complex interactions between different agencies and between the local and the national levels, deriving from different interests. The main Bulgarian agency was an élite group with good internal and political networks combined with external commercial links. The Austrian partners had money and saw the joint venture as providing a strategic base for expansion into Bulgarian and other East European markets. The goal of the trade union at national level was to preserve as far as possible employment in the enterprise. Initially this involved seeking to conciliate in the disputes between the Austrian management and the workforce, and subsequently supporting the campaign to secure national support for the enterprise. The role of the trade union at the district level and of its local leader was of a different kind. The latter was the prime mover in the campaign, at district and national levels, against the Austrians, which became defined in terms of promoting local Bulgarian interests against those of foreigners. The principal researcher for this case judged that the labour-relations conflicts which became central to the case were as much the result of mobilization by the local trade-union leadership as of spontaneous workforce dissatisfaction. The Austrians were unhappy with the internal labour-relations institutions, but the attempt to transfer an Austrian model of a works council was not successful. Although there was some restructuring of management, there was no transformation of the labour process before the termination of the joint venture. Ethnic conflicts and the interaction of local and national political interests have continued to shape the situation of the enterprise.

Promed and Foundry Compared

An essential similarity between these cases was that prototype joint ventures were initiated by the organizations as the central features of their survival strategies. Further, in both cases, these joint ventures were terminated as the result of emerging conflicts of interest between the indigenous and foreign partners. A major difference between the two enterprises was the salience of labour-relations issues. At Promed, the trade union was not an active agency and the institutions of collective labour relations withered. At Foundry, the trade union was an agency, articulating the interests of the workforce, and the transferred mechanism of the works council did not take root.

CONTRASTING OUTCOMES IN AIR TRANSPORT

National airlines in Eastern Europe have been élite organizations and as bearers of national prestige their expansion and development were strongly supported by the state. Their employees, especially the flying staff, were privileged through their access to valued foreign goods and currency as well as travel, and in consequence the opportunity for employment in them could be facilitated through personal or even political connections. The staff were also well aware of the salary structures and other terms and conditions operated in Western airlines. The aircraft were almost entirely those made in the Soviet Union. In earlier years these had been relatively advanced technologically, but by the later 1980s they were not equivalent to the aircraft of their Western competitors in terms of fuel efficiency and other technical aspects. The prospects following the political changes of 1989 were influenced by different factors. To operate competitively in international markets meant that the marketing and route strategy would need to be reviewed and that more efficient Western aircraft would have to be acquired. This was likely to involve acquisition of significant shares in the company by foreign airlines. However, the issue of the extent of foreign control over a prestige asset was an important political issue and inevitably national political considerations would be involved in the discussions about restructuring and the form of privatization and joint venture. By the standards of Western competitors the manning levels were high and staff reductions would in time become a major issue. In the shorter term, however, wage costs would remain lower because of the lower wage rates.

The similarities in business and organizational structures make these cases of Hungair and Bosair a matched pair which can provide significant comparisons about the processes of restructuring and ownership change and the dynamics of change in labour relations. It was originally anticipated that Bosair would be an early candidate for privatization and a series of schemes have been developed over the years accompanied by discussions with various potential foreign partners. The political decisions have, however, repeatedly postponed major changes in ownership. By contrast, in Hungair there has been major restructuring accompanied by foreign partnerships. It is, therefore, logical to consider Hungair first, so that the 'counterfactual' aspects of the comparison are sharpened to show what has happened in Hungair and what has not happened in Bosair but might have occurred if the extent of ownership change had been more substantial.

Hungair

The first event changing the structure of labour relations was the fragmentation of union organization. This occurred as one outcome of the 1988 Act on Associations, which allowed the formation of political and other organizations, including independent trade unions. At one stage there were thirteen different trade-union organizations within the company representing different sectional, occupational, and other interests. In part this process was a consequence of external actions—the new trade unions which later became associated with the *Liga* targeted leading companies and set out to recruit membership within them. This process of fragmentation took place before any significant change had occurred in the management of the enterprise.

The initial change in management came with the appointment by the ministry of a new Managing Director in 1990. The long-term aims were to preserve it as a national company and to develop its range of activities and improve its value. The immediate aims were to separate the company from the socialist planned economy and its ministry controls and to increase its market value for privatization so that in time partnership with a foreign company for investment could be achieved. At this time there was seen to be a major issue of business strategy: whether to stay within the European market and to remain as a relatively small organization or to combine long- and short-haul business and increase its size. The latter was the goal of the new Managing Director. Internally it was recognized that significant organizational restructuring and the development of modern accounting and information systems, which would provide an accurate base for decision-making and the collection of revenue, were required. Restructuring would involve retraining and, over time, substantial staff reductions and increases in productivity. The coming of the new Managing Director was in itself divisive, because it split employees into those who favoured change and those who were opposed to it.

During 1991 there were parallel developments in the privatization and restructuring strategies accompanied by significant conflicts in labour relations, of which some came to centre on the role of the Managing Director. In June 1991 a steering committee made up of representatives of the State Property Agency, the Ministry and the enterprise was set up to manage the privatization process. The first step was to prepare the project for the transformation of the enterprise into a single-person share company with all shares held by the state property company, which was an essential precondition for privatization. The first draft of this was finished at the end of 1991. At the same time drafts of articles of association, and tenders and draft contracts for potential foreign partners were prepared; preliminary bids were received at the beginning of 1992. In July the single-person share company was formally created on terms which provided for a Hungarian majority holding and management. At the end of 1992 a foreign airline bought a 30 per cent share in the company.

During 1991, in addition to the restructuring of ownership, there were other significant changes in the structure of the enterprise: the separation of the technical and maintenance department through the creation of a foreign joint venture with labour-relations consequences explained below; the separation of airports from the company; and plans for the internal development of cost/profit centres. In terms of labour relations, 1991 was a year of conflict between the Managing Director and the trade unions and groups within the company (old managers against new managers), primarily related to the threat of staff reductions. (The Managing Director had plans for a reduction of about 15 per cent.) At this period there were seven trade unions in the company (the other unions had either disintegrated or been unable to show they were representative). Three of them (including the successor to the former sole union) formed an association affiliated to MSzOSz, the national successor confederation which had the largest membership. There were two unions, the Technicians' Union and the Union of Economic Experts, affiliated to the *Liga*, while the trade unions for cabin staff and for pilots had no national affiliation. There were many tensions and uncertainties between the different unions and elements of competition which hindered cooperation. Nationally the different confederations had established a round table as a forum for coordination and developing common policies. The trade unions in the company had followed this model, but rivalry and uncertainty initially prevented its effective operation. In January, management took the initiative to set up an 'interest conciliation forum' at which issues would be discussed between representatives of both sides, but, because of the divisions on the trade union side, it did not become operational until August.

This was a period of great uncertainty for workers in which rumours and gossip about management's intentions shaped their perceptions. The salient management–union issue at this period was that of jobs and the Managing Director's intentions for reducing them, together with the proposal to separate the maintenance organization into a joint venture. In August 1991 the seven trade unions issued a statement attacking management behaviour which united them. There was a campaign against the personal behaviour and character of the Managing Director using the legacy of inherited connections and informal channels with the ministry and other organizations and the company newspaper. (Union representatives had gained access to a confidential letter from the Managing Director to the Ministry of Labour asking for guidance on procedures for mass dismissals.) The Managing Director responded by saying that the newspaper must be hung up in every workplace as a means of appealing to the mass of employees on the assumption that the campaign was the work of a group of union activists and lacked mass support. Subsequently the Managing Director resigned, acknowledging that in part he was responsible for the conflicts which had occurred.

The separation of the maintenance organization and the creation of a joint venture with a foreign partner were seen as a means of getting foreign capital and technology and developing the business of maintaining the aircraft of other airlines. Thus, the maintenance organization, as a limited company, had more autonomy over its business. The new management's aim was to reduce total employment and to improve productivity by changing the organization of work. The main union representing the technical staff campaigned against this privatization, using the press to argue against foreign ownership. In June 1992 there was a mass meeting (spontaneous rather than union organized) at which the workers threatened to leave the company because their incomes were threatened by the ending of shift work which would prevent them moonlighting to the second jobs which about half the workers had. Their demand was, therefore, to remain with the parent company. In subsequent negotiations management conceded a substantial annual wage increase—the result of united-worker rather than trade-union action.

The issue of redundancy emerged when the management first appreciated the scale of the costs of compensation which had been provided for in the collective agreement. When it sought to negotiate a reduction in the collective agreement to the level provided in the Labour Code, the trade unions resisted.

In August 1993 there was a longer stoppage over wages which was broken by management bringing in foreign workers. In July 1993 there was a warning strike by pilots on a wage claim backed by others. There was demand for a new collective agreement—the 1989 one was still in force and in the dispute management recorded the names of strikers.

The Hungair case provides illustrations of the development and decay of labour-relations institutions and mechanisms and of the process by which they operated. As shown above, the relations between the trade unions in the main company were initially characterized by competition and uncertainty and this influenced the way in which they operated. For the successor unions there was at first an issue of legitimacy. Thus, it was the issue of job loss linked to the Managing Director's strategy which brought both the Trade Union Round Table and the Interest Conciliation Forum into operation. In the mobilization and handling of labour relations issues, the evidence suggests some conclusions. An analysis of the handling of issues showed that there was a tendency for them to be taken through different stages of the procedure to the top and this was explained as the reluctance of lower managers to take responsibility for decisions in conditions of uncertainty. Several contested issues were taken outside the company to be decided by the Labour Court.

The Labour Code of 1992 provided for works councils with consultative/advisory powers to be elected by the workforce, and these elections eventually took place in May 1993. In the intervening period since the enactment of the Labour Code in July 1992 participation rights in Hungair had been exercised by the Trade Union Round Table. This raised the issue for the trade unions of how they should respond to the elections. Initially the trade unions did not promote the elections as an issue, because they were uncertain about the number of their members and the degree of membership support. They were also concerned about the possibility of their functions being narrowed. In fact in the elections there were no non-union candidates, so that the central Works Council and the five divisional councils became in effect institutions for the trade unions to use.

In this period of restructuring the industrial relations situation was influenced by a number of factors on the trade-union side. Thus, the mixture of old and new trade unions facilitated conflicts. There was an issue of trade-union representativeness and uncertainty about the status of agreements. The successor unions had a legacy of structures and experience which resulted in better organization and the loss of fewer members, and they had a better appreciation of the balance of power than the new ones. There was, at this period, for all unions a need to prove their legitimacy as organizations in a different political and economic environment.

The strategic choice of a foreign partner in this case was shaped by the managerial and ministerial élites. The organizational and managerial restructuring which preceded the agreement with the foreign partner produced major industrial conflicts. The labour process in the maintenance division was restructured following the foreign acquisition, but the labour process in Hungair itself remains substantially unchanged.

Bosair

Bosair was the largest airline in Eastern Europe outside the Soviet Union. As an organization it comprised all the functions associated with air transport, and management was strongly centralized. The initial changes in labour relations at Bosair were remarkably similar to those at Hungair. In the period of political and economic crisis at the end of 1989 Bosair was one of the enterprises where there was instantaneous and autonomous fragmentation of the trade-union organization. This fragmentation was mainly on sectional and occupational lines (pilots, cabin, and ground staff) and not simply of the division between *Podkrepa* and the established union, which was the most usual structure of fragmentation.

The issue of organizational restructuring became salient during 1990, and in 1991 the existing conglomerate was dissolved and replaced by ten companies independent of the ministry, of which Bosair was one. However, this left Bosair as the major constituent, including the airports and ground staff, and with increased autonomy as a limited company with the state as the only shareholder. Although this reorganization was officially under the control of the ministry, there were internal groups, especially the pilots, who articulated their interests in relation to the form of restructuring and had asserted their interests in 1990 with a strike. The unions demanded the dismissal of the Director and an audit of the organization's accounts. A key figure was an ex-pilot, the deputy controller, who subsequently became Director. He was seen as a position-holder with extensive networks of relations within the organization. These were mobilized around the restructuring issue against the plans put forward by the ministry. Inter-personal and group networks were thus a significant factor in the power structure of the organization and in relation to the formal institutional power exercised by the ministry. Thus, the process of initial restructuring was influenced by group interests. The restructuring was followed by the leasing of modern foreign aircraft.

At this time the company faced major strategic issues of choice of market segment and the replacement of the ageing Soviet aircraft. Technological modernization would ideally have been facilitated by an injection of foreign capital. However, as a flagship enterprise, potentially profitable, and of national importance, the issue of privatization was politically important and sensitive, especially in relation to the proportion of shares for the different stakeholders—state and foreign. During 1992 the issue of the form and content of privatization was the salient issue for the organization. At the end of 1992 foreign consultants had prepared a privatization project as a basis for attracting declarations of interest from foreign partners. The initial expectation was that privatization could be completed in 1993. At this time the privatization of the enterprise with the participation of a foreign partner was seen by top management as the crucial event on which the future of the organization and its development in an increasingly competitive world market would turn. It was considered that privatization would ensure survival by optimizing routes, by the use of joint routes, by expansion of activities, and the renewal of airport and other services. Transfer of Western know-how, the weakest feature of Bosair, would strengthen the case for foreign investment. The purchase of up to 20 per cent of the shares at preferential rates by employees was provided for in the privatization proposal, but it became apparent that only the pilots would have sufficient earnings to acquire many shares and the expectation was that employee share participation would probably be only 5–6 per cent. Trade-union representatives met a representative of the consultants to discuss share participation when the proposal was announced, but it was not a contested issue.

In fact there was no significant development with this project by 1997 and the expectation was that privatization might be delayed for up to five years. The exclusion of this event was mainly due to the activities and interests of political and other groups at higher levels above the enterprise. This prevented major restructuring despite the leasing of some more modern aircraft and some airport modernization. The responses inside the organization to the expected privatization within the enterprise were mixed and did not correlate with membership of specific professional or status groups. Typical perceptions were: privatization is good and although a lot of people will lose their jobs those remaining will work under normal conditions and be well paid; privatization is the next under-the-table deal for laundering money; the new owner will take over the flights and take over the airline. Inside the enterprise the impression was one of the articulation of sectional and occupational interests. The basic division was between flying and other staff and the pilots were the leading group—they were professionals seeking power in the organization and gaining it to some extent.

The process of collective bargaining began in 1992 and a major issue was the structure of representation, which was complex and reflected the basic division between flying and ground staff. At one stage there were seven organizations, but this was later reduced to five, with an average density of about 60 per cent. CITUB and *Podkrepa* both had organizations with separate occupational sections—for example, for stewardesses and administrative staff. Unaffiliated were the Union of Pilots and the Union for Engineering and Technical Personnel. The legal requirement for recognition for collective bargaining was that unions must be affiliated to a national confederation. Despite this, *de facto* recognition was accorded to the pilots and the engineers for the collective agreements. A revised wage structure was a major outcome of collective bargaining in 1993. However, the organization of *Podkrepa*, which mainly represented the ground staff, disintegrated. Changing aircraft meant that retraining became an issue, as did the custom of making payments in foreign currency to flying staff. Temporary contracts were issued to some stewardesses, but the major reduction in staff had not taken place by the end of 1996.

During 1994 the financial position of the company deteriorated as a result of foreign competition and cost inflation which made the charges for the leasing of the modern aircraft unprofitable. Some long-distance routes were suspended and the General Director was fined by the ministry for the unsatisfactory performance of the company; he left when his contract expired. In 1994 attempts to arrange an acceptable privatization involving a foreign partnership and capital on terms which were politically acceptable were unsuccessful. An alternative scheme for mainly Bulgarian ownership was also abandoned and in February 1995 the privatization agency announced that the company was not for sale. The trade unions were excluded from information about discussions with the foreign companies on grounds of confidentiality; their crisis package involving organizational restructuring, state subsidies, and a reduction of perhaps 15–20 per cent of the staff was reported to be under consideration by the privatization agency, the management, and the government. In a published article the new Director stressed the need for a 'sound corporate spirit' to integrate the efforts of the different professions and groups.

Comparison of Hungair and Bosair

Although there are inevitably differences in detail, there is a remarkable parallel in the course of events in this matched pair of cases up to 1992. The initial fragmentation of the trade unions into professional and sectional interest groupings followed closely from political changes and suggests that the previous structures of political and organizational control had restrained latent pressures for the articulation of interests and their institutional representation.

In both cases, organizational restructuring was the salient issue in 1991 and was accomplished. Restructuring had both internal and external aspects; its imminence created both threats and opportunities for mobilization. In both cases, the process was accompanied by changes of managing director, mainly as a result of internal opposition within the enterprise. In both organizations there were informal groupings with established network connections which were operationalized in the mobilization process, though at Bosair the alternative candidate was internal. At Hungair the process of organizational restructuring in 1991 was followed by the logical step of the establishment of foreign partnerships in 1992. This led to conflicts which were unanticipated by management. Labour relations had not been a key part of the management's restructuring agenda. The process was one in which there was a great deal of uncertainty, but one outcome was the consolidation and development of the institutions of labour relations—that is, of the trade unions and of management specialists for the organization for labour relations and of the procedures for management–union relations. At Bosair a management specialist was appointed for labour relations and institutions were developed. The salience of labour relations was such that the main negotiations with the trade unions were conducted with the Managing Director. However, the central labour-relations issue of employment reduction was not pursued during this period.

One of the most important differences between Hungair and Bosair lies in the effects of the decision-making process in the political arena. In Hungary the political process made it possible to follow through the general strategy of restructuring and ownership change, whereas in Bulgaria it did not. In Hungary, although the organization was not independent, there was sufficient autonomy to pursue organizational restructuring from within. In Bulgaria decisions about Bosair were dependent on the constellation of political forces outside the enterprise at specific moments. This is shown by the succession of changes in the position of Managing Director, which were the result of external decisions without the involvement of internal forces.

A major hypothesis is that privatization through foreign acquisition would lead to further important restructuring and the reduction of employees. On this basis the foreign acquisition of Hungair would have been followed by a substantial restructuring of a kind which has not yet been attempted at Bosair. The Hungair case does not confirm this hypothesis, since by the end of 1995 such restructuring had not occurred. The question is how is this to be explained. There are two major reasons. The first is the nature of the partnership and the basis on which the foreign partner operates. One possibility is that it may be an acquisition to combine forces in a competitive environment but not requiring a high level of organizational integration. Another possibility is that of takeover and complete domination by the foreign partner. In the case of Hungair, the acquisition was of the former type and the partner was still owned by the state. However, there is still the strategic issue of the choice of partner. In the Hungair case it is plausible to conclude that the management agencies had sufficient influence and leverage in the political arena to prevent a predatory takeover and secure a partner of a different type. Of course there may be internal political pressures for restructuring deriving from the situation of the company and its profitability or otherwise. However, the legacy of the serious industrial conflicts of 1991–2 which were prominent in the public arena can be seen as a constraint on government pressure for further restructuring, running the risk of confrontation in a key enterprise.

SUMMARY OF FINDINGS

The cases presented here show that foreign ownership can have very different consequences for organizations and for labour relations. Although the cases discussed here are a small sample, and in no sense representative of all foreign direct investment in Eastern Europe, the cases caution against the assumptions that foreign ownership is necessarily a uni-directional process. The Promed and Foundry cases, although they are clearly atypical, demonstrate that foreign direct investment is reversible. However, the nature of the foreign owner's organization and of its relationship to local organization is of great importance. Thus, Slovcar has been in the process of becoming a wholly owned subsidiary and an integral part of the parent plant's business strategy, but with local operational management and labour relations. In Promed the foreign interest was in market access and financial returns rather than direct operational management. At Foundry the foreign interest was for strategic market access combined with expatriate operational management. (The problems encountered with the Austrian management of a joint venture in the Hungarian steel industry are indicated in Furedi (1994).) At Hungair the fact that the partner was a state-owned company and that it did not aim at operational management was important.

The various countries in Eastern Europe and Russia have taken different views about the desirability of foreign direct investment and this is reflected in variations in the proportions of acquisitions, joint ventures, and greenfield sites (see Kogut 1996: 298–321). As in any other part of the global economy, the strategies of multinational companies and overseas investors can vary from case to case. In relation to employment and labour-relations strategies, Ferner (1997: 32) has suggested that the nature of the sector may be one important factor affecting the strategies of multinational companies. In industries with global markets, such as cars, individual plants are more likely to be integrated into a company-wide corporate strategy. Where overseas investment is directed at capturing new domestic markets, the individual plant may be managed in relative isolation from the parent company. Where foreign owners, such as in the Slovcar case, seek to introduce methods of HRM brought in from elsewhere, as Kogut (1996: 297) points out, this can provide 'a template of the feasibility of alternative modes of organization adapted to the domestic environment. It has a quasi-public good characteristic insofar as other firms may observe the successful outcome of organizational experiments from proven companies.' However, diffusion of 'good practice' in this manner, given the relatively small scale of foreign direct investment so far, may take a considerable time and the expectation of a substantial imitation or spillover effect, in the context of Eastern Europe and Russia, may underplay the continued politicization of issues around foreign ownership.

The significance of networks in the process of transforming the economies of Eastern Europe has been emphasized recently (Grabher and Stark 1997). Four of the cases presented here show their importance in the process of restructuring and ownership change. The outcome of the prototype ownership change at Promed was determined by the mobilization of existing and competing political networks. Foundry was an example of early ownership change in Bulgaria and the initial change similarly depended on specific national networks within the political élite. In the airline cases linkages between the enterprises and the ministries were especially important in the initial stages and in the case of Hungair was important in the choice of the foreign partner. Subsequently the Foundry case shows the introduction of new networks with multiple institutions and levels. In both airlines and in Foundry subsequent decisions became primarily dependent on processes in the political arena. Thus, at Bosair the postponement of ownership change largely separated the enterprise as an active agent.

In both airlines trade-union and occupational representation was significant in the initial process of organizational restructuring and the development of trade unions as representative organizations is apparent. Subsequently they reverted to wage-bargaining agencies. At Foundry the union was an active agency in shaping the exclusion of the foreign partners. Trade unions have been willing and able to try to mobilize forces outside their enterprise to secure their preferred ownership outcomes. The highly politicized nature of four of the cases of foreign involvement discussed here (Promed, Foundry, Hungair, and Bosair) suggests that even the most apparently straightforward forms of privatization, where capital and know-how is available through direct foreign investment, can be difficult to accomplish in the context of Eastern Europe.

The effectiveness of transferring labour-relations institutions from one country to another has long been a topic of academic debate. These cases provide two examples of the unsuccessful transfer of works councils. On the other hand, the successful transfer and implementation of the *kaizen* philosophy at Slovcar was achieved with the consent of the workforce and transformed the labour process more radically than in the other cases. This suggests that the effect of foreign investment on labour relations in Eastern Europe and Russia is likely to be as varied as in any other part of the global economy, contributing to the increasing heterogeneity of labour-relations dynamics in the transformation period and beyond.

9

The Limitations of Transference, Imitation, and Imposition

This final chapter concludes the exploration of the nature of change and development in Eastern European and Russian labour relations. It combines an assessment of the processes of transference, imitation, and imposition which have accompanied the transformation of labour relations in the countries under consideration with an evaluation of the strategies of the principal agents. As throughout the volume, the impact of legacies from the previous regimes are examined, at the levels of power and authority, institutions and behaviour and beliefs. The discussion is drawn together by assessing, in the light of these considerations, the extent of institutionalization of new labour-relations models and whether the countries have begun to move in the direction of Western-style labour relations.

COMPARATIVE TRANSFORMATIONS

In assessing what has happened in Eastern Europe it is appropriate to discuss the features which distinguish it from other transitions and which influence the trajectories of labour relations. As noted in Chapter 3, the IFI consider the transformations in Eastern Europe as one of several taking place in the global economy which includes Latin America, sub-Saharan Africa, and east Asia. In other transitions, with the exception of China, varying forms of capitalism and capitalist institutions were already established, though to different degrees, and their economies were open to world markets and prices. Such institutions were absent in Eastern Europe, where the socialist system meant the integration of political control with command over the management of the economy. Although agriculture was important, all the economies of Eastern Europe were highly industrialized. Industrialization had been a primary political goal and all the economies were integrated through CMEA. A highly developed and distinctive model of labour relations had been created congruent with the organization of the economy. As Slomp (1990: 170) characterized it, 'the subordination of labour relations to Communist Party politics, [was] the central characteristic of the Soviet model'.

The relationship between political and economic changes in Eastern Europe and Russia contrasts with that of other regions and countries. All of the countries faced a growing economic crisis in the late 1980s (see, e.g., Hethy 1991: 345–6). Reforms to decentralize economic management of the economy and develop mechanisms of 'self-management' in enterprises differed from country to country but were typical of the last years of socialist regimes. However, such attempts at change did not deliver significant economic results. Thus, in Russia, Gorbachev took the view that effective economic change required political reform, whereas in China significant economic reform has been promoted without political pluralism. Political change in other socialist countries of Eastern Europe was conditional on Soviet assent (or dependent on changes in the Soviet Union), but the rapid political changes of 1989 were accompanied everywhere by acceptance of the market economy as the model to pursue. This simultaneity of transformations in economic and political spheres (Offe 1996: 32–6) has no parallels in other transitions, such as in Latin America, where the economic changes have been more gradual and less closely linked to political changes and where a capitalist class already existed. A condition common to Eastern Europe and to other transitions has been the role of the IFI as agencies of the developed capitalist countries and upon which Eastern Europe was heavily dependent for financial assistance. The IFI's lack of support for the regional integration provided by the CMEA contributed substantially to the industrial crises experienced throughout Eastern Europe. Nevertheless, the IFI imposed the neo-liberal model more or less simultaneously over the region as a whole (see also Vickerstaff and Thirkell 1997).

In terms of labour relations in Eastern Europe, the predominant institutional model has been that of Western Europe—an influence deriving from contiguity, historical and cultural affinity, and a sense of the need, by countries such as Poland, Hungary, and the Czech Republic and Slovakia, to return to the European fold. In the field of labour relations there has been transference and imitation of institutions from the West. This contrasts sharply with other transitions, where external transference has derived more typically through the agency of multinational companies. Closer to the Eastern European experience is the case of Spain in the post-Franco period. From the late 1970s and into the middle 1980s governments and unions actively pursued a northern European neo-corporatist model (Martinez Lucio 1992; Crouch 1993: 267). However, unlike Eastern Europe, this was in the context of an already existing capitalist economy, albeit built on 'late and dependent patterns of industrialization' (Martinez Lucio 1992: 495).

All of these opening comments reinforce the argument for looking at developments in Eastern Europe through their own historically specific circumstances and cautions against a too ready assumption that patterns of development elsewhere will simply be replicated there. Nevertheless, the strategic choice throughout Eastern Europe to opt for a market economy gives rise to the question as to whether any other forms of economic organization and labour relations were feasible. Towards the end of the 1980s discussions about 'market socialism' as an alternative form of economic organization were current among economic reformers (see Lavigne 1995: 244–5).

These were prefigured to some extent in the early 1980s by Solidarity's conception of the 'self-governing enterprise' (Morawski 1997: 302). Later, in the Soviet Union, there was discussion about the relevance of the New Economic Policy (NEP), while at the end of 1988 the Hungarian Academy of Sciences secured papers from twenty-seven Hungarian and foreign economists for a 'Discussion on Socialist Market Economy' (*Acta Oeconomica* 1989). The general assumption was in favour of a more decentralized economy with market forces but with the main enterprises remaining in public ownership. The accompanying structures of labour relations were generally hypothesized within the paradigm of self-management, with forms of industrial democracy as in Russia, Poland, Hungary, and Bulgaria. Although, following the political transition, there were occasional discussions about a 'third way' between capitalism and socialism, this model never gained widespread political support.

Frydman, Gray, and Rapaczynski (1996*a*: 4) suggest it may have been less of a risk to borrow from the 'standard portfolio' of capitalist institutions than attempt to create completely new ones. Kornai (1992: 512), who was sceptical of a 'third way', notes that there was 'a kind of renaissance of market socialism' among anti-communist reformers that 'a democratic system must induce real market behaviour in state owned firms' in a way which the Party state failed to do. Such ideas persisted, as in the programme of Zyuganov and the Communist Party in the 1995 Russian election. However, market socialism was shaped as a response to bureaucratic control; it has disappeared because it was displaced politically by the prospect of Western consumer goods offered by neo-liberalism and its associated economic and institutional reforms. The hegemony of the neo-liberal project, supported by governments of all political backgrounds over the last seven years, has effectively consigned a market-socialist project to the margins of politics, at least for the time being. However, the legacy of decentralized economic management and self-management from the 1980s has continued to influence the strategies and scope for reform in the period of transformation—for example, in the different forms of privatization prevalent in the region.

TRIPARTISM

A common trend in many of the post-communist societies of East and Central Europe is the emergence of some form of tripartite or neo-corporatist process for forging political agreement on the transition agenda for economic and social reform. The prototype was established in Hungary in 1988 whilst the Socialist Workers' Party was still in power. In Bulgaria tripartite collaboration began in 1990 with the creation of the National Commission for the Coordination of Interest. Similar developments occurred in Czechoslovakia in the autumn of 1990 and have persisted with the division of the country. In

Poland, it was not until 1992 that the Kuron Pact brought the prospect of tri-partism. In Russia, federal and some branch tripartite commissions were established at the end of 1991 and the beginning of 1992.

These developments have been, and continue to be, encouraged by a range of agencies outside the countries. International institutions and Western academics, such as Przeworski (1993), have drawn analogies with the processes of political transition in southern Europe and Latin America, although the existence of capitalism and its institutions in these regions restricts its relevance to Eastern Europe, where such institutions were absent. The principal issues to be discussed here are the nature and functions of tripartite processes in Eastern Europe, whether they are merely a phenomenon of the transition, or if there are possibilities for a more permanent institutionalization, and, if so, what conditions are necessary for this to occur.

In trying to move quickly from a state-driven to a market-led system, the legitimacy of the East and Central European states as organizations was weak but the capacity and legitimacy of the market were still undeveloped. The only immediately available basis for consensus-building has been the existing functional organizations. Corporatism or tripartism in Eastern Europe has emerged as a government response to the real or perceived threat of political and industrial instability (Thirkell *et al.* 1994: 93). In the early phase of transformation in Eastern Europe, in the context of weak political parties, the trade unions, as the only organizations with a mass base, have played a crucial role in helping governments to establish some legitimacy for reform agenda.

The functions of the ensuing tripartite process have to be considered in relation to the development of economic reforms in Eastern Europe and the different phases of the neo-liberal policies promoted by the IFI and their associates within the countries. In all countries the process of macro-stabilization involving liberalization of prices and trade became the dominant policy issue and there was encouragement of the tripartite process to secure social consent. Although wage policy has always been at the core of tripartism, the political importance of concertation and the range of issues covered have varied significantly between countries and over time within countries. Thus, wage policy has often taken place in the contexts of tripartite discussions on broader issues of economic and social policy.

As explained in Chapter 2, the prototype of tripartism was established in Hungary initially in relation to the decentralization of wages, which had been recognized as an issue before the political changes. It was an autonomous development by the state, although it is possible that there was some imitation of the Austrian model, but the subsequent assistance and endorsement of the ILO was, in the Hungarian case, also accompanied by the support of the World Bank. In Bulgaria, on the other hand, the system of peak-level corporatism adopted in the revised Labour Code of 1993 was as a result of the political power of the trade unions and partly under the guidance of the ILO, though the World Bank and the IMF favoured a different approach (Hill *et al.* 1997: 236). A common factor in the initial development of tripartite processes, with the exception of Hungary, was the need for macro-stabilization and liberalization of the economies and the involvement of the IFI in this process. The reduction of living standards and employment, which derived from the stabilization packages, threatened the guarantee of employment which had been one of the building blocks of socialism. Within the different countries there were expectations that, as a result of stabilization, and especially in response to the effects of shock therapy, the social peace needed for the development of capitalism might be threatened. Consequently, in varying degrees and at varying times it could be said that 'governments feared the workers'. Thus, in 1992, a key informant in Bratislava acknowledged that a public-transport strike would bring the city economy to halt and the government would be very concerned to avoid such a threat. The taxi drivers' strike in Hungary in 1990 was a dramatic event which became a turning point in the development of tripartism. For such pragmatic reasons the IFI endorsed the involvement of trade unions. As an example, in 1991, in Bulgaria, IMF financial aid was conditional on the agreement of the trade-union centres to support the principle of social peace, which was maintained for nine months. The ILO, on the other hand, has a longer-term and less pragmatic commitment to social partnership with tripartism as the main institutional structure for its implementation. Thus, tripartism was a model with a lot of external backing but it also fitted both with local exigencies—the need to secure social peace—and, arguably, with local predilections—in the sense of building on a legacy of corporativist or socialist corporatist organization in which branch corporations were key economic and social organizations (Hausner, quoted in Hausner and Morawski 1994: 34–5; see also Hethy 1994: 315; Gorniak and Jerschina 1995) and in which cooperation between management and workers was encouraged.

Although, broadly speaking, the functions of tripartism were similar everywhere, the timing and way in which tripartism has developed in the different countries have varied according to the specific local economic and political context. The risks of the stabilization crisis in Poland were clearly recognized by Balcerowicz when the government made the strategic choice of shock therapy. Solidarity's role as the leading agency of political change in Poland led to its assuming the role of umbrella for the stabilization crisis, and to drawing on its political credit to legitimate the transformation. Here the process was fundamentally based on bipartism. However, the extent of the crisis eroded Solidarity's credit and its membership. Strikes, resistance, and delays in privatization resulted in the Enterprise Pact of 1992, which established tripartite institutions. The Pact covered privatization as well as wage policy and in this respect widened the scope of tripartite negotiations more than in other countries.

In Hungary, as noted above, the move towards tripartite negotiation had begun before the regime changed. Although its genesis was earlier and it is now more institutionalized than in the other countries, its development has not been an entirely smooth incremental process. The range of issues covered in the 1992 Agreement extended beyond wage regulation to employment policy, social policies, and benefits (for text and summary of measures implemented, see Hethy 1995: 97–104). The Pension and Health Insurance Boards (to which employers' representatives were delegated and union representatives were elected by the whole population) were established in 1993 and constituted a very important step in the institutionalization of the social partners' role in social policy. However, this incremental development of tripartite machinery was threatened in 1995. The Horn-led Socialist Government, elected in May 1994, was committed to the negotiation of a comprehensive tripartite social pact. The idea was abandoned, however, after half a year of bargaining provided no agreement (Hethy 1995). The increasingly unsettled economic position undercut the scope for genuine political exchange. In other countries macroeconomic stabilization was judged as an essential precondition for the economic transformation, and the adverse consequences for the economic welfare of the population were considered to threaten the social peace regarded as necessary for the capitalism. In Russia, Gaidar's imitation of the Polish model of shock therapy was closely linked to the establishment of tripartite institutions. In Bulgaria, the political and industrial turbulence led to the IFI demanding trade-union consent to social peace as the essential precondition for a loan in 1991.

The divergences in the trajectories of tripartism in the Czech Republic and Slovakia illustrate the influences of political and economic contexts and their interrelationship. In Czechoslovakia, and subsequently in the Czech Republic, the initial acceptance by the government of the tripartite process was succeeded by the clear strategic choice of Klaus to restrict the significance of tripartism as much as possible in the Czech Republic. In 1994 Klaus announced that in the Czech Republic the economic transformation was complete and would be followed by the social transformation, especially affecting pensions, social insurance, and other aspects of social policy. In practice, tripartism ceased to function. In general, trade unions have opposed changes in the social-policy sphere and this has made them reluctant to engage in the tripartite process. Paradoxically, in Slovakia, with steady development of the economy, the operation of the tripartite process was one of continuing *de facto* institutionalization. However, in March 1997 the tripartite process came to a halt over public-sector pay, while in the summer of 1997 the economic crisis in the Czech Republic led Klaus to revive the tripartite process.

As explained in Chapter 5, the control of wage policy to meet the criteria imposed by the IFI has been a central feature of neo-liberal policy. At the same time, the role of the state budget influences living standards through its control of key prices of services—such as energy and public transport as well as the pay of state employees. Consequently, bargaining about such different aspects of the state budget has been a significant component of the tripartite process in, for example, Hungary and Slovakia. Under the centrally planned economy, the locus of key economic decisions was the state plan; in the transitional market economy the focus has shifted to the state budget, which has been a concern of the IFI as well as the trade unions.

Governments concerned with promoting economic reform face a strategic choice; according to Przeworski (1991: 182) either they must 'seek the broadest possible support from unions, opposition parties, and other encompassing and centralized organizations, or they must work to weaken these organizations and try to make their opposition ineffective'. In practice, the two alternatives are not necessarily separated and indeed may coexist, as Connor (1996: 22) argues in relation to Russia: 'Over the years 1991–1993, it might be said (and the government would) that it had tried the first; those who did not like the government's line would, from the outset, accuse it of doing the second. And in spring 1994, a Russian deputy finance minister would tell the author that, in essence, both were correct.' A similar process was seen in Hungary under the Antall government, when the institutional development of tripartism was fostered within a social-market philosophy but the government tried to weaken the trade unions in the Labour Code and in relation to the issue of property.

The nature of a tripartite process is such that, in general, there will be a tendency for two of the parties to act in coalition against the third, although the alliances will alter in relation to different issues and in the context of different political and economic environments. It has been widely remarked that independent organizations of employers have been slow to develop in Eastern Europe. The substantial role of the state in relation to the economy has influenced the nature of the tripartite bargaining process. Thus, in 1994, Melikian, the Russian Minister of Labour, commented that in Russia 'the trade unions and the employers are on one side and the government is on the other' (quoted in Connor 1996: 161), and this was reported still to be true in 1997 (M. Voeikov, personal communication). This has certainly been the case in some other countries in Eastern Europe. In Bulgaria, bipartite relations between trade-union centres and the organizations of employers have been more active—for example in producing joint policy documents—than the tripartite relations with government involvement. There have been episodic examples of employers and trade unions jointly lobbying the state—for example, on behalf of the mining industry in the Czech Republic and in Bulgaria. However, attempts to foster a tripartite (local government, employers, and trade unions) approach to problems of local employment have not generally led to institutionalization, with the possible exception of Russia, where regional and branch agreements are more common (Gerchikov 1995: 158–62).

From this discussion it can be concluded that the three parties to tripartite agreement have nowhere reached a stable accommodation in the continuing conditions of economic crisis and political turbulence. The continuing role for the state as a key economic agent impacts upon the development of tripartite machinery. As Dittrich and Haferkemper (1995: 140) have noted, 'unlike in the West the state plays a different role . . . and there is not the separation of state and economy. . . . That means that the institutional prerequisite of organized social regulation by organized interests, as defined by Dahrendorf (1957) and others, does not exist.'

In the countries of Eastern Europe, where tripartism has functioned effectively it has operated at two levels: peak-level policy concertation, with structures of policy implementation and articulation to the lower levels. The functional requirements for effective institutionalization have been well-organized and cohesive representative structures and transmission mechanisms for relations between levels. In Western and Northern Europe, an established social-democratic tradition has been a major element of the political context in which tripartite processes were created and developed, and, as Streeck and Schmitter (1991: 145) have argued, neo-corporatism has been a fair-weather mechanism:

some sort of effective Keynesian-expansionist capacity seems indispensable for the kind of corporatist concertation and social contract bargaining that was to stabilize non-American capitalism in the 1970s . . . under the rules of corporatist bargaining a state that cannot with any reasonable prospect of success promise to apply its fiscal and monetary policy tools to alleviate unemployment cannot possibly hope to gain concessions from unions or to influence settlements between unions and employers by, for example, offering to improve the terms of the bargain through a corresponding economic policy.

It is clear that the political context for the development of tripartism in Eastern Europe has not been a favourable climate and that its development as a political shell for a neo-liberal economic strategy further distinguishes it from the success stories of neo-corporatism in Western Europe.

The future prospects for tripartism have to be considered in relation to the factors which have favoured the operation of the tripartite process and peak-level concertation. The perceived threat (and actual threats in Bulgaria and Poland) to social peace in response to macro-stabilization were significant factors in the early development of tripartite processes, so that governments made strategic choices, encouraged by the IFI, to co-opt trade unions into the tripartite process. Subsequently, the continuation of the role of the state in the running of the economy, which has restricted the separation of politics from economics, has given a basis for the continuation of the tripartite dialogue. Conditions of economic crisis, as in Bulgaria in 1996/7 and in the Czech Republic in 1997, tend to foster the need for consent through tripartism whilst also making agreement more difficult, as was seen with the failed social pact in Hungary in 1994/5. In Russia, the crisis affecting many workplaces has led to a continuing pattern of protest strikes, especially in relation to the non-payment of wages. These have not threatened the economy in the way which the earlier miners' strikes did but represent pressures to which the state has to some extent to respond.

In the future the factors influencing government's choices will partly depend on economic and social stability and of course the extent of trade-union fragmentation and weakness. In conditions of stability, governments may conclude that they no longer need trade-union consent. However, the economic and political developments in the Czech Republic in 1996 and 1997 show how the political legitimacy and popular support enjoyed by the Klaus government, which facilitated its downgrading of the tripartite process, could be eroded. Institutionalization of the tripartite process requires the establishment of patterns of interaction which are regular and relatively stable in their functioning as well as having the necessary organizational structures and mechanisms. As practices of interaction become established, the parties can draw upon these traditions when relations are threatened. Currently such institutionalization appears most evident in Hungary and to some extent in Slovakia. As countries in Eastern Europe converge towards the EU, some of the latter's traditions of social partnership may have an influence on the processes of tripartism developed during the transformation.

Alternatively, tripartism may persist as an empty process which is not underpinned by the downward articulation of its results and the process may become unstable. Such an outcome holds threats for the trade unions. The case of Spain may provide a relevant parallel. The trade unions were reconstructed after Franco's death and played a key part in the struggle to overthrow his successors. Trade-union membership rose to almost 50 per cent in 1979/80. Between 1977 and 1986 the trade unions were involved in concertation with government: 'The unions supported concertation, first, as a means of consolidating democracy. Second, however, they saw it as a way of legitimizing themselves as actors within the new regime, of achieving their own consolidation as organizations, and of institutionalising the rules of industrial relations' (Martinez Lucio 1992: 505). Wage control was traded by the unions for reforms—for example, in trade-union law and policies on job creation and social policy. However, it is agreed that, although wage controls were generally implemented, increasingly the social reform was not. This process was not without costs for the unions in terms of membership: 'But the change of national union strategy in 1977, towards national political compromise and concertation, led to a widely noted phenomenon of *desencanto*—"disenchantment"—among workers who saw the transition and its nascent organizations in terms of material and economic improvement rather than merely democratic consolidation' (Martinez Lucio 1992: 489). By 1988 trade-union membership was estimated at 16.5 per cent. Although by no means wholly attributable to tripartism, the unions' decline was related to the fact that, as Miguelez (1995: 84) commented, 'Spanish trade unions are relatively strong in society but weak in companies.'

In the Spanish case neo-corporatism or concertation was a strategy used by different actors at different times for different reasons. The weakness of the state in the immediate transition period, as in Eastern Europe, forced the concertation dimension. The relative institutionalization of Spanish trade unions at a national level has insulated them from declining membership, but it is not a safe assumption that such an outcome, if achievable, would be assured in Eastern Europe. It has already been argued by some that the focus on the national political arena has led unions in Eastern Europe to neglect their base and fail to try and organize workers in new firms in the emerging private sector (Thirkell *et al.* 1995*a*: 25–6; Pollert 1997: 223–4). However, in conditions of continuing economic turbulence and diminishing union membership, trade unions may face the strategic choice of whether to seek survival in institutionalization in tripartite mechanisms of regulation at a national level or to face increasingly harsh realities at the level of the enterprise. Such a choice could be characterized, following Martinez Lucio's (1992: 500–1) discussion of the Spanish case, as that between 'a "voters' trade unionism" rather than a "members' trade unionism"'.

As the preceding discussion has shown, the trajectories of the tripartite processes have varied between the different countries and in some cases have altered over time within the countries themselves, which makes prediction about future prospects very uncertain. In the processes of ownership change and privatization, with the exception of the Kuron Pact in Poland, there was not the external endorsement for tripartite involvement, whilst the reforms in social policy led to conflicts with the trade unions and in some cases withdrawal.

TRADE UNIONS

The issue of trade-union strategies for the future is a subject worthy of further discussion. Their strategies are influenced by the nature and continuation of the economic reform and the political and institutional contexts. The refusal of trade unions to give their support to the social-policy reforms of the neo-liberal model which constituted the second stage of the 'transition' and their reluctance to give commitment to long-term social contracts reflect some membership pressure for a stronger, hardline position. Consequently, most trade-union centres distanced themselves from the aims and substance of the second structural stage of the reforms. After 1994 tripartism, social partnership and most governments underwent a crisis reflected in the interruption of national-level dialogue (in the Czech Republic in 1994, in Hungary in 1994 and 1995, in Bulgaria in 1993, 1994, and 1995). In the Czech Republic from 1995 the dialogue virtually ceased. In these countries and in Poland there was an increase in strikes and other forms of industrial and social protest, showing that the initial consensus on the reform process between the partners had been broken.

The policies of the IFI in relation to trade unions have combined both ideology and pragmatism. The trade unions, initially accepted as supporting structures and as agents of change, were later considered as a potential obstacle to the reform process and even as a retrograde force which should have no place in political processes. (The position of Klaus in the 1996 election was quoted in Chapter 2.) The World Bank has expressed generalized concern about the negative effects of trade union demands and positions in the course of the reforms as a result of their 'monopolistic behaviour' and 'opposition to the reforms' (World Bank 1995: 81). However, the possibility for unions to contribute to improving the competitiveness of the economy (especially at the level of the company) is recognized. Although the overall analysis has aimed at rejecting or limiting the macroeconomic or strategic role of trade unions, there is a pragmatic acceptance of their position in practice.

The question of the opportunities for East European trade unions to create successful strategies has to be considered in relation to the short- and medium-term perspectives and the distinction between adaptive and innovative strategies (Leisink *et al.* 1996: 1–3). In the current situation unions are pushed to the periphery of decision-making on the reform process and threatened with marginalization in relation to it. Unions are deprived of the possibility to be strategic actors. In these conditions union strategies in Eastern Europe are necessarily of the adaptive type. The focus of trade-union strategy has to be on correcting or refuting the current reform policies where the erosion of labour standards and the social consequences have been greatest. However, the opportunities for innovative trade-union strategies in the medium term depend upon theoretical criticism of the neo-liberal model in terms of its inappropriateness for its principal purpose of transforming the economies to a market basis and leading them out of the crisis. At the start of the reforms there was not enough evidence to produce a theoretical analysis and critique. There is as yet no indication in the conditions prevailing in Eastern Europe of a political project capable of producing a significant modification of the neo-liberal model to take account of national specificities and the modification of its wage policies. It therefore seems unlikely that there will be space for trade unions to operate as strategic agents of change except in times of economic crisis, as in Poland in 1992, Hungary in 1994/5, and to some extent in the Bulgarian crisis of 1996. When economic conditions have been more stable, the tendency is towards the marginalization of trade unions at the political level.

Since the separation of the established trade unions from the communist parties, the relations between trade unions and political parties have varied significantly. These relationships have shifted in different directions over time, reflecting the changing salience of issues in the political arena and the outcomes of the electoral process. In principle the main alternatives are: separation; limited coalitions over specific issues; or partnership. From about 1992 a common pattern was one of separation from political parties. Thus, after the victory of the UDF opposition in Bulgaria in 1991, *Podkrepa*, which had been a founding constituent of the UDF in 1989, sought to separate itself from the political organization. However, with the return of the Socialist Party to power from 1994 to 1997, *Podkrepa* reverted to a more overtly political role. In Poland, the roles of Solidarity have been complex also: 'Solidarity (the movement) spawned parties but Solidarity (the trade union) did not allow them scope . . .' (Waller and Myant 1994: 175). From about 1995, however, trade-union centres in several countries have made strategic choices to try to develop or re-establish links with political parties. In Hungary and the Czech Republic leading trade unionists are MPs or participate in parliamentary commissions, while in Russia FITUR has attempted to associate with the Social Democrats.

In other cases trade union centres have formed political parties (the OPZZ has sixty MPs) or attempted to form them, like Solidarity in Poland or CITUB in Bulgaria. This trend has been influenced by the restriction of tripartism; underlying such choices has been the recognition that the power resources have now shifted into the party political arena rather than in the tripartite processes. Privatization and economic restructuring are processes which tend to reduce trade-union membership. The strategic choice here is whether to initiate the diversification of trade-union functions to include the provision of services to members—for example, through pensions and investment funds—and thus sustain a role that way. The trade unions face a tension between possible roles at different levels. In the early period of transformation it has been necessary for trade unions to orient themselves to the national political stage, but it is not clear that this strategy will ensure their survival as mass organizations. The alternative—to respond to members' interests at the level of the enterprise by bargaining with management and/or developing other services which members want—is difficult in conditions of economic recession. If the trade-union role in the politics of transformation is a contradictory mixture of threats and opportunities, this is no less so for the state itself.

THE STATE

In the initial stage of the political transformation the emergence of social movements and political parties into the new political space meant that state institutions and their bureaucracies were relatively less active. The failure of the socialist system to meet the economic expectations of East European populations meant that there was considerable doubt about the state as an effective agency for economic and social reform. Governments have been profoundly hampered in the implementation of the reform agenda by the weakness of the state in terms of financial crises (Owsiak 1995), poor regulatory control (for example, in tax collection), and internal strife between ministries and other state agencies. In Hungary, Poland, and Russia these problems were exacerbated by the policies of the 1980s, which had already weakened ministry control over the economy through measures which encouraged some decentralization of economic management to enterprises (see, e.g., Bruszt 1995: 269–72). Thus, before the state could try to withdraw from the economy, through marketization and privatization, it had to recentralize control over enterprises in some cases. This exemplifies a major contradiction of the neo-liberal blueprint: its neglect of the vital role of the state in steering political and economic change. The neo-liberal model of a minimal state and decentralized economy has not been achievable as central state agencies have necessarily continued to exercise state power over privatization and investment. Policies have been determined top down through ministries and special agencies created to oversee the privatization process. Some have argued that this has resulted in a recentralization of power (Bruszt 1995: 275–6).

An important contrast of the contemporary situation with the politics of the socialist system is that the removal of party control, operating through its parallel structure, has created space for the state bureaucracy to expand its influences. Old structures were dismantled quickly but new institutions have been slow to develop. The political parties in pluralist governments have not reproduced the structures of control over ministries operated by their predecessors. At the same time the still predominant role of the state in the running of the economy has been noted by researchers in several countries of Eastern Europe. Thus, Sylwestrowicz (1995) (cited in Chapter 2 above) showed how this functioned in Poland, McDermott (1997) emphasizes the control of governments over the nominally independent banks and hence over the running of privatized enterprises in the Czech Republic, while Stark (1993) has shown the importance of networks linked to the state privatization agency in Hungary.

In conditions of continuing economic crisis and the necessity of negotiating assistance from the IFI it is hardly surprising that the finance and economic ministries of the state tend to hold centre stage over the labour and social-policy ministries (Hethy 1991: 349). This feature of the transformation stage is further reinforced by the inherited underdevelopment of social administration and employment policy from the Soviet period, when full employment and welfare policy were delivered by enterprises. Other received characteristics are also visible in the internal politics of the post-Soviet state. In Russia, partly as a consequence of geographical scale, concentrations of power in regional governments have remained important. Thus, Hanson (1997: 416) has illustrated the importance, in 1996, of national and regional industrial lobbies pressing for regional government action on energy prices in Samara. Kabalina *et al.* (1994) have similarly pointed to concentrations of regional power in Russia. The branch structure, so central to the planning system in the past, remains as a basis for organized pressure on the government.

The legacy of institutional and behavioural patterns in relation to the role of the state has been enhanced by the contradictions deriving from the neo-liberal blueprint which seeks to confine the state to public order and tax-gathering, downgrading its role as an agency of economic development. The hegemony of the neo-liberal model has served to characterize any argument for more state intervention in the economy as a step back to the Communist past. As Lavigne (1995: 155) characterized it, any mention of industrial policy is easily castigated 'as nostalgia for the old system'. Thus, rather than encourage the rapid development of 'normal' labour relations, the neo-liberal strategy and its attendant continuing economic crises have tended to forestall the depoliticization of labour-relations institutions and hence to hinder the development of bargaining relationships between employers and trade unions at lower levels. The continuing role of the state in the economy and labour relations is likely to keep tripartite concertation on the agenda as an expedient for all parties, whilst also tending to undercut its institutionalization at levels below the national.

The combination of continuing economic crisis, fear of social unrest, and a neo-liberal dogma which forestalls adequate discussion of how to reform the state results in a tendency to ignore (or underplay) the real and persistent pressures on governments to respond to pressure to preserve the economy and enterprises within it. Taking a line of least resistance should not be diagnosed as a lack of will and/or capture of the state by vested interests (e.g., Aslund 1994; ECE 1997: 81, conclusions about the Bulgarian crisis), but rather as an intrinsic feature of post-Soviet states in transition. Born in a crisis, with an inheritance of bureaucratic structures and ingrained habits of regulation and control, growing up in a period of continuing economic and political crisis, and faced with a massive task of economic restructuring and social transformation in which a key task is limiting its own power and role, it is hardly surprising that the post-Soviet state struggles to meet the challenge.

OWNERSHIP CHANGE

It was widely assumed in much early writing on transformation, both within and outside Eastern Europe, that privatization would be a central mechanism for the economic transition and the reform of enterprise-level labour relations. Following on from macroeconomic stabilization policies, privatization was seen as a key policy for 'normalizing' the economy. It was expected that 'real owners' would require management to adopt plans for restructuring which would involve new and tougher attitudes to employees. In other words, it was expected that the pressures of the market would break up the indulgent style of labour relations thought to have existed in the past. In fact, as was explored in Chapter 4, the concept of privatization has served to obscure the diversity of ownership forms that have developed with their resulting myriad forms of corporate governance. The idea that privatization could be accomplished or completed quickly, thereby creating a market economy, now gives way to the realization that the dynamics of ownership change will continue to influence both economic and political development for some time to come.

The dominant form of privatization in Eastern Europe and Russia has been insider dominated, with ownership shifting from the state to employees and managers of the enterprises (Earle and Estrin 1996: 50), although the exact form of such privatization varies significantly from one country to another. The Czech Republic and Slovakia have been notable as the exceptions, where voucher privatization, on a mass basis, provided no explicit encouragement for employee ownership. It is clear from a comparison of privatization strategies in the different countries that this, unlike many other features of the neoliberal approach, was an area in which governments had some discretion over both the pace and the form of policies. The strategies adopted also illuminate the differences between countries in other respects. In practical terms it has proved difficult for Russian, Hungarian, Polish, and Bulgarian governments to push through privatization projects without the consent of enterprise stakeholders. In the cases of Russia and Hungary, enterprise managers have been in a strong position to affect and profit from ownership changes (what Schleifer and Vasiliev (1996: 69) have termed 'manager-friendly' privatization). In both of these cases, but especially in Russia, it has also been the case that the absence of a strong independent labour movement has further strengthened enterprise managers' positions. In Poland and Bulgaria, by comparison, the very strength of the trade unions has provided the main countervailing power to governments' privatization projects at the level of individual enterprises.

All of these cases suggest that the enduring legacy of the Soviet enterprise as the social, political, and economic centre of peoples' lives has been difficult to eradicate simply through privatization measures. Instead, governments have been forced to respond to pressures for employee ownership. The dominance of such 'rights-based approaches' (Offe 1996: 108) can be seen as an enduring legacy of expectations from the past which may foreclose upon, or at least significantly delay, the progress towards ownership forms more characteristic of mature capitalist societies.

The Czech and Slovak cases appear to be different from the other countries discussed. In the absence of organized opposition, the early Klaus governments were able to speed ahead with a mass privatization scheme based on vouchers which resulted in an outsider-dominated pattern of ownership change. After the separation of the two countries, the process in Slovakia slowed and diverged in form. Early praise for the voucher strategy has more recently turned to criticism, as it appears that many of the investment funds which effectively dominated the voucher privatization are managed or controlled by domestic banks and doubts exist as to their motivation or ability to encourage enterprise restructuring (Takla 1994: 160–6). Notwithstanding this critique, it is possible to suggest that the voucher strategy may still prove a more flexible method for future development of ownership forms and systems of corporate governance, in contrast to the insider-dominated models.

Privatization has not taken the forms nor had the effects that were initially expected in Eastern Europe. The idea that shifting state-owned enterprises into private hands would contribute rapidly to the creation of the 'normal' 'boundary between politics and economics' (Aslund 1992: 70) has proved illusory and perhaps naïve in the light of the institutional, ideological, and political legacies of the former regimes and the continuing economic and political turbulence. This can be characterized as part of the broader transition fallacy—namely, that the switch from a planned to a market economy would be a simple unilinear process driven by economic reform. The new forms of corporate governance arising from different ownership forms (with the exception of foreign ownership) have as yet failed to have the expected impact on the pace of restructuring in many enterprises. Even foreign investment has been subject to considerable political pressures, as illustrated by some of the cases discussed in Chapter 8.

The link between ownership change and restructuring has not been as straightforward as many expected or hoped. Many large state-owned enterprises have been broken up into smaller parts, some of which have been privatized, taken over, or merged with other organizations. These processes are continuing. In other enterprises ownership change has not led immediately to organizational restructuring or reductions in the numbers employed. It might be argued that there is simply a delayed response, that privatization has not yet been completed (or even started in some cases) and that therefore the impacts on managerial and enterprise behaviour are yet to be fully realized. Although this is plausible, it tends to underestimate the impact of current developments on future possibilities. It also sustains the assumption that the effect of policies in Eastern Europe will faithfully mirror the impacts of privatization experienced in other countries. There is, at the very least, reasonable ground for assuming that, where privatization has been insider dominated, it will be difficult to move rapidly to alternative forms of outsider-dominated ownership (the preferred outcome of the heralds of neo-liberalism). The most recent Economic Survey from the ECE (ECE 1997: 83–4) argues that without investment to update technology the future for state-owned enterprises is bleak. It therefore recommends that financial assistance from the IFI is now directed towards some state-owned enterprises. Hitherto, the IFI have been implacably opposed to such a strategy because it was seen as propping up old socialist dinosaurs.

The ownership forms that have emerged have been severely hampered also by the initial absence, and subsequent faltering development, of the normal financial institutions of capitalist economies—namely, a legal framework guaranteeing shareholders' rights, an independent and dependable banking system, a reasonable and effective taxation system, and accounting rules. This reinforces the point that the East European and Russian transformations are unique in attempting a simultaneous transformation of both economic and political systems and cautions against the attempt to theorize a basic commonality of experience with other societies undergoing a political transformation.

LEVELS OF REGULATION AND COLLECTIVE BARGAINING

The marketization of the economy in the countries of Eastern Europe and Russia is expected to lead to substantial changes in the institutions of distribution, and of the values shaping the structures of rewards. A common assumption about the likely trajectory of development in these countries was that the depoliticization of labour relations brought about by privatization would lead to the establishment of 'normal' labour relations, which meant in effect collective bargaining or other mechanisms of conflict resolution between independent employers and trade unions, and a structure of differentials dictated by the market. In practice, as discussed above, the process of privatization has been considerably more diffuse and the maintenance of centralized wage policies has kept governments at the centre of distribution issues.

In Eastern Europe and Russia collective bargaining is a foreign import with only an indirect legacy which necessarily raises questions about the extent to which it can be rapidly institutionalized. Although the transference of collective-bargaining models was occurring in Eastern Europe in the context of economic crisis, the independence of trade unions, the right to strike, and the establishment of bargaining machinery were widely seen as essential features of democratization, as well as being 'normal' features of market economies. Thus, the legal frameworks for collective bargaining were established relatively early. However, this rewriting of labour regulations was largely preemptive, in the sense that it was legislating for a liberal-market economy which did not yet exist. It has also been the case that labour legislation and codes have been issues of contention in all countries (Kyloh and Hethy 1995: 18–20).

A central question in relation to any system of collective bargaining is the relative salience of different levels—national, branch/sectoral, regional, and enterprise—and the degree of articulation between them. In the developed capitalist economies there are well-known variations between countries. The extent of centralization characteristic of the socialist system and the post-socialist commitments to a market economy poses the question of how the balance will shift between levels. It was prefigured in most legislation in Eastern Europe that the enterprise should become the key unit for collective bargaining as the necessary corollary of privatization and the decentralization of economic management. This raises the issue as to whether there is a continuing role for the branch or sector.

The evidence from countries is varied, reflecting the different political and economic trajectories. Thus, the postponement of privatization in Bulgaria, combined with tax-based wage control, has contributed to the continuation of the branch as a significant level of intermediate regulation. In Russia, as remarked above, there is a combination of inertia and institutional recombination which keeps the branch as an important mediator. In the Czech Republic, the policy of Klaus has been to decentralize to the enterprise; on the other hand, in Slovakia branch-level agreements have been and continue to be a significant level of regulation and are no longer purely dependent on tripartite agreements. (At the end of 1996 leading branches had concluded their agreements in advance of the national tripartite agreements.) In Hungary and the Czech Republic trade-union centres have seen the extension of branch agreements as a means of ensuring that non-union workplaces are linked to the standards negotiated through collective bargaining, but so far without significant success. In 1995 the achievement of more branch agreements was an objective of Solidarity (interview with Solidarity official). However, the very limited results of the national policy to promote branch-level bargaining in Hungary indicate the difficulties for this level, except in the budget sector. The Hungarian case is of special interest when seen as a case of attempted imitation and transference. As Neumann (1997: 189) explains, 'For the government it was a way to copy European (and especially German) industrial relations procedures.'

It appears that there are three possibilities for the structure of collective bargaining to coexist within a country: first, there may be a continuation of previous forms of bargains, as in some Russian cases; secondly, there could be erosion of the old system but with no new system replacing it, as a result of economic crisis and/or growth of the non-unionized sector; thirdly, there is persistence of old elements in new developments, resulting in hybrid forms or adaptation. The branch continues to be significant in Bulgaria, Slovakia, and Russia. The hybrid forms appear to be common in larger, formerly state-owned enterprises. The transformed enterprise or branch collective agreement now includes wages and other items which were excluded from its socialist predecessor, but health and safety and social-fund items still exist in Bulgaria, the Czech Republic, Slovakia, and Russia.

Trade unions now have the right to bargain, but the continuing recession undercuts the scope for bargaining. At the same time there are increasing numbers of non-unionized workplaces where employers are apt to take a unitarist strategy and government is still the ghost at the bargaining table by virtue of centralized wage policy. The countries of Eastern Europe and Russia are thus some way away from institutionalizing new collective-bargaining systems along Western European lines.

EMPLOYEE COUNCILS AND PARTICIPATION IN MANAGEMENT

The theory of the socialist enterprise was that those who worked in it should have the opportunity to participate in its management within the framework of the planning process. There were, therefore, the typical institutions of a general assembly of all employees or their representatives and an elected council with varying functions and powers. Especially during the 1980s councils of various kinds were promoted, sometimes accompanied by elections of supervisors (under the brigade organization of work) and of managers and directors. At the time of regime change there was, therefore, an institutional legacy, and a central question was how these pre-existing institutions would relate to the independent trade unions, now recognized as representatives of workers' interests and as wage negotiators.

Since the political transformation, the question of councils and their powers and functions has been an issue in the political arena, with varying significance over time. One early pattern was to abolish them, as in Czechoslovakia, as 'a relic of socialism' or, as in Hungary, as a constraint on privatization. An alternative pattern has been to promote councils as bargaining agents, often with the idea of limiting the powers of the trade unions, a strategy which trade unions have opposed. In Russia, proposals of this kind raised at the national level in 1991 were soon dropped, but at enterprise level there are cases where councils have been used as alternatives to trade unions.

The works councils as bargaining agents, legitimated by the German Works Council system as a Western model to be imitated, were proposed by the governments of Hungary and Bulgaria for inclusion in the new Labour Codes. This was successfully resisted by the trade unions, although works councils were introduced in Hungary as a mechanism for consultation. The prospect of trade-union opposition in Slovakia initially prevented the government from pursuing a strategy of reviving the councils which had been abolished in 1990, though in 1997 there was some possibility of the revival of this proposal. The Polish case illustrated that the salience of the council question can alter over time. The establishment of enterprise councils with managerial powers was a central aim of Solidarity in the 1980s. However, with the political transformation, although the consent of the Employees' Council was required to legitimate privatization, once this had been secured the council was liquidated, leaving the trade union(s) as sole representatives of employee interests. Towards the end of 1996, however, political leaders were expressing the hope that councils could be reinstated in order to reduce the influence of trade unions, and in 1997 a bill to effect this was in preparation despite the objections of Solidarity and OPZZ.

The outstanding case of direct transfer and imposition of both trade unions and works councils is eastern Germany. Hyman has concluded that neither the trade unions nor the councils have been able in practice to replicate the patterns of activity typical in west German firms. He explains this as a result of the lack of any legacy of activism combined with the scale of the economic crisis in eastern Germany (Hyman 1996). Toth (1997) similarly argues that the imitation of works councils in Hungary has resulted in their modification to local circumstances. However, Hegewisch, Brewster, and Koubek (1996: 57–8) suggest that the close relationship between works councils and management was a feature of the initial period of transformation and that in the future works councils in the east of Germany may behave more like their western counterparts.

THE ENTERPRISE

As this discussion of ownership change and the mechanisms for bargaining suggests, the legacy of the Soviet enterprise has continued to influence reform strategies and modify attempts to marketize the enterprise. The importance of the enterprise as a fundamental social, political, and economic unit in Soviet society has been remarked upon throughout this volume. The socialist enterprise was the point of entry into society and into the employment guaranteed by that society. Although there was differentiation between sectors, the conception of the enterprise as a community was strengthened by its function in the distribution (mainly through the trade union) of many benefits to its employees. These commonly included housing, holidays, recreational and other social, educational, and cultural activities, consumer services, and sometimes health care. In Russia, larger enterprises owned farms which produced food for the canteens and for the workers, and a range of consumer goods were allocated through the enterprise. The planning criterion of even development favoured the distribution of enterprises according to social, geographical, and political criteria and not simply economic ones. In company towns the links between the enterprise and the territorial community were naturally close. The neo-liberal project to normalize the economy and turn enterprises into 'purely economic institutions' (Hill *et al.* 1997: 242) has met with both institutional and behavioural resistance. This is most clearly seen in Russia and Bulgaria, where social funds and the social assets of the enterprise have been retained to a significant degree, but it is also visible in Slovakia.

The legacy of the enterprise can be distinguished at two levels: institutions and interests. The continuing influence of such legacies do not merely reflect a time lag in development or a slowness of behaviour change (although it is true enough that behaviour is difficult to change (Morawski 1997: 299)); it also reflects incentives in the current environment to maintain the role of the enterprise (Gough and McMylor 1995: 16; Le Cacheux 1996: 21–7). There are rational reasons for sustaining some of the social assets of the organization under present conditions: the absence of comprehensive and effective state welfare systems and the difficulties for local authorities to replace the system of enterprise provision; cooperation between enterprises and local authorities where an enterprise is effectively *the* industry in the town; insider-dominated forms of ownership change which encourage maintenance of the enterprise; market failures which make payment in kind highly desirable to employees; tax regimes which may encourage payment in kind as a means for avoiding either corporate tax or personal-income tax; and the use of social assets as a management tool in retaining and motivating employees (Gough and McMylor 1995: 16; Le Cacheux 1996; Mudrakov 1996; Hill *et al.* 1997). The dominance of insider forms of privatization in many countries further maintains the continuing behavioural legacy in which enterprise insiders have sustained the view that the enterprise is there for them.

In this light the slowness of economic restructuring, especially in Russia, Poland, and Bulgaria, appears less as an aberration and more as a predictable outcome of the current constellation of political interests and forces. Governments are reluctant to face the political and social consequences of a rapid growth in unemployment; enterprise managers keep workers on the books as a safety valve, either for future needs or to maintain employee support; and individual workers may prefer underemployment or disguised unemployment if it sustains their access to enterprise welfare systems. Thus, the centrality of the enterprise is an enduring legacy, not merely because old habits die hard, but because in the current conditions there are incentives encouraging and reinforcing the social and political significance of the enterprise. In the Soviet period there was an enforced, but real, community of interest amongst enterprise insiders as directors battled with the ministries to get good plan targets and thus secure good social assets for the enterprise community. It was expected that privatization and market forces would rapidly alter the basis for interest articulation by differentiating managers as the representatives of 'real' owners from the workers. In fact, in many insider-dominated forms of privatized enterprise there is not as yet a clear differentiation of interest between managers and employees *vis-à-vis* outsiders, although workers are aware of the growing differentials in pay between management and themselves. There is still a basis for a community of interest within the enterprise as it battles for survival in harsh economic circumstances.

TRANSFERENCE, IMITATION AND IMPOSITION

The institutions of the Soviet labour-relations model have been destroyed or transformed, although attitudes and expectations persist. Some institutions of labour relations found in Western market economies have been transferred and embodied in legislation. The most complete case of imposition is that of eastern Germany, where not only labour-relations institutions have been transferred, but 'the wholesale adoption of west German economic models' has taken place (Hegewisch *et al.* 1996: 61). Here, with the relative strength of the west German economy underpinning the imposition, the prospects for institutionalization of Western labour relations is much greater. However, in the other countries of Eastern Europe, consideration of such institutional imports and imitation has to take greater account of the conditions both of the societies from which institutions and mechanisms were transferred and of those societies into which they have been transplanted. The institutions come from societies which had experienced both sustained economic improvements over a long period and stable political environments. The societies into which they have been imported were experiencing simultaneous transformations in both the political and economic fields. The transfer of institutions took place at an early stage both of the political transformation crisis and at the outset of what Kornai (1994) has termed the transformational 'recession'.

It is appropriate to review the political and economic contexts in which the developments in labour relations have been and are taking place. In the field of politics the principal conclusion is that political pluralism, which was a pre-requisite for trade-union independence, has not been reversed. On the other hand, in the field of economics the two principal conclusions are: first, that the massive economic crisis associated with stabilization has not been automatic-ally succeeded by more stable ('normal') economic growth—rather there has been the persistence of transformation crisis, especially in Bulgaria and Russia; secondly, the variations in the trajectories of economic development from country to country have been affected, in unpredicted ways, by periodic economic shocks. Thus, in Central Europe at the time of the political trans-formation the legacy of economic reform and the absence of economic crisis in Hungary would have indicated the probability of steady progress in economic development and the possibility of the incremental development of the market economy. In contrast, in Poland the legacy of economic crisis and of industrial conflict would have suggested a more troubled trajectory of economic devel-opment. However, in Hungary, despite attracting a large share of foreign direct investment initially, with particular significance for the transfer and adaptation of labour-relations ideas from outside, the economic crisis of 1995 slowed economic reform with its attendant implications for labour relations. In Poland, on the other hand, in 1997 economic development appeared more secure. To take another case, the crisis of 1997 in the Czech Republic, which saw a rise in industrial unrest and the withdrawal of support from the govern-ment, was an unanticipated interruption in the trajectory of marketization which, since the velvet revolution, was judged to be proceeding smoothly and steadily on the basis of the political consent of the population. As a recent ECE report (EEC/UN 1997: 81) noted: 'The Bulgarian economic crisis under-lines the possible fragility of the process of transition from plan to market in a number of countries and points to some unexpected hurdles to be overcome.'

The continuing economic crisis and resulting instability have reinforced some legacies and inhibited others. As indicated above, legacies do not persist autonomously from their surroundings; the current environment may provide new incentives to behave in apparently old ways. Some legacies have been negative, some positive. The legacy of economic misdevelopment and bureaucratic state management continues to be a constraint on change and restructuring. The search for 'a model' and the imitation of institutions from elsewhere perhaps confirm the old design-led approach to change, and have been reinforced by the oversimplistic model of 'transition' fostered by the IFI. As Hethy (1991: 356) commented early on:

Developments are often based on isolated interventions, motivated by the urgent need to find solutions for new problems or simply by the urge to follow Western European models. The appearance of models of industrial relations systems that fit well into the fabric of the emerging political and economic systems and that are, at the same time, based on the historical and cultural traditions of the individual countries in the region will probably be a lengthy process. Such models cannot be 'imported'; they can only be developed on the spot.

It was expected that the existing managers of state-owned enterprises would lack the appropriate skills for operating successfully in a market economy. As the case studies discussed in Chapter 7 indicated, there has been turnover amongst managers and at times change was contingent upon the election or appointment of new directors; however, there is also considerable continuity in management. From the late 1980s onwards many directors were using moves towards more decentralized forms of economic management as a lever for increasing their own autonomy, and these strategies have continued in the process of ownership change. In mobilizing enterprise insiders for particular privatization schemes and in negotiating with privatization agencies, many directors have been continuing to use skills learnt and networks developed during the last decade of the planned economy.

The hope of copying Western methods of privatization have also proved unrealistic. The insider-dominated forms of privatization that have characterized the early years of transformation bear the legacy of moves to decentralize economic management in the 1980s and experiments with self-management. On the basis of earlier reforms, insiders have been able to engineer forms of ownership change that, in the short term at least, seem to maintain the interests of the enterprise insiders. The enterprise for many in the present remains the best (or the only) source of certain economic and social goods. Survival of the enterprise continues as a basis for a community of interest *vis-à-vis* outsiders. Patterns of corporate governance common in capitalist societies have not resulted from much of the ownership change that has happened so far, and further the configuration of ownership that has ensued is likely to inhibit the rapid development of ownership by outsiders. The most dramatic changes in labour relations at enterprise level have typically occurred in the 'new economy'—that is, in foreign-owned firms and new small entrepreneurial undertakings.

In the light of the role of new trade unions in the first phase of political transformation, it was expected that such movements were likely to become a major constituent of the new labour-relations arena. In fact, the new unions were not able to consolidate their position by building structures of representation in the face of the old trade unions. The established trade unions have weathered the transformation so far, perhaps surprisingly well. The legacy of support and connection to the Party has been broken, but leaders have been able to use inherited structures and resources to recreate new organizations capable of operating in the new environment. However, they face difficult choices over the direction to pursue in the future.

In all of the countries in the region there is continuing potential for crisis; the prognosis of an early return to a 'normal economy' was part of the transition fallacy and has proved illusory. Consequently, labour relations remain in a state of change and continuing development. The future trajectories and forms of labour relations are likely to depend: first, on whether, when, or to what extent, economies emerge from the transformational recessions; secondly, on the future dynamics of ownership change and any resulting restructuring; thirdly, on the rate of growth of the 'new economy'—that is both small private firms but also the impact of foreign ownership; fourthly, on the ability of the trade unions to halt the decline in membership, which is a prerequisite for the establishment of genuine collective bargaining. The context of economic uncertainty and the diversity of ownership forms emerging from the processes of commercialization, privatization, foreign takeovers, and the establishment of new private businesses can be expected to lead to increasingly heterogenous outcomes in labour relations. Just as aspects of West European models have been transposed and adapted in the specific context of East European transformation, there is the persistence and modification of institutions and attitudes from the past. This combination is unlikely to result in the early consolidation of market economies and labour-relations systems along West European lines.

Appendix A. Methodological Note and Core Case-Study Enterprises

The main body of empirical work which underpins the discussion in this book was conducted as part of the project 'Labour Relations in Transition—Restructuring and Privatization' funded by the Economic and Social Research Council (ESRC) (Grant no. L309253027) as part of its East–West Initiative. The project was designed and the methodology agreed by an international research team at the outset. Teams of local researchers were commissioned to undertake the case-study research. In addition, members of the British team visited the enterprises during the course of the research. The case-study enterprises were identified in the six countries and visited over a three-year period. In the initial visits key informants were identified at each level in the enterprise: senior, middle, and junior management, trade-union leaders, and other workers' representatives and employees. In return visits researchers were able to attend management meetings and workers' meetings and to observe production processes. (For a full discussion of the research process, see Thirkell *et al.* 1995: 2–6.) The following provides a brief overview of the research in each country. The British team consisted of Richard Scase, John Thirkell, and Sarah Vickerstaff, all at the University of Kent at Canterbury. Listed below are the core cases discussed in this volume. The research project included other enterprises which are not discussed here.

BULGARIA

Research Consultants

Professor K. Petkov, Professor of the Sociology of Work at the University of Sofia and President of the Confederation of Independent Trade Unions (CITUB); Grigor Gradev, Director of Research, CITUB.

Case Studies

BOSAIR
  An enterprise in the air-transport industry; state owned.
    Principal researchers: Professor K. Petkov and G. Gradev.

FLEXTOOLS
  An enterprise producing hand tools and motors; state-owned joint stock company.
    Principal researchers: Professor K. Petkov and G. Gradev.

FOUNDRY
  A foundry; became a joint venture and then returned to state ownership.
    Principal researchers: Professor K. Petkov and G. Gradev.

CZECH REPUBLIC AND SLOVAKIA

Research Consultant

Ludovit Cziria, Deputy Head of Research at the Slovak Institute of Labour, Family and Social Affairs, Bratislava.

Case Studies

SPRINGS
Enterprise producing mechanical springs; privatized by the voucher method in the first wave of privatization.
Principal researchers: L. Cziria, F. Lipták, and V. Mravec.

SLOVCAR
Car manufacturer; privatized by foreign ownership.
Principal researchers: L. Cziria and B. Michalik.

HUNGARY

Research Consultant

Dr Lajos Hethy, Director of the Labour Research Institute, Ministry of Labour, Budapest.

Case Studies

HUNGAIR
Air transport company; privatized with part foreign ownership in 1992.
Principal researchers: F. Ternovszky and G. Kauscsek.

PROMED
Enterprise making medical equipment and protective equipment; holding company sold to a French investor in 1990; JV (one division of the company) was privatized with 50 per cent foreign ownership.
Principal researchers: F. Ternovszky and M. Adorján.

POLAND

Research Consultant

Professor Witold Morawski, Professor of Sociology at the Institute of Sociology, Warsaw.

Case Studies

MEDEX
  Medical-equipment manufacturer; leased from the state in the form of a stock company.
  Principal researcher: Dr Michał Federowicz.

POLTOOLS
  Manufacturer of industrial tools; no ownership change up to 1995.
  Principal researcher: Dr Michał Federowicz.

COLDCUTS
  Food manufacturer, meats; leased from the state, plan for privatization agreed in 1996.
  Principal researcher: Professor Wiesława Kozek.

RUSSIA

Research Consultant

Dr Vladimir Gerchikov, Senior Researcher at the Institute of Economic and Industrial Engineering, Siberian Academy of Sciences, Novosibirsk.

Case Studies

SIBERTURB
  Engineering plant manufacturing large electrical machines; leased from the state in 1990 and management/employee buyout in 1992/3.
  Principal researchers: N. Barkhatova and E. Gorbunova.

LEBAGS
  Manufacturer of leather haberdashery; became a leasehold company in 1990 and then a joint stock company of the closed type.
  Principal researchers: N. Barkhatova and E. Gorbunova.

MATOOLS
  Machine-tools enterprise; became a leasehold company in 1991 and then a joint stock company of the open type.
  Principal researchers: L. Truth and M. Demenshko.

Appendix B. Additional Research

In addition to the original case-study-based research, the analysis presented here has benefited also from the following additional research: non-standard interviews with Russian industrial-relations researchers in Moscow in the summer of 1995 and in Canterbury in February 1996, and work from the project 'The Management of Production in Some Russian Enterprises' funded by a Nuffield Foundation Grant in 1996/7. The latter research was undertaken by John Thirkell and John Sharp of the University of Kent at Canterbury and Professor M. Voeikov, Institute of Economics, Russian Academy of Sciences. This study visited manufacturing enterprises in Tver, Nizhni Novgorod, and Moscow.

REFERENCES

Acta Oeconomica (1989), 'Discussion on Socialist Market Economy—Answers to an Inquiry' 40/3–4: 179–283.

Adam, J. (1995), 'Transition to a Market Economy in the Former Czechoslovakia', in Hausner *et al.* (1995), 193–217.

Aganbegnyan, A. (1988), *The Challenge: The Economics of Perestroika* (London).

Amsden, A. H., Kochanowicz, J., and Taylor, L. (1994), *The Market Meets its Match: Restructuring the Economies of Eastern Europe* (Cambridge, Mass.).

Aro, P., Abadjiev, E., Neikov, I., Neikova, S., and Repo, P. (1996), *Collective Agreements under the New Regulations in Bulgaria* (Brussels).

Ashwin, S. (1997), 'Shopfloor Trade Unionism in Russia: The Prospects of Reform from Below', *Work Employment and Society*, 11/1: 115–31.

Aslund, A. (1992), *Post Communist Economic Revolutions: How Big a Bang?* (Washington).

——(1994), 'Lessons of the First Four Years of Systematic Change in Eastern Europe', *Journal of Comparative Economics*, 19: 22–38.

Balccrowicz, L. (1995), *Socialism, Capitalism, Transformation* (Budapest).

Bangert, D., and Poor, J. (1993), 'Foreign Involvement in the Hungarian Economy: Its Impact on Human Resource Management', *International Journal of Human Resource Management*, 4/4: 817–40.

Barr, N. (1994) (ed.), *Labour Markets and Social Policy in Central and Eastern Europe* (Oxford).

——and Harbison, R. W. (1994), 'Overview: Hopes, Tears and Transformation', in Barr (1994), 1–28.

Batt, J. (1994), 'Political Dimensions of Privatization in Eastern Europe', in Estrin (1994*b*), 83–91.

Berg, A. (1994), 'The Logistics of Privatization in Poland', in Blanchard *et al.* (1994), 165–88.

Berki, B., and Lado, M. (1995), 'Moves towards Free Wage Bargaining in Hungary', in Vaughan-Whitehead (1995), 163–217.

Berlanger, B. (1995), 'The Substance of IMF Program Design in Transition Economies of Central and Eastern Europe', paper presented to IMF Conference for Central and Eastern European Trade Leaders, Baden bei Wien.

Bim, A., Jones, D., and Weisskopf, T. (1994), 'Privatization in the Former Soviet Union and the New Russia', in Estrin (1994*b*), 263–6.

Bird, G. (1993), 'Does the World Still Need the IMF?', in Murshed and Raffer (1993), 166–80.

Blanchard, O. J., Froot, K. A., and Sachs, J. D. (1994), *The Transition in Eastern Europe*, ii. *Restructuring* (Chicago).

Brady, J. (1997) (ed.), *Central and Eastern Europe—Industrial Relations and the Market Economy* (Dublin).

Bristow, J. A. (1996), *The Bulgarian Economy in Transition* (Cheltenham).

Bronstein, A. S. (1995), 'Societal Change and Industrial Relations in Latin America: Trends and Prospects', *International Labour Review*, 134/2: 163–86.

Bruszt, L. (1995), 'Reforming Alliances: Labour, Management and State Bureaucracy in Hungary's Transformation', in Hausner *et al.* (1995), 261–86.

Buketov, K. (1995), 'Russian Trade Unions in 1994', *Labour Focus on Eastern Europe*, 50: 24–40.

Bulgarian State Gazette (*Durzhaven Vestnik*) (1994), 'Transformation and Privatization of State-Owned and Municipal-Owned Enterprises Act', 51: 1–9.

Burawoy, M., and Krotov, P. (1992), 'The Soviet Transition from Socialism to Capitalism: Worker Control and Economic Bargaining in the Wood Industry', *American Sociological Review*, 57.

——and Lukacs, J. (1992), *The Radiant Past: Ideology and Reality in Hungary's Road to Capitalism* (Chicago).

Carlin, W. (1994), 'Privatization and Deindustrialization in East Germany', in Estrin (1994*b*), 127–53.

Canning, A., and Hare, P. (1994), 'The Privatization Process—Economic and Political Aspects of the Hungarian Approach', in Estrin (1994*b*), 176–217.

Camdessus, M. (1996), 'The Impact of Globalization and Regional Integration on Workers and their Trade Unions', speech to ICFTU and ETUC in Brussels, mimeo, ETUC.

Centre for Labour Market Studies (1995), *Formation of Social Partnership in the Russian Federation* (Institute of Economics, Russian Academy of Sciences, Moscow).

Cichon, M. (1995), 'Social Protection Reform in Central and Eastern Europe: Status and Requirements for Programs', paper presented to IMF Conference for Central and Eastern European Trade Union Leaders, Baden bei Wien.

——and Samuel, L. (1995) (eds.), *Making Social Protection Work: The Challenge of Tripartism in Social Protection Governance for Countries in Transition* (Budapest).

Clague, C. (1992), 'Introduction: The Journey to a Market Economy', in Clague and Rausser (1992), 1–22.

——and Rausser, G. C. (1992) (eds.),*The Emergence of Market Economies in Eastern Europe* (Cambridge, Mass.).

Clarke, O., and Niland, J. (1991), 'The Dynamics and Dimensions of Change', in Niland and Clarke (1991), 164–82.

Clarke, S. (1993), 'Privatization and the Development of Capitalism in Russia', in Clarke *et al.* (1993), 199–241.

——(1995) (ed.), *Management and Industry in Russia* (Aldershot).

——and Fairbrother, P. (1993*a*), 'Beyond the Mines: The Politics of the New Workers Movement', in Clarke *et al.* (1993), 121–44.

————(1993*b*), 'The Origins of the Independent Workers' Movement and the 1989 Miners' Strike', in Clarke *et al.* (1993), 145–60.

————(1993*c*), 'The Strikes of 1991 and the Collapse of the Soviet System', in Clarke *et al.* (1993), 161–72.

————(1993*d*), 'After the Coup: The Workers' Movement in the Transition to a Market Economy', in Clarke *et al.* (1993), 173–98.

————(1994*a*), 'Does Trade Unionism Have a Future in Russia?', *Industrial Relations Journal*, 25/1: 15–25.

————(1994*b*), 'Post-Communism and the Emergence of Industrial Relations in the Workplace', in Hyman and Ferner (1994), 368–97.

——and Kabalina, V. (1994), 'Privatization and the Struggle for Control of the

Enterprise in Russia', paper presented to the Conference Russia in Transition: Elites, Classes and Inequalities, 15–16 Dec., Cambridge.

—— Fairbrother, P., Burawoy, M., and Krotov, P., (1993), *What About the Workers?* (London).

—— —— Borisov, P., and Bizyukov, P. (1994), 'The Privatization of Industrial Enterprises in Russia: Four Case Studies', *Europe–Asia Studies*, 46/2: 179–214.

Coffee, J. C. (1996), 'Institutional Investors in Transitional Economies: lessons from the Czech experience', in Frydman *et al.* (1996*b*), i. 111–86.

Cohen, S. F. (1973), *Bukharin and the Bolshevik Revolution: A Political Biography 1888–1938* (New York).

Communist Party of the Russian Federation (1995), *Materiali i Dokumenti* (Moscow).

Connor, W. D. (1996), *Tattered Banners: Labor, Conflict and Corporatism in Postcommunist Russia* (Boulder, Colo.).

Cook, P., and Kirkpatrick, C. (1995) (eds.), *Privatization Policy and Performance: International Perspectives* (Hemel Hempstead).

Cooter, R. (1992), 'Organization as Property: Economic Analysis of Property Law Applied to Privatization', in Clague and Rausser (1992), 77–97.

Cox, T. (1994), 'Privatization and Social Interest in Eastern Europe', *Journal of European Public Policy*, 1/3: 395–412.

Crawford, I., and Thompson, A. (1994), 'Driving Change: Politics and Administration', in Barr (1994), 322–52.

Crouch, C. (1993), *Industrial Relations and European State Traditions* (Oxford).

Cziria, L. (1995), 'Tripartism in the Slovak Republic', in Kyloh (1995), 146–63.

Dabrowski, J. M., Federowicz, M., and Levitas, A. (1991), 'Polish State Enterprises and the Properties of Performance: Stabilization, Marketization, Privatization', *Politics and Society*, 19/4: 403–37.

Dahrendorf, R. (1957), *Soziale Klassen und Klassenkonflikt in der Industriellen Gesellschaft* (Stuttgart).

Deppe, R., and Tatur, M. (1995), 'Trade Union Configurations and Transformation Policy in Poland and Hungary', paper presented to the ICCEES 5th World Congress, 6–11 Aug., Warsaw.

Dittrich, E. J. (1994), 'Economic Transformation and Labour Relations', in Moerel (1994*b*), 149–86.

—— and Haferkemper, M. (1995), 'Industrial Relations in the Making—Bulgaria, Hungary, Poland and the Czech Republic', in Dittrich *et al.* (1995), 137–62.

—— Schmidt, G., and Whitley, R. (1995) (eds.), *Industrial Transformation in Europe* (London).

Domànski, H., and Heynes, B. (1995), 'Toward a Theory of the Role of the State in Market Transition: From Bargaining to Markets in Post-Communism', *Archives Européennes de Sociologie*, 36/2: 317–51.

Driscoll, D. D. (1994), *The IMF and the World Bank. How Do They Differ?* (Washington).

Dunlop, J. T. (1958), *Industrial Relations Systems* (New York).

Earle, J. S., and Estrin, S. (1996), 'Employee Ownership in Transition', in Frydman *et al.* (1996*b*), 1–61.

—— Frydman, R., and Rapaczynski, A. (1993) (eds.), *Privatization in the Transition to a Market Economy* (London).

ECE (1992): Economic Commission for Europe, *Economic Survey of Europe in 1991–2* (New York).
——(1993), *Economic Survey of Europe in 1992–3* (New York).
——(1994), *Economic Survey of Europe in 1993–4* (New York).
——(1997), *Economic Survey of Europe in 1996–7* (New York).
Ellman, M. (1994), 'Transformation, Depression, and Economics: Some Lessons', *Journal of Comparative Economics*, 19: 1–21.
Ericson, R. E. (1995), 'The Russian Economy since Independence', in Lapidus (1995), 37–77.
Ernst, M., Alexeev, M., and Marer, P. (1996), *Transforming the Core: Restructuring Industrial Enterprises in Russia and Central Europe* (Boulder, Colo.).
Esping-Andersen, G. (1996) (ed.), *Welfare States in Transition: National Adaptations in Global Economies* (London).
Estrin, S. (1994a), 'Economic Transition and Privatization: The Issues', in Estrin (1994b), 3–30.
——(1994b), *Privatization in Central and Eastern Europe* (Harlow).
ETUI (1995): European Trade Union Institute, *Labour Markets, Wages and Social Security in Central and Eastern Europe* (Brussels).
Fagan, G. (1991), 'Hungary: The Collapse of Kadarism', *Labour Focus on Eastern Europe*, 40: 23–32.
Fairbrother, P. (1994), 'Privatization and Local Trade Unionism', *Work Employment and Society*, 8/3: 339–56.
Federowicz, M. (1994), *Poland's Economic Order: Persistence and Transformation* (Warsaw).
Ferner, A. (1997), 'Country of Origin Effects and HRM in Multinational Companies', *Human Resource Management Journal*, 7/1: 19–37.
——and Collins, T. (1991), 'Privatization, Regulation and Industrial Relations', *British Journal of Industrial Relations*, 29/3: 391–409.
——and Hyman, R. (1992), *Industrial Relations in the New Europe* (Oxford).
Filtzer, D. (1994), *Soviet Workers and the Collapse of Perestroika: The Soviet Labour Process and Gorbachev's Reform 1985–1991* (Cambridge).
Fisher, J. (1996), 'Democracy and Reform', *Worldlink* (Mar.–Apr.), 22–3.
FITUR (1996), 'Globalization and Collective Bargaining: the Russian Case', report presented to the FITUR Congress (Moscow).
Flanders, A. (1975), *Management and Unions* (London).
Fretwell, D., and Jackman, R. (1994), 'Labour Markets: Unemployment', in Barr (1994), 160–91.
Frydman, R., Rapaczynski, A. J., Earle, J. S., *et al.* (1993a), *The Privatization Process in Russia, Ukraine and the Baltic States* (London).
————(1993b), *The Privatization Process in Central Europe* (London).
——Gray, C. W., and Rapaczynski, A. (1996a), 'Overview of Volumes 1 and 2', in Frydman *et al.* (1996b), 1–19.
————(1996b) (eds.), *Corporate Governance in Central Europe and Russia*, i: *Banks, Funds and Foreign Investors*; ii. *Insiders and the State* (Budapest).
——Pistov, K., and Rapaczynski, A. (1996), 'Investing in Insider-dominated Firms: A study of Russian Voucher Privatization Funds', in Frydman *et al.* (1996b), i. 187–241.
Furedi, G. (1994), 'New Requirements for the Human Resource Management in Joint Venture Management', in Mako and Novoszath (1994b), 113–22.

Gerchikov, V. (1995), 'Russia', in Thirkell *et al.* (1995*b*), 137–68.

Gomulka, S., and Jasinki, P. (1994), 'Privatization in Poland 1989–1993', in Estrin (1994*b*), 218–51.

Gorbachev, M. S. (1987), *Perestroika* (London).

Gordon, L. A., and Klopov, E. V. (1992), 'The Workers' Movement in a Post Socialist Perspective', in Silverman *et al.* (1992), 27–52.

Gorniak, J., and Jerschina, J. (1995), 'From Corporatism to . . . Corporatism: The Transformation of Interest Representation in Poland', in Hausner *et al.* (1995), 168–89.

Gortat, R. (1994), 'The Feud Within Solidarity's Offspring', in Waller and Myant (1994), 116–24.

Gough, I., and McMylor, P. (1995), *Enterprise Welfare in Russia and the Transition to the Market Economy* (CID Studies No. 8; Copenhagen).

Grabher, G. (1995), 'The Elegance of Incoherence: Economic Transformation in East Germany and Hungary', in Dittrich *et al.* (1995), 33–53.

——and Stark, D. (1997) (eds.), *Restructuring Networks in Post-Socialism: Legacies, Linkages, and Localities* (Oxford).

Grime, K., and Duke, V. (1992), 'A Czech on Privatization', *Regional Studies*, 27/8: 751–7.

Haggard, S., and Kaufman, R. (1992) (eds.), *The Politics of Economic Adjustment: International Constraints, Distributive Conflicts and the State* (Princeton).

Hall, M. (1994), 'Industrial Relations and the Social Dimension of European Integration: Before and After Maastricht', in Hyman and Ferner (1994), 281–311.

Hanson, P. (1997), 'Samara: A Preliminary Profile of a Russian Region and its Adaptation to the Market', *Europe–Asia Studies*, 49/3: 407–29.

Hausner, J. (1995), 'The State Enterprise Pact and the Potential for Tripartism in Poland', in Kyloh (1995), 105–29.

——and Morawski, W. (1994), 'Tripartism in Poland', paper presented to the Tripartism in Central and Eastern Europe Round Table Conference organized by the Hungarian Institute of Labour Research and the ILO, 26–7 May, Budapest, vol. ii.

——Jessop, B. and Nielson, K. (1995) (eds.), *Strategic Choice and Path-Dependency in Post-Socialism: Institutional Dynamics in the Transformation Process* (Aldershot).

Hayashi, T. (1997) (ed.), *The Emerging New Regional Order in Central and Eastern Europe* (Sapporo, Japan).

Hegewisch, A., Brewster, C., and Koubek, J. (1996), 'Employee Relations in the Czech Republic and East Germany', *Industrial Relations Journal*, 27/1: 53–64.

Henderson, J., Whitley, R., Lengyel, G., and Czaban, L. (1995), 'Contention and Confusion in Industrial Transformation: Dilemmas of State Economic Management', in Dittrich *et al.* (1995), 79–108.

Hethy, L. (1991), 'Towards Social Peace or Explosion: Challenges for Labour Relations in Central and Eastern Europe', *Labour and Society*, 16/4: 345–58.

——(1992), 'The Reconstruction of Industrial Relations in Hungary', in van Hoof *et al*, 33–48.

——(1994), 'Tripartism in Eastern Europe', in Hyman and Ferner (1994), 312–36.

——(1995), 'Anatomy of a Tripartite Experiment: Attempted Social and Economic Agreements in Hungary', *International Labour Review*, 134/3: 361–76.

——and Csuhaj, I. V. (1990), *Labour Relations in Eastern Europe* (Budapest).

Hethy, L., and Kyloh, R. (1995), 'A Comparative Analysis of Tripartite Consultations and Negotiations in Central and Eastern Europe', in Kyloh (1995), 1–48.

Hill, S., Martin, R., and Vidinova, A. (1997), 'Institutional Theory and Economic Transformation: Enterprise Employment Relations in Bulgaria', *European Journal of Industrial Relations*, 3/2: 229–51.

Hyman, R. (1994*a*), 'Introduction: Economic Restructuring, Market Liberalism and the Future of National Industrial Relations Systems', in Hyman and Ferner (1994), 1–14.

—— (1994*b*), 'Changing Trade Union Identities and Strategies', in Hyman and Ferner (1994), 108–39.

—— (1996), 'Institutional Transfer: Industrial Relations in Eastern Europe', *Work Employment and Society*, 10/4: 601–39.

—— and Ferner, A. (1994) (eds.), *New Frontiers in European Industrial Relations* (Oxford).

ILO (1984): International Labour Office, *The Trade Union Situation and Industrial Relations in Hungary* (Geneva).

—— (1996), *Yearbook of Labour Statistics 1996* (Geneva).

ILO-CEET (1994): International Labour Organisation, Central and Eastern European Team, *The Bulgarian Challenge: Reforming Labour Markets and Social Policy* (Budapest).

—— (1996): International Labour Office, Central and Eastern European Team, *Trade Union Experiences in Collective Bargaining in Central Europe*, Report of the ILO Survey in Bulgaria, Czech Republic, Hungary, Poland, and Slovakia, mimeo (Budapest).

Jackman, R., and Rutkowski, M. (1994), 'Labour Markets: Wages and Employment', in Barr (1994), 121–59.

Jones, D., and Rock, C. (1994), 'Privatization in Bulgaria', in Estrin (1994*b*), 311–24.

Kabaj, M. (1995), 'Searching for a New Results-Oriented Wage Negotiation System in Poland', in Vaughan-Whitehead (1995), 219–54.

Kabalina, V., Fairbrother, P., Clarke, S. and Borisov, V. (1994), 'Privatization and the Struggle for Control of the Enterprise in Russia', paper delivered to the ESRC East–West Programme Seminar, London.

Kadar, J. (1984), *Socialism and Democracy in Hungary* (Budapest).

Kerr, C., Dunlop, J. T., Harbison, F. H., and Myers, C. A. (1960), *Industrialism and Industrial Man* (Cambridge, Mass.).

Khasbulatov, R. (1993), *The Struggle for Russia: Power and Change in the Democratic Revolution*, trans. R. Sakwa (London).

Kilminster, A. (1995), 'Privatization in Eastern Europe', *Labour Focus on Eastern Europe*, 51: 86–105.

Kiss, Y. (1992), 'Privatization in Hungary—Two Years Later', *Soviet Studies*, 44/6: 1015–38.

Kloc, K. (1994), 'Trade Unions and Economic Transformation in Poland', in Waller and Myant (1994), 125–32.

Kochan, T. A., Katz, H. C., and McKersie, R. B. (1986), *The Transformation of American Industrial Relations* (New York).

Kogut, B. (1996), 'Direct Investment, Experimentation and Corporate Governance in Transition Economics', in Frydman *et al.* (1996*b*), i. 293–332.

Konecki, K., and Kulpinska, J. (1995), 'Enterprise Transformation and the Redefinition of Organizational Realities in Poland', in Dittrich *et al.* (1995), 234–54.

Kornai, J. (1980), *Economics of Shortage* (2 vols.; Amsterdam).
—— (1990), *The Road to the Free Economy* (New York).
—— (1992), *The Socialist System: The Political Economy of Communism* (Princeton).
—— (1994), 'Transformational Recession: The Main Causes', *Journal of Comparative Economics*, 19: 39–63.
—— (1995), 'The Principles of Privatization in Eastern Europe', in Poznanski (1995), 31–56.
Kozek, W., Federowicz, M., and Morawski, W. (1995), 'Poland', in Thirkell *et al.* (1995*b*), 109–35.
Kubinkova, M. (1996), 'The Legal Basis of Collective Agreements in the Czech Republic', paper presented to the ILO Conference, Prague.
Kuznetsov, A., and Kuznetsov, O. (1996), 'Privatization, Shareholding and the Efficient Argument: Russian Experience', *Europe–Asia Studies*, 48/7: 1173–85.
Kyloh, R. (1995) (ed.), *Tripartism on Trial: Tripartite Consultations and Negotiations in Central and Eastern Europe* (ILO and Eastern European Team, Budapest).
Lado, M. (1994), 'Tripartism and/or Bipartism in Hungary', paper presented to the IIRA Congress, Helsinki.
Lapidus, G. W. (1995) (ed.), *The New Russia: Troubled Transformation* (Boulder, Colo.).
Lavigne, M. (1995), *The Economics of Transition: From Socialist Economy to Market Economy* (London).
Le Cacheux, J. (1996), 'The Current Situation and Key Issues for the Long-term', in OECD (1996), 17–29.
Leisink, P., van Leemput, J., and Vilrokx, J. (1996) (eds.), *The Challenges to Trade Unions in Europe: Innovation or Adaptation?* (Cheltenham).
Lenin, V. I. (1970), *On the Trade Unions* (Moscow).
Locke, R., Kochan, T., and Piore, M. (1995), 'Reconceptualizing Comparative Industrial Relations: Lessons from International Research', *International Labour Review*, 134/2: 139–61.
McDermott, G. A. (1997), 'Renegotiating the Ties that Bind: The Limits of Privatization in the Czech Republic', in Grabher and Stark (1997), 70–106.
McFaul, M. (1995), 'Agency Problems in the Privatization of Large Enterprises in Russia', in McFaul and Perlmutter (1995), 39–55.
—— and Perlmutter, T. (1995) (eds.), *Privatization, Conversion and Enterprise Reform in Russia* (Boulder, Colo.).
McShane, D. (1981), *Solidarity: Poland's Independent Trade Union* (Nottingham).
—— (1994), 'The Changing Contours of Trade Unionism in Eastern Europe and the CIS', in Hyman and Ferner (1994), 337–67.
Major, I. (1993), *Privatization in Eastern Europe* (Aldershot).
Mako, C., and Novoszath, P. (1994*a*), 'Multinational Firms and the Heterogeneity of Labour Relations', in Mako and Novoszath (1994*b*), 145–68.
—— —— (1994*b*) (eds.), *Convergence versus Divergence: The Case of the Corporate Culture* (Budapest).
—— —— (1995), 'Employee Relations in Multinational Companies: The Hungarian Case', in Dittrich *et al.* (1995), 255–76.
Marginson, P., and Sisson, K. (1994), 'The Structure of Transnational Capital in Europe: The Emerging Euro-Company and its Implications for Industrial Relations', in Hyman and Ferner (1994), 115–51.

Marginson, P., and Sisson, K. (1996), 'Multinational Companies and the Future of Collective Bargaining: A Review of the Research Issues', *European Journal of Industrial Relations*, 2/2: 173–97.

Markoczy, L. (1993), 'Managerial and Organizational Learning in Hungarian–Western Mixed Management Organizations', *International Journal of Human Resource Management*, 4/2: 277–303.

Martin, R. (1992), *Bargaining Power* (Oxford).

—— Vidinova, A., and Hill, S. (1996), 'Industrial Relations in Transition Economies: Emergent Industrial Relations Institutions in Bulgaria', *British Journal of Industrial Relations*, 34/1: 3–24.

Martinez Lucio, M. (1992), 'Spain: Constructing Institutions and Actors in a Context of Change', in Ferner and Hyman (1992), 482–523.

Mason, B. (1995), 'Industrial Relations in an Unstable Environment: The Case of Central and Eastern Europe', *European Journal of Industrial Relations*, 1/3: 341–67.

Miguelez, F. (1995), 'Modernization of Trade Unions in Spain', *Transfer: European Review of Labour Research*, 1/1: 1–15.

Mikhalev, V. (1996), 'Restructuring Social Assets: The Case of Health Care and Recreational Facilities in two Russian Cities', in OECD (1996), 61–94.

Moerel, H. (1994*a*), 'The Study of Labour Relations', in Moerel (1994*b*),1–34.

—— (1994*b*) (ed.), *Labour Relations in Transition* (Nijmegen).

Morawski, W. (1997), 'Society as an Economic Actor: Three Patterns of Institutionalization (Systemic Change in Poland)', in Hayashi (1997), 293–315.

Mudrakov, V. I. (1996), 'Social Protection and Social Infrastructure in Enterprises', in OECD (1996), 31–6.

Murrell, P. (1992), 'Evolution in Economics and in the Economic Reform of the Centrally Planned Economies', in Clague and Rausser (1992), 35–53.

Murshed, S. M., and Raffer, K. (1993) (eds.), *Trade Transfers and Development: Problems and Prospects for the Twenty-First Century* (Aldershot).

Myant, M. (1993), *Transforming Socialist Economies: The Case of Poland and Czechoslovakia* (Aldershot).

Nagy, L. (1984), *The Socialist Collective Agreement* (Budapest).

Neikova, S. (1996), 'Major Problems of the Collective Bargaining Practices in Bulgaria (1993–95)', paper distributed at the ILO Conference, Prague.

Nelson, L. D., and Kuzes, I. Y. (1994), *Property to the People* (New York).

Neumann, L. (1992), 'Workplace Industrial Relations of Joint Ventures in Hungary', paper presented to the First European Conference of Sociology (Working Group 111/4), Vienna.

—— (1996), 'Workplace Industrial Relations in Joint Ventures in Hungary', mimeo, paper presented at the first European Conference of Sociology (Working Group Roman 3/4), Vienna.

—— (1997), 'Circumventing Trade Unions in Hungary: Old and New Channels of Wage Bargaining', *European Journal of Industrial Relations*, 3/2: 183–202.

Nielsen, K., Jessop, B., and Hausner, J. (1995), 'Institutional Change in Post-Socialism', in Hausner *et al.* (1995), 3–44.

Niland, J., and Clarke, O. (1991) (eds.), *Agenda for Change: An International Analysis of Industrial Relations in Transition* (Sydney).

Nuti, D. M., and Portes, R. (1993), 'Central Europe—The Way Forward', in Portes (1993), 1–20.

O'Connell Davidson, J. (1993), *Privatization and Employment Relations* (London).

OECD (1996): Organization for Economic Cooperation and Development, *The Changing Social Benefits in Russian Enterprises* (Paris).

Offe, C. (1995), 'Designing Institutions for East European Transitions', in Hausner *et al.* (1995), 47–83.

——(1996),*Varieties of Transition: The East European and East German Experience* (Cambridge).

Owsiak, S. (1995), 'Financial Crisis of the Post Socialist State: The Polish Case', in Hausner *et al.* (1995), 149–67.

Peev, E. (1995), 'Separation of Ownership and Control in Transition: The Case of Bulgaria', *Europe–Asia Studies*, 47/5: 859–75.

Pereira, L. C. B., Maravall, J. M., and Przeworski, A. (1993) (eds.), *Economic Reforms in New Democracies* (Cambridge).

Perotti, E. (1994), 'Corporate Governance in Mass Privatization Programmes', in Estrin (1994*b*), 54–68.

Petkov, K., and Thirkell, J. (1991), *Labour Relations in Eastern Europe: Organizational Design and Dynamics* (London).

Plant, J. (1994), *Labour Standards and Structural Adjustment* (Geneva).

Pollert, A. (1997), 'The Transformation of Trade Unionism in the Capitalist and Democratic Reconstruction of the Czech Republic', *European Journal of Industrial Relations* 3/2: 161–81.

——and Hradecka, I. (1994), 'Privatization in Transition: The Czech Experience', *Industrial Relations Journal*, 25/1: 53–63.

Portes, R. (1993), *Economic Transformation in Central Europe* (London).

——(1994), 'Transformation Traps', *Economic Journal*, 104: 1178–89.

Poznanski, K. Z. (1995) (ed.), *The Evolutionary Transition to Capitalism* (Boulder, Colo.).

Przeworski, A. (1991), *Democracy and the Market: Political and Economic Reforms in Eastern Europe and Latin America* (Cambridge).

——(1993), 'Economic Reforms, Public Opinion, and Political Institutes: Poland in the Eastern European Perspective', in Pereira *et al.* (1993), 132–98.

Radygin, A. (1995), 'The Russian Model of Mass Privatization: Government Policy and First Results', in McFaul and Perlmutter (1995), 3–18.

Raffer, K. (1993), 'International Financial Institutions and Accountability: The Need for Drastic Change', in Murshed and Raffer (1993), 151–65.

Rausser, G. C., and Simon, L. (1992), 'The Political Economy of Transition in Eastern Europe: Packaging Enterprises for Privatization', in Clague and Rausser (1992), 245–70.

Ruble, B. A. (1981), *Soviet Trade Unions* (Cambridge).

Rudolph, H. (1995) (ed.), *WZB Jahrbuch 1995* (Berlin).

Rusnok, J., and Fassman, M. (1995), 'The True Effects of Wage Regulation in the Czech Republic', in Vaughan-Whitehead (1995), 123–62.

Rutland, P. (1994), 'Privatization in Russia: One Step Forward, Two Steps Back?', *Europe–Asia Studies*, 46/7: 1109–31.

——(1997), 'The Antinomies of Privatization in Eastern Europe', in Grabher and Stark (1997), 276–89.

Schleifer, A., and Vishny, R. W. (1994), 'Privatization in Russia: First Steps', in Blanchard *et al.* (1994), 137–64.

Schleifer, A., and Vasiliev, D. (1996), 'Management Ownership and Russian Privatization', in Frydman *et al.* (1996*b*), 62–77.

Schmidt, G. (1995), 'Europe in Flux: Change in East and West', in Dittrich *et al.* (1995), 1–10.

Schwartz, G. (1995), 'Privatization in Eastern Europe: Experience and Preliminary Policy Lessons', in Cook and Kirkpatrick (1995), 31–47.

Silverman, B., Vogt, R., and Yanowitch, M. (1992) (eds.), *Labour and Democracy in the Transition to a Market System* (New York).

Simoneti, M. (1993), 'A Comparative Review of Privatization Strategies in Four Former Socialist Countries', *Europe–Asia Studies*, 45/1: 79–102.

Slomp, H. (1990), *Labour Relations in Europe* (New York).

——(1992), 'Westbound or the Southern Trail?' in van Hoof *et al.* (1992), 9–31.

Stallings, B. (1992), 'International Influence on Economic Policy: Debt, Stabilization and Structural Reform', in Haggard and Kaufman (1992), 41–88.

Standing, G. (1995*a*), *Enterprise Restructuring in Russian Industry and Mass Unemployment* (Employment Department, ILO, Geneva), 3–9.

——(1995*b*), 'Challenges for the Governance of Social Protection in the 1990s', in Cichon and Samuel (1995), 29–40.

——(1996), 'Social Protection in Central and Eastern Europe: A Tale of Slipping Anchors and Torn Safety Nets', in Esping-Andersen (1996), 225–55.

——and Vaughan-Whitehead, D. (1995), *Minimum Wages in Central and Eastern Europe: From Protection to Destitution* (Budapest).

Stark, D. (1990), 'Privatization in Hungary: From Plan to Market or From Plan to Clan?', *East European Politics and Societies*, 4/3: 351–92.

——(1993), 'Recombinant Property in Eastern European Capitalism', Discussion Paper FS I 93-103, Social Science Research Centre (WZB) (Berlin).

——(1997), 'Recombinant Property in East European Capitalism', in Grabher and Stark (1997), 35–69.

Steele, J. (1994), *Eternal Russia* (London).

Streeck, W. (1992), 'National Diversity, Regime Competition and Institutional Deadlock: Problems in Forming a European Industrial Relations System', *Journal of Public Policy*, 12/4: 301–30.

——and Schmitter, P. C. (1991), 'From National Corporatism to Transnational Pluralism: Organized Interests in the Single European Market', *Politics and Society*, 19/2: 133–64.

Sylwestrowicz, J. (1995), 'Capitalist Restoration in Poland: A Balance Sheet', *Labour Focus on Eastern Europe*, 53: 31–9.

Szabo, M. (1992), 'The Taxi Driver Demonstration in Hungary: Social Protest and Policy Change', in Szoboszlai (1992), 357–81.

Szoboszlai, G. (1992) (ed.), *Flying Blind: Emerging Democracies in East Central Europe* (Budapest).

Szomburg, J. (1993), 'The Decision Making Structure of Polish Privatization', in Earle *et al.* (1993), 75–85.

Takla, L. (1994), 'The Relationship between Privatization and the Reform of the Baking Sector: The Case of the Czech Republic and Slovakia', in Estrin (1994*b*), 154–75.

Thirkell, J., and Tseneva, E. (1992), 'Bulgarian Labour Relations in Transition: Tripartism and Collective Bargaining', *International Labour Review*, 131/3: 355–66.

——Atanasov, B., and Gradev, G. (1994), 'Trade Unions, Political Parties and Governments in Bulgaria, 1989–92', in Waller and Myant (1994), 98–115.

——Scase, R., and Vickerstaff, S. (1995*a*), 'Changing Models of Labour Relations in Eastern Europe and Russia', in Thirkell *et al.* (1995*c*), 7–29.

————(1995*b*), 'Models of Labour Relations: Trends and Prospects', in Thirkell *et al.* (1995*c*), 169–86.

————(1995*c*) (eds.), *Labour Relations and Political Change in Eastern Europe* (London).

Toth, A. (1997), 'The Invention of Works Councils in Hungary', *European Journal of Industrial Relations*, 3/2: 161–81.

Touraine, A., and Geisicka, G. (1983), *Solidarity: The Analysis of a Social Movement* (Cambridge).

Toye, J. (1995), *Structural Adjustment and Employment Policy* (Geneva).

Tratch, I., Rein, M., and Worgotter, A. (1996), 'Social Asset Restructuring in Russian Enterprises: Results of a Survey in Selected Russian Regions', in OECD (1996), 95–111.

Tzanov, V. (1995), 'For a Negotiated Alternative to Tax-Based Incomes Policy in Bulgaria', in Vaughan-Whitehead (1995), 87–122.

van Brabant, J. M. (1990), *Remaking Eastern Europe On the Political Economy of Transition* (London).

van Hoof, J. (1992), 'Between Corporatism and Contestation', in van Hoof *et al.* (1992), 97–108.

——Slomp, H., and Verrips, K. (1992) (eds.), *Westbound?* (Amsterdam).

Vaughan-Whitehead, D. (1995) (ed.), *Reforming Wage Policy in Central and Eastern Europe* (Budapest).

——(1997), 'Employee-Share Ownership in Central and Eastern Europe or The Privatization Method by Default', in Brady (1997), 201–52.

Vickers, J., and Yarrow, G. (1988), *Privatization: An Economic Analysis* (Cambridge, Mass.).

Vickerstaff, S., and Thirkell, J. (1997), 'Eastern European Labour Relations: Transference, Imitation and Imposition', in Brady (1997), 15–36.

Voeikov, M. I. (1996) (ed.), *Ekonomicheskol Polozhenie Rossii I Trudovie Otnosheniya* (Moscow).

——(1997), Personal Communication.

——and Milovankina, N. I. (1996), 'Ekonomicheskaya i Trudovaya Situatsiya v Rossii (ekonomiko-statisicheskii obzor)', in Voeikov (1996), 86–103.

von Hirschhausen, C. (1995), 'From Privatization to Capitalization: Industrial Restructuring in Post-Socialist Central and East Europe', in Dittrich *et al.* (1995), 54–78.

Voros, P. (1996), 'The Situation of Collective Bargaining in Hungary', paper presented to the ILO Conference, Prague.

Voszka, E. (1993), 'Spontaneous Privatization in Hungary', in Earle *et al.* (1993), 89–107.

Waller, M., and Myant, M. (1994), *Parties, Trade Unions, and Society in East-Central Europe* (London).

World Bank (1995), 'Workers in an Integrating World', *World Development Report* (Oxford).

Yakovlev, R. A. (1995), 'Income and Wages Distortions in Russia and Strategies for Reform', in Vaughan-Whitehead (1995), 301–24.

Zaslavskaya, T. (1986), 'Cheloeschskii faktor razvitiya ekonomiki: Sotsialnaya spravedliv', *Kommunisto*, 13: 61–73.

INDEX